*The
American
Community*

The American Community

BY

BLAINE E. MERCER *University of Colorado*

RANDOM HOUSE · NEW YORK

323.35
M53a

341 72
October, 1956

TO *Arlene and Cathy*

PREFACE

THIS BOOK does not, of course, say everything that might be said about the American community. But it does say many things which are important and, the author hopes, may be interesting and challenging to anyone concerned about social living in his, and other people's, communities.

The sociologist is at once a scientist and a citizen. In the first role, he need not be concerned with what is done with his objective description and predictive ability, but in the second role, as a citizen with special training and knowledge, he ought to be very much concerned. This is the proper place of values. The trick, however, is to keep these roles separate to the extent that one's values as a citizen do not interfere with his objective vision as a scientist—but not to the extent that his method of seeking truth fails to serve him in his responsibility as a citizen.

The author has probably been able to accomplish such role-separation only imperfectly in writing this book, but an honest attempt has been made. Without some expression of value-orientations—the ideals, fears, and hopes of its author —a book on a social subject is likely to make rather dull, and possibly misleading, reading. There are plenty of facts in this volume to stuff a reader: statistics and other factual word-maps, case studies, and reports of the findings of scientific researches. There are theoretical discussions and conceptual analyses. There are, too, expressions of opinion and of hope and fear.

This volume is designed for the layman interested in the American community (and that ought to include a great many adults) as well as for the college student. It is particularly planned, however, for courses which deal with communities and community life, either as their major interest or as one aspect of a broader study. This volume has been deliberately made a short and concise one so that it can readily be supplemented by readings from the existing literature on communities. A list of suggested references is included at the end of each chapter. Where possible, inexpensive and readily available reprint editions are cited in bibliographies and footnotes.

The writer is indebted to many people for the ideas expressed herein: to the long list of scholars and authors cited in text and footnote, but especially to Max Weber, Talcott Parsons, Robert K. Merton, Kingsley Davis, Robert M. MacIver, Charles Horton Cooley, Franklin H. Giddings, John Dewey, A. R. Radcliffe-Brown, Ralph Linton, Ruth Benedict, Margaret Mead, W. Lloyd Warner, Robert E. Park, Robin M. Williams, Jr., and many others whose writings have inspired, provoked, or informed; to his colleagues at the University of Colorado, for discussion and intellectual stimulation, especially to Jiri Nehnevajsa, Edward L. Rose, Judson B. Pearson, Howard Higman, Gordon H. Barker, Laird J. Dunbar, James L. Busey, Gordon Hewes, and Clay P. Malick; to his students who so kindly passed judgment on some of the chapters; to some great teachers for inspiration they may little know about, Colin Goodykoontz, Karl Muenzinger, Morris Garnsey, and Joseph Cohen, all of the University of Colorado, and Douglas G. Haring, Marguerite

J. Fisher, and Edward Palmer, of Syracuse University; and, most of all, to David L. Hatch, of Madison College, teacher, mentor, and friend, and Charles H. Page, of Smith College, whose patience and aid were extended far beyond the call of editorial duty. Thanks are due Mrs. Francis Robinson for secretarial help in preparing the manuscript. Whatever merits the book has belong to them, one way or another, but its faults are owned by the author alone.

BLAINE E. MERCER

CONTENTS

PART ONE

Community
Structure
and Function

CHAPTER 1

Social Structure and Social Function

1. Social Structure

The task of the sociologist in modern society is to study human social relationships as social. No other student does this; not the economist, who deals with the segment of wealth-getting, -distributing, and -consuming relations; not the political scientist, who analyzes governmental and power relations; not the historian nor the anthropologist nor the psychologist, all of whom focus more or less exclusively on some narrower aspect of man and his life in a social and physical environment or are to be distinguished by some other characteristic of subject or method.[1] Whatever their methods, whatever their interests, however, social scientists are, as are philosophers, generally agreed that the goal of all their work is knowledge of man. Man, they agree, as the Ancients were the first to realize, can be understood only in the context of his social and political life. Man has his very being in his social relationships.[2] And the study of human social relationships is the study of a process associated with a

[1] MacIver, R. M., and Charles H. Page, *Society*, Rinehart and Company, Inc., New York, 1949, p. v.

[2] Cassirer, Ernst, *An Essay on Man*, Doubleday and Company, Inc., Garden City, New York, 1953, pp. 17, 87.

structure, just as the study of a biological organism includes analysis of both its physical structure and the processes associated with it.

Social structure and *social function* are abstractions designed to make communicable a myriad of ideas concerning the nature of human relations. Abstract as they are, these two concepts, when properly employed, bring a fresh insight into the complexities of human social behavior and social groupings.

It appears to be one of the universals about human beings and their lives that they become aware of one another and organize themselves into groups, large or small. "A separate individual," as Charles Horton Cooley so aptly put it, "is an abstraction unknown to experience." The fact is, further, that most human groups are more than mere physical aggregations of individual organisms; they are cemented together and defined by a pattern of relationships which influence the individual's views of himself and of others and which guide his individual activities. This arrangement of individuals in patterns of interrelationship, defined and controlled by a complexity of standards, values, norms, beliefs, customs, mores, habits, myths, and the more concrete facts of technology and material things they share, is what we mean by *social structure*.

We must be wary of using analogies uncritically in sociology,[3] but it seems safe to say that just as the biological organism has a structure of parts—of tissues, cells, fluids, organs, and limbs—so also any social group has a structure of parts. But the human social group is marked by a structure of *institutions*, that is, of recognized conduct patterns which

[3] For an interesting and masterful discussion of the proper use and abuse of the image of society as an organism, see Vinding Kruse, *The Community of the Future*, Oxford University Press, London, 1950, pp. 387-8.

people, to a greater or lesser degree, approximate in their daily activities. They come also to expect of other people a general approximation to these behavior norms. Moreover, just as the biological organism displays a process which we call life and which is in fact a functioning (or inter-contributory) process relating parts of the structure, so a basic feature of any human group is the process we call social life. This, too, is a functioning process tying together the system's related parts which, taken in their totality, are its structure.

Social structure has a sectional as well as a general character. The members of each subgroup in a community possess cultural and other attributes in common which they do not share, *in toto,* with members of other groups. The uniformities resulting from the sharing of characteristics are maintained by social pressures which involve leadership and the subordination of followers to leaders. In turn, the members of any one group share *some* attributes with all persons in the social structure, be it a small local community or a large society.[4]

A *social structure,* then, is an arrangement of persons whose relationships with one another are defined by *institutions,* normative patterns which guide individual behavior. A *social system* is a network of institutions and establishes the limits within which *most* of the social behavior of the group takes place; behavior not falling within these defined limits is usually called *deviant behavior. Society* is a more inclusive concept, subsuming both social structure and social system; it is the total organization man creates, the constantly changing "system of usages and procedures, of authority and mutual aid, of many groupings and divisions, of controls of human behavior and of liberties." [5] Patterns of inter-

---

[4] Wilson, Godfrey, and Monica Wilson, *The Analysis of Social Change,* Cambridge University Press, Cambridge, England, 1945, p. 51.

[5] MacIver, R. M., and Charles H. Page, *op. cit.,* p. 5.

action between persons or groups in a society are called *social relationships*. Such relationships result from reciprocal expectations and predictions of behavior of the other or others; these expectations are defined by the social system.[6] Social relationships and social behavior in general are, for particular individuals, expressions of *status* and *role*. A *status* is a pattern of privileges and responsibilities and represents a person's position in the value hierarchy of his society. *Role* is what one *does* in his society and is the dynamic aspect of status.[7] These definitions will be used consistently throughout this volume.

Terms such as *social structure, social system,* and *society* are "constructs"; this means, as Donald K. Adams says, that "they are not directly perceived but are, rather, notions invented to account for the phenomena (things, events, processes) which we do perceive."[8] Any one individual can directly perceive only such human relationships as he somehow experiences; he cannot form an *accurate* mental image of a social structure in all its numberless details. From his limited experience, his partial perception, the individual "constructs" a social structure, *his* view of the total arrangement of people in his society, and bases actions upon this view.

It is not necessary to its persistence that a social structure (or a social system) be seen whole by the individual members of a society. Barring destruction by external forces, a social structure will persist and a social system "work" as long as people are trained to function in their respective roles.[9]

[6] For an excellent discussion of these concepts, see Ely Chinoy, *Sociological Perspective,* Short Studies in Sociology, Random House, Inc., New York, 1954, pp. 19-27.

[7] Linton, Ralph, *The Study of Man,* D. Appleton-Century Company, Inc., New York, 1936, pp. 113-4.

[8] Adams, Donald K., *The Anatomy of Personality,* Papers in Psychology, Random House, Inc., New York, 1954, p. 2.

[9] Gillin, John, *The Ways of Men,* D. Appleton-Century Company, Inc., New York, 1948, p. 352.

2. Function

We have already used the concept of *function* several times in discussing social structure. Structure, as we have used it, is most meaningful as related to the complementary idea, *function*.

Function, as an analytical construct for the study of natural phenomena, including human relationships, was one of the important contributions of Darwinian biology. It represents the shifting of attention of scientists from the study of substance to the study of relationships, from unchanging composition to dynamics. As a concept, function came into general use before the turn of the century[10] and still retains its significance, not only in sociology and anthropology, but in economics, biology, psychology, and many fields outside the social sciences. As a preliminary explanation, it may be stated that functionalism and functional analysis are concerned with the contribution of an item to the continuity, the persistence, of a larger system of which it is a part. Such an approach is applicable to the study of human groups.[11]

Before the beginning of the present century, a great American sociologist insisted that his colleagues ought to turn their attention from what then may have been an almost sterile study of group structures to the study of functional interrelations. He said: "My thesis is that the subject matter of sociology is human *achievement*. It is not what men are

[10] Kallen, Horace M., "Functionalism," *Encyclopaedia of the Social Sciences,* vol. 6, The Macmillan Company, New York, 1932, p. 525.

[11] Function is "vital or organic processes considered in the respects in which they contribute to the maintenance of the organism" (Robert K. Merton, *Social Theory and Social Structure,* The Free Press, Glencoe, Illinois, 1949, p. 23) or "a contribution to the existence of a given structure, be it a personality, an institution, or a society" (Kingsley Davis, *Human Society,* The Macmillan Company, New York, 1949, p. 124).

but what they do. It is not the structure but the function." [12] We believe now, however, that the concept of function is of little use without the complementary concept of structure. Accordingly, we refer to our approach to the study of community as one which emphasizes "structural-functional" analysis; we shall not hesitate, however, to draw upon other approaches or emphases wherever we find them applicable.

We have described structure as the arrangement of individuals in relationships defined and controlled by patterns of standards, values, customs, or behavioral norms. We have defined function as the processes associated with the structure, or, more specifically, those contributions of a part to the continuity and ordered change of the larger whole to which it belongs. Now we shall attempt to bring the two together into meaningful relationship. But let one of the outstanding functionalist scholars speak for us:

For me, as for many others, there is such a thing as social structure. The theory of social evolution depends on this concept, since that theory is that in human life there has been a development of different types of structural systems by divergence or variation, and a development of more complex systems from simpler ones. A social structure is an arrangement of persons in relationships defined and regulated by institutions; and an institution is an established pattern of conduct, or a set of patterns, relating to some feature of social life. The process that is connected with social structure is social life, the interactions and joint actions of persons who are brought into relation by the structure. The concept of function, as I employ it, is used to describe the discoverable interconnections of the social structure and the processes of social life. The social life is determined by the structure; the structure is maintained in existence by the

[12] Ward, Lester F., *Pure Sociology*, Second Edition, The Macmillan Company, New York, 1911, p. 15.

social life, or undergoes modification through the events of the social life (such as a war, for example). The function of an institution, custom or belief, or of some regular social activity, such as a funeral ceremony, or the trial and punishment of a criminal, lies in the effects it has in the complex whole of social structure and the process of social life.[13]

The study of function, then, involves the understanding of the contributions which a social or cultural element (including institutionalized behavior patterns) makes toward such conditions as the preservation of group solidarity, reduction of friction between individuals, training of individuals in specific statuses, co-ordination of the activities of persons, the provision of the group with leadership guidance,[14] and whatever else is required for social continuity.

3. Modifications of the Concept of Function

Before we go on to point out in more detail what is known about the requirements for social stability to the degree that the group continues to exist rather than tear apart, we should pause to note that the construct of function, although used quite uncritically by some students, bears careful analysis as to its possible alternative meanings. Robert K. Merton, an American sociologist, has turned his searching insight to the concept and, with the distinction between "manifest" and "latent" functions and between function and dysfunction, has modified the original concept and enlarged its usefulness.[15]

Merton points out that investigators have often confused

[13] Radcliffe-Brown, A. R., "Functionalism: A Protest," *American Anthropologist*, April-June, 1949, pp. 320-3. Used by permission of *American Anthropologist*.
[14] Linton, Ralph, *op. cit.*, pp. 412, 260-2, 299.
[15] For Merton's discussion, see *op. cit.*, pp. 61-81.

"subjective motivations" with "objective functions"—that is, individual motives to social action with functional consequences for a social system. Confused interpretations of data result from this, and, in order to eliminate this problem, it is necessary to distinguish carefully between the categories of subjective, conscious motivation and objective, observed consequences. The constructs of *manifest* and *latent* functions are designed to accomplish this distinction.

Manifest function refers to intended and recognized consequences for a specific person, subgroup, social system, cultural system, or social structure, of any cultural or behavior item. *Latent function* refers to unintended or unrecognized consequences. This distinction, as Merton says, has several analytical uses: it makes possible the analysis of what appear to be irrational social patterns, calls attention to neglected or fruitful areas for research, adds to knowledge through discovery of hitherto unrecognized latent functions, and substitutes objective analysis for naïve moral judgments.

Another of Merton's significant contributions to clarification of the idea of function is his criticism of certain widely held theories in this mode of analysis. One of these theories is called the "postulate of the functional unity of society," and implies that standardized social activities or cultural items are functional for the entire social or cultural system. Merton marshals considerable evidence to dispute this formulation and substitutes for it the requirement that there be a definite "specification of the units for which a given social or cultural item is functional." For the "postulate of universal functionalism," which holds that all cultural items have positive functions, he substitutes the idea that any item, if it is to persist, must have a "net balance of functional consequences" for the society as a whole or for a sufficiently powerful subgroup within it. Finally, he substitutes for the "postulate of indispensability," which holds that every cultural item has some vital function and is indispensable to a society, the idea of "functional alternatives." A single item may have a number of functions and one function may be filled by a number of items.[16]

In our analysis of the structure and function of the American community, we follow Merton's modifications of the term, *function*. Not all functional contributions of a local community as a whole to the larger society of which it is a part, or of parts of a community to the community as a system, are evident. Some consequences are hidden deeply in people's subjective motivations for their actions, and some are clearly unintended and perhaps unrecognized. While this approach makes our task more difficult than simple description, it also makes it more interesting and sociologically realistic. For to understand a community thoroughly requires inquiry into latent as well as manifest functions of groups and institutions.

Moreover, standardized social activities or cultural items do not necessarily have the same functional consequences for the entire social structure or social system of which they are parts. We believe, with Merton, that it is useful in the study of an institution or a behavior pattern that there be clear specification of the parts of the society for which the institution or behavior complex is functional. A cultural or social item is not necessarily completely functional; for some people in the structure or for some institutions in the system, it may be non-functional or even dysfunctional.[17] If the item is to persist, however, it must serve the needs or interests of some persons or the community as a whole to the extent that people do not, consciously or unconsciously, forget or ex-

[16] *Ibid.*, pp. 27-38.
[17] *Ibid.*, p. 41, and note, p. 51.

tinguish it.[18] Finally, no specific cultural or social unit is indispensable. Functional *alternatives* are generally present.[19]

4. Functional Requisites

A social structure is maintained in existence by the functional contributions of the parts which make it up, and it seems that we should know something of the requirements for existence which characterize such structures. We do know something of this matter, but, unfortunately, not as much as thorough sociological analysis requires. Perhaps the major reason for this is that societies "live" longer than the people who live in them; they so seldom "die" to permit a "social autopsy" to see what was lacking. When we analyze communities, however, we are on somewhat surer ground, for communities do spring up and disappear, sometimes within the lifetime of one man, and hence do permit such autopsies.

Societies do not have "needs"; only organisms have needs, and societies are not organisms. The idea of *functional requisites* is preferable to that of *needs* in the analysis of social structures and social systems. Needs refer to specific requisites; lack of their provision results in disappearance of the structure. *Functional requisites,* as we use the term, are much less specific, for they refer to general conditions which may change with the changing society, and the failure to fulfill them does not necessarily mean disappearance of the so-

[18] *Extinction* is the process of "dropping out" a habit because of absence of reward for the behavior for which it calls. Similarly, a cultural item (value, belief, or material "thing," for example) or a social item (such as a particular relationship between two people) may be dropped from daily thought and behavior without being truly forgotten. Should cultural or social change be such that the item once more becomes functional (or rewarding to some people), it may become part of the social system or social structure again.

[19] Merton, Robert K., *op. cit.*, pp. 35-6.

cial structure, but may merely produce in it ordered change along some predictable pattern.[20]

There are various ways of classifying these requisites for societal existence; the following examples indicate what we have in mind. One writer outlines "social necessities" as

I. Maintenance of the population
   a. Provision of nutriment
   b. Protection against injury
   c. Reproduction of new organisms
II. Division of function among population
III. Solidarity of the group
   a. Motivation of contact between members
   b. Motivation of mutual tolerance and resistance to outsiders
IV. Perpetuation of the social system.[21]

Another lists societal requirements as (1) securing of social order through institutions, folkways, mores, and a system of authority, (2) provision for the fulfillment of needs for sustenance, (3) provision for population renewal, (4) provision for induction of children into the culture, that is, cultural transmission, and (5) a system of rituals for reaffirmation of the value system of the society.[22]

Still another sociologist, Talcott Parsons, names the following conditions as the "functional prerequisites" of a society: satisfaction of certain psychological and biological needs for a sufficient proportion of the membership, the pro-

---

[20] We follow here Marion J. Levy, Jr., *The Structure of Society,* Princeton University Press, Princeton, New Jersey, 1952, p. 62: "A *functional requisite* . . . is a generalized condition necessary for the maintenance of the unit with which it is associated, given the level of generalization of the definition of that unit and the most general setting of such a unit."

[21] Davis, Kingsley, *op. cit.,* p. 30. Used by permission of The Macmillan Company.

[22] Wilson, Logan, and William L. Kolb, *Sociological Analysis,* Harcourt, Brace and Company, New York, 1949, pp. 513-4.

vision of order and co-ordination of individual actions, and the provision of adequate motivation to the performance of essential social roles.[23]

Marion J. Levy, Jr., lists the following *functional requisites:* (1) "Provision for an adequate physiological relationship to the setting and for sexual recruitment." (In general, satisfaction of the biological needs of the individual, not only for survival, but to the end of "an adequate level of operation," and reproduction of the species at a "sufficient" rate.) (2) "Role differentiation and role assignment." (Some system of allocating privileges, obligations, and performances expected of individuals.) (3) "Communication." (A means of conveying ideas or feelings from person to person.) (4) "Shared cognitive orientations." (Shared understanding or knowledge of *some* phenomena, for example, measuring units, such as "gallon" or "yard," but not of *all* phenomena.) (5) "A shared articulated set of goals." (Agreement as to *some* desirable goals or states of affairs, and articulation of them to ensure societal persistence.) (6) "The regulation of the choice of means." (Prescription—and proscription—of means or methods to attain the desired goals.) (7) "The regulation of affective expression." (Control of the expression of emotion between individuals.) (8) "Adequate socialization." (Sufficient "inculcation of the structure of action of a society on an individual . . . to permit the effective performance of his roles.") (9) "Effective control of disruptive forms of behavior." (Especially, the control of force and fraud.) (10) "Adequate institutionalization." (The existence of institutions or normative patterns guiding behavior.)[24]

[23] Parsons, Talcott, *Essays in Sociological Theory Pure and Applied*, The Free Press, Glencoe, Illinois, 1949, pp. 6-7.
[24] Levy, Marion J., Jr., *op. cit.*, pp. 149-97.

Although the sociologists mentioned above have carefully and logically defined their constructs, it is not yet clear, in an empirical sense, *exactly* what is meant by such terms as *"minimum* biological and psychological needs," *"adequacy* of motivation," *"adequate* socialization," or *"adequate* institutionalization." Thus far, sociologists have not formulated a satisfactory inductive methodology by which researchers can determine empirically the functional requisites of a given social structure or social system. Nonetheless, the concept of functional requisites is suggestive and, awaiting the development of testing and measuring techniques, provides a thought-provoking orientation to the study of social groups of large size.

Structural-functional analysis in sociology is the attempt to learn empirically (1) what structures (uniformities) are involved in human interrelationships, (2) what positive and negative contributions to its persistence and ordered change (that is, functions and dysfunctions) are associated with a structure, and (3) what specific functions and dysfunctions are associated with what particular aspects or segments of a social structure.[25] We shall use this mode of analysis in our study of community. Our major questions in the next two chapters will be: What is the nature of the structure of a community? and, What is the nature of the functional process associated with this structure, including functional requisites for persistence and ordered change?

[25] Cf. *ibid.*, pp. 27-8. Our formulation differs significantly from Levy's, in part because of our more restricted definition of the concept of *function.* (For Levy's definition and several other terms derived from it, see *ibid.*, pp. 56-7.) Moreover, we include the third part of our definition as a means of emphasizing the analytic usefulness of spelling out the contributions of specific social or cultural items to the persistence and ordered change of a social structure.

SELECTED REFERENCES

Chinoy, Ely, *Sociological Perspective,* Studies in Sociology, Random House, Inc., New York, 1954. The student will find this inexpensive and readable short study especially valuable for definitions and concepts.

Davis, Kingsley, *Human Society,* The Macmillan Company, New York, 1949. Davis' introductory textbook is an example of the structural-functional approach and contains many excellent discussions of sociological concepts.

Hertzler, Joyce O., *Society in Action,* The Dryden Press, New York, 1954. Hertzler's recent volume contains several excellent chapters on the structural-functional view of human society and is a thoroughgoing functionalist study.

Levy, Marion J., Jr., *The Structure of Society,* Princeton University Press, Princeton, New Jersey, 1952. Levy's thoughtful volume on the scope and method of structural-functional analysis in sociology is worth careful study. The chapter on "functional requisites" is especially useful to students of community.

Linton, Ralph, *The Study of Man,* D. Appleton-Century Company, Inc., New York, 1936. This widely read volume in anthropology contains good chapters on society, social system, and function, and can be read profitably in its entirety.

Merton, Robert K., *Social Theory and Social Structure,* The Free Press, Glencoe, Illinois, 1949. "Manifest and Latent Functions," the first paper of this collection of essays by a leading structural-functional analyst should be carefully studied. The entire book is scholarly and thoughtful.

Parsons, Talcott, *Essays in Sociological Theory Pure and Applied,* The Free Press, Glencoe, Illinois, 1949. This devious but scholarly book on structural-functional analysis should be studied as a companion volume to Merton's *Social Theory and Social Structure,* cited above.

Parsons, Talcott, *The Social System,* The Free Press, Glencoe, Illinois, 1951. Parsons' study is highly abstract and often tedious to read, but is a "must" for the serious student of society.

Parsons, Talcott, and E. A. Shils, *Toward a General Theory of Action,* Harvard University Press, Cambridge, Massachusetts, 1951. For the advanced and serious student, this book can be helpful as an introduction to structural-functional analysis.

Wilson, Logan, and William L. Kolb, *Sociological Analysis,* Harcourt, Brace and Company, New York, 1949. Wilson and Kolb's large collection of readings emphasizes the structural-functional mode of analysis in sociology.

CHAPTER 2

Community Structure

1. The Biotic Community

Many years ago, in explaining the complex interrelationships of living things in their habitats, Darwin used the descriptive term "the web of life." This succinct phrase describes very well indeed our concept of community. It is a "web of life" within which live its members.

Communities are of many sorts, but fundamental to the understanding of all of them is understanding of the "biotic" community, a construct long in good standing among biologists and now adopted by sociologists. This concept refers to any distinguishable "configurations of relationships" among living organisms. These relationships are complex, but they are neither random nor beyond analysis. It is possible to distinguish and to categorize these configurations according to the varying essentials of their organization, for the biotic community is made up of *specific* relationships in *specific* places and at *specific* times. "Life," as Amos Hawley puts it, "is a space-time phenomenon; just as there is differentiation to constitute units of the physical environment, there is also differentiation to constitute unities of associated life. These unities are described as communities." [1]

The biotic community is made up of the webs of inter-relationships of animals and plants living in a particular area at a particular time. It is a community because it occupies a habitat and exhibits (perhaps not collectively, but certainly as the sum of the individual ends of its members) goals related to the common requirement of adaptation to the environment in which it exists.[2] Biotic communities are more than mere aggregates of biological organisms, just as human communities are more than mere aggregations of human individuals. The functional interrelations of these individual units are as significant for the understanding of community as are the individual units themselves.

The biological concept of "niche" or "functional role" is of assistance to us at this point in our attempt to depict clearly the meaning of the biotic—and, indeed, any kind of community. This concept calls attention to what organisms do rather than to their morphological structure.

Individual organisms in the biotic community make specific contributions to the continuity and ordered development of the community as a whole. If the community contains trees and mosses, for example, the trees may contribute the necessary shade for the mosses to grow, and the mosses may contribute to the water-holding character of the terrain so necessary for the trees to grow. A breakdown of the functional contribution of the trees would, undoubtedly, result in the destruction of the mosses, which, in turn, would mean the disappearance of the biotic community as such. Failure of the mosses to perform their functional role might or might not result in the destruction of the community, but the fact

[1] Hawley, Amos, *Human Ecology: A Theory of Community Structure,* The Ronald Press Company, New York, 1950, p. 41.

[2] *Ibid.,* pp. 41-2.

of the matter is that as long as trees and mosses are living together in time and space, they are functionally related.

In any biotic community, one or more of the organisms—the trees in our example—may be *dominant:* they are able to "control" the community and other species must adapt to their presence. The presence of dominants, in other words, determines whether certain other organisms do or can live in the community. Mosses of certain kinds evidently cannot live in certain places without the trees which provide the shade necessary to them. The mosses may be termed *influents,* and live, figuratively and literally, in the shade of the trees, playing lesser "functional roles" which are largely determined by the dominant organisms.[3]

Again, a word of caution is in order with regard to the uncritical adoption by analogy of biological terms and thought patterns, but it is safe to state, we believe, that in the study of any human community, however defined, the concepts of dominants and influents may be profitably employed. For in each human community certain institutions, groups, or individuals play dominant functional roles, and other institutions, groups, or individuals play the roles of influents. In a particular community, for example, family may be the dominant institution, the chamber of commerce the dominant organized group, and the town banker the dominant individual, while education, Boy Scouts, or the local bum are influents. Such relationships do not remain static, and roles are often reversed, a dominant becoming an influent and an influent becoming a dominant.

2. Integration, Specialization, and Complexity

Biologists have noted that there is a "drive to integration" among living things. This characteristic is present in a bio-

[3] *Ibid.,* pp. 44-5.

logical organism and the relationships among its physical parts, in insect societies, and in biotic communities of plants and animals. This tendency toward integration is never the only drive, nor is integration ever complete, even in individual biological organisms. Indeed, some living things are so loosely integrated that certain of their parts appear to operate independently of other parts. The sea anemone is such a loosely integrated creature; in moving from one place to another, it sometimes seriously injures itself by leaving behind a portion of its foot, still fastened to a rock.[4]

Whether there is a drive toward integration in human communities analogous to the tendency in biotic ones is debatable. There is, however, a movement in some human communities from a diffuse social structure to a more compact one, and to more uniformity in behavior of members. Moreover, some communities as wholes exhibit a trend in the direction of functional specialization, as exemplified by residential suburb developments and communities which have changed from many-industry to one-industry towns. The manner in which this is taking place in contemporary American communities will be discussed later in this book. Suffice it to say here, for some communities as well as for animals and plants, the matter of survival value of integration and specialization may well explain these trends.[5] Furthermore, if there is a drive to integration in communities (perhaps akin to the meaning of William Graham Sumner's old phrase, "strain for consistency" as applied to human cultures), it may be interfered with. The last great war was

---

[4] Parker, G. H., *The Elementary Nervous System*, quoted in Robert K. Merton, *Social Theory and Social Structure*, The Free Press, Glencoe, Illinois, 1949, pp. 28-9.

[5] For a discussion of specialization and integration in animal and human communities, see Caryl P. Haskins, *Of Societies and Men*, George Allen and Unwin, Ltd., London, 1952, *passim*, especially pp. 39-41. On specialization and generalization in organisms, see William Howells, *Mankind So Far*, Doubleday and Company, Inc., New York, 1947.

fought in part to stop the Nazi move in the direction of a certain form of integration.

For most communities, the current trend is toward greater complexity in such matters as size, density of population, and interlacings of the relationships of individuals. Small towns come within the orbit of growing cities or become large and complex urban centers themselves. Rural hamlets disappear, their people moving away to pursue specialized functions in more heavily populated places. As communities become larger, the variety of socially acceptable behaviors usually becomes greater. Individuals and groups with different backgrounds contribute new customs and ideas to an expanding community culture. But, as time goes by and people are exposed to a pervasive communication system and share experiences, populations become more homogeneous, and within the complexity of many communities there develops, in turn, a trend toward uniformity in thought and behavior.

In most communities at least two trends, then, are observable in many of their particulars: first, toward functional specialization of the community as a whole and toward uniformity among people, which is partially a result of this specialization, and, second, toward complexity in social relationships and individuality among people. An important aspect of the study of community change is the analysis of these trends in terms of the modifications they produce in the structure and function of the community. The processes of change are patterned and ordered, as is community structure. This is not to say that a community "functions" in a manner as orderly as the tissues of a living organism. Communities are not in fact organisms and the "orderliness" of the processes associated with a community and an organism should not be equated.[6]

[6] Cf. Jessie Bernard, *American Community Behavior*, The Dryden Press, New York, 1949, p. 15, for such analogy and comparison.

3. The Human Community

Now, just what is a human community? It has, first of all, an external structure. The structure of any specific community, due largely to its specialized function within the society, is uniquely its own. The external appearance of different communities from the air illustrates this point: an observer from a plane has no difficulty in noting the contrasts between the external structural appearances, the buildings, roads, and rail lines, for example, of industrial centers, financial centers, governmental centers, and trading centers. The skylines of cities symbolize their functional roles in the society. New York, Chicago, and Pittsburgh all tell in their skylines part of the story of their functional emphases.[7]

The external physical structure of the community is important to the understanding of the less easily discerned "internal" aspects which interest us most: the complex webs of relationships which are unique for each community and distinguish one from another, but which also have much in common.

We have already considered the biotic community. As applied to human groups, this conception refers to the *ecological* community. Human ecology is the study of the relationships of human organisms and their environments, and emphasizes analysis of discoverable connections between social life and patterns of man's distribution in space. The ecological structure of a community results in part from competition and cooperation among people who share a common geographic setting. Population composition (as to age, sex, race, or national origin, for example), settlement, dispersion, and increase or decline of size are major elements in the

[7] MacIver, R. M., and Charles H. Page, *Society*, Rinehart and Company, New York, 1949, pp. 285-87.

ecological order. Some comprehension of the ecology of a community is prerequisite to understanding it as a social structure. In addition to its geographical and ecological aspect, a community is an arrangement of people who live together and whose relationships are largely defined by a set of interests, values, culture standards, and behavior norms more or less commonly held.

Terms such as "community of interest" and "community of value" are seen in newspapers and popular magazines, and social scientists sometimes utilize constructs such as "school" community and "church" community. Segmentalized definitions are quite sufficient for certain specialized analyses. But our concern is with the community as an "ideal type," and our concept must be highly generalized. Consideration of existing general definitions at this point will prove helpful in the development of our own.

Community, MacIver and Page point out, should be understood with reference to other sociological concepts. Society, they state, is a web of relationships involving mutual awareness of individuals. There are both likeness and difference in a society: a "consciousness of kind," as F. H. Giddings put it, and complementary interdependency growing out of the fact of difference. Further, man seems to have an inherent "need" for society, or, as we prefer to put it, group living makes man human. A community is a group having the characteristics ascribed to a society, a sharing of the "basic conditions of common life," and a territorial locality. A community may be small as a rural hamlet or large as a nation—with a world community probably in the making. MacIver and Page make it clear that a community need not be self-sufficient; as they say, "The wholly self-contained community belongs to the primitive world." At the same time, "the mark of a community is that one's life *may* be lived wholly within it . . . that all one's social relationships *may* be found within it." [8]

Kingsley Davis presents a similar definition. One must consider both the "territorial proximity" and the "social completeness" in defining a community, he writes. People cluster together for protection, contact, organization, group integration, and for the purpose of exploitation of a particular region, and, secondly, "the community is the smallest territorial group that can embrace all aspects of social life." [9]

Dwight Sanderson, speaking of the rural community, states that it "consists of the social interaction of the people and their institutions in the local area in which they live on dispersed farmsteads and in a hamlet or village which forms the center of common activities." [10] Kimball Young defines a community as "a group of people of all ages having a more or less common culture and living in a limited region in which they find a geographical center for most of their common interests and actions." [11]

These references are sufficient to indicate that, taken collectively, such generalized definitions of community involve a number of clearly discernible elements. These elements are: (1) an aggregate of people, (2) a geographic locality, (3) a common culture, (4) a social system which guides and defines social behavior, (5) social structure, and (6) functional interdependency of individuals and groups. Any concept of community as an "ideal type" must, it should be em-

[8] *Ibid.*, pp. 8-11. Quotations are from pp. 10 and 9.

[9] Davis, Kingsley, *Human Society*, The Macmillan Company, New York, 1949, pp. 310-13.

[10] Sanderson, Dwight, *The Rural Community*, Ginn and Company, Boston, 1932, p. 481.

[11] Young, Kimball, *Sociology*, Second Edition, American Book Company, New York, 1949, p. 20.

phasized, do injustice to the relative significance of respective elements. From our point of view, a community is an aggregate of people exhibiting the following characteristics:

(1) A *geographic area,* whether wholly contiguous or not. A common living space for the group is an essential element of community.

(2) An *existence in time.* Communities, like all reality, exist in a framework of space and time. In some cases they may be studied as dynamic entities from origin to disappearance.

(3) A *culture* more or less commonly known and shared. Cultures vary in their *total* composition from community to community.

(4) A *social system* and a *social structure.* The behavior norms which make up the social system are cultural rather than inherited and people, therefore, are arranged into a social structure in terms of selected aspects of their total culture.

(5) *Functional interdependence.* In general, the people of a community are functionally related: individuals and groups make contributions to the persistence of the social system and social structure.

(6) An *awareness by the people that they have enough in common to set them off from other aggregates.* What they have in common, and do not share *in its totality* with other aggregates, is their pattern of living, their unique "web of life." This pattern is based in the physical aspects of the environment, the flatland, hill land, mountains, lakes, and rivers provided by nature, and the material things man himself makes, as well as the non-material values, interests, beliefs, customs, folkways, and mores which guide the behaviors of people, define their status and other structural arrangements, and determine the nature of their contributions as

individuals and groups to the persistence of the community. Connected with the awareness of separate identity is the sense of "belonging" most people feel toward their communities.

A human community is a functionally related aggregate of people who live in a particular geographic locality at a particular time, share a common culture, are arranged in a social structure, and exhibit an awareness of their uniqueness and separate identity as a group.

The fundamental distinction between the concepts of *society* and *community* is the geographical or territorial aspect of the latter. One may be a member of a society and not live in it (for example, be an American and live in France), but to be truly a member of a community implies residence. The community is, then, the "habitat of the society." [12] It is due largely to the recognition of the relationship of geographical locality and social organization that the study of community to such a considerable extent has been ecological. Our particular concern is with variations and uniformities in the social life of American communities, and throughout this volume, unless otherwise indicated, we shall use the term *community* to refer to distinguishable entities exhibiting some degree of common culture, interests, and social structure. Such entities vary in size from the smallest rural hamlet to the largest metropolis, and include states and regions. Community boundaries are sometimes roughly coincident with political boundaries; the reason for this is that political units often result from a real or imagined commonality of interests. Conversely, though, one of the continuing sources of common interests for the people of a community may be the fact that they live in the same political entity. A com-

---

[12] Park, Robert Ezra, *Human Communities,* The Free Press, Glencoe, Illinois, 1952, pp. 180-82.

munity may, however, cut across artificial political boundaries; the various regions of the country exemplify this situation. The people of the Rocky Mountain region, for example, have a functional relatedness and many common concerns: use and conservation of water, timber, minerals, and other natural resources, communication and transportation, and economic development in general. The city of Denver may be thought of as the economic (but not political) hub of a large community which not only includes Colorado, but cuts across state boundaries to include portions of Nebraska, Wyoming, Utah, and New Mexico; a vast web of social relationships unique in its totality is gradually evolving. The exact social structure of the Rocky Mountain region is not duplicated elsewhere. And, within the vague boundaries of this great community exist other, smaller communities, each a social entity in itself, varying to a greater or lesser degree from its neighbors.

4. Spatial Organization and Size

Community organization in the United States is currently of three major types: the *trade area,* the *urban community,* and the *region*.

(1) *The trade area.* The small town in the United States typically is a trade and service center. It merges into what has been called the trade area, a community composed of the town or village and the outlying district which it serves. Such communities are exemplified by the midwestern rural village and the surrounding farm families who habitually obtain in the village services and commodities not produced at home. Communities of this sort may also be found in recreational and resort areas where certain small towns offer specialized vacation facilities, sports, and other entertainment. While

agricultural trade areas are generally fairly stable of population and their people conservative in attitude toward change, resort communities often experience radical shifts in population and activity from one season to another.[13]

The small service center with its surrounding trade area is ordinarily dependent upon larger centers for many services and goods; if a larger city is not too far distant, residents of small villages or towns may carry on some "community" activities there. They may live in the small town, send their children to school and buy many daily necessities there, but seek recreation, employment, and professional services, and purchase large items in the city. The pull of the city in such matters as these probably varies inversely with the distance of the smaller community and directly with its own size.

(2) *The urban community.* Urban communities develop as a result of the growth of trade areas. The larger and more heavily populated the trade area becomes, the more specialized and concentrated the services supplied for it become.

In terms of population size, urban communities may be classified according to the system used by the United States Bureau of the Census. In 1950, there were 4270 *urban places,* incorporated and unincorporated towns or cities with a population of 2500 or more. *Urbanized areas* are cities of 50,000 or more population plus contiguous outlying territory related to the city by economic or commercial ties and having certain required population densities. (Towns of 2500 or more persons are included if they are incorporated and exhibit a minimum density of 100 or more dwelling units and 500 persons for each square mile; unincorporated areas are included if they have a density of 500 or more persons for each square mile.) Occasionally, territory which is not con-

[13] Cf. J. Ellis Voss, *Summer Resort: An Ecological Analysis of a Satellite Community* (Ph.D. dissertation), University of Pennsylvania, Philadelphia, 1941.

tiguous is included if it meets other requirements. *Standard metropolitan areas* are cities of 50,000 or more population and the outlying territories which are closely related to them economically. The 1950 Census reported that a total of 84,-500,680 people lived in 168 standard metropolitan areas. These large centers are growing in population size more rapidly than smaller communities: the total population of standard metropolitan areas increased 22.0 per cent from 1940 to 1950, while the increase for all other communities was 6.1 per cent for the same period. The rate of increase for the entire United States during the ten-year period was 14.5 per cent.

(3) *The region.* The federal government has used scores of different regional classifications; for most of its statistical work, however, the Bureau of the Census divides the United States into nine regions: New England, Middle Atlantic, South Atlantic, East North Central, East South Central, West North Central, West South Central, Mountain, and Pacific. These regions are distinguishable mainly by their ecological characteristics.

Social scientists have come to realize the potentialities of the study of these great communities and have developed "regional" emphases in a number of disciplines, notably sociology and economics. As the authors of a recent textbook put it, "One of the most important contributions that social science can make is to determine the relative degrees of interdependence of the various areas that are now separated by arbitrary political boundaries. Unless social organization coincides at least roughly with the 'natural areas' upon which the basic livelihood of a group depends, unnecessary hardships, tensions, and conflict are inevitable." [14] Nowhere is

[14] Lundberg, George A., Clarence C. Schrag, and Otto N. Larsen, *Sociology*, Harper and Brothers, New York, 1954, p. 138.

the truth of this statement more vividly illustrated than in the attempts by certain Western states—especially Colorado and California—to deal separately with a growing water shortage, a problem which can be met only by regional planning and action. Attempts to solve the problem through action by political units—states—thus far have been productive largely of threats, litigations, angry shoutings, and frustration.

5. Spatial Organization in Urban Communities

Three basic theories have been used to explain the spatial organization of cities, *concentric zone* theory, *sector* theory, and *multiple nuclei* theory.

(1) *Concentric zone theory.* Ernest W. Burgess based his zonal theory on studies of Chicago. This theory is that cities are organized in zones which may be schematically portrayed as concentric circles. Zone I is the central business district, the location of department stores, banks, large hotels, many business offices, and theaters. Adjacent to the central business district is Zone II, an area of deteriorated residences, rooming houses, slums, light manufacturing, and warehouses—a transitional area being encroached upon by business. Still farther from the center of the city is Zone III, made up largely of lower-class workmen's homes, mostly older buildings. Zone IV contains better type residences and expensive apartments. Zone V is the suburban district, generally lying partially within the political boundaries of the city and partially outside them; it is the location of middle-class homes, some large estates, and, here and there, commercial and industrial establishments.[15]

[15] Park, Robert E., Ernest W. Burgess, and Roderick D. McKenzie, *The City*, University of Chicago Press, Chicago, 1925, pp. 47-62. This chapter is by Ernest W. Burgess.

(2) *Sector theory*. From a study of rent differences in 142 cities, Homer Hoyt discovered that most cities have one or more high-rent areas which take the shape of wedge-shaped sectors from the center of the city to its environs; there are, also, high-rent districts in suburbs. The sector theory is that high-rent residential sectors tend to follow transportation lines from the center of the city toward its environs, and include areas of desirable natural features such as lake and stream frontages in demand for residential locations.[16]

(3) *Multiple nuclei theory*. Some observers have noted that cities have not one influential nucleus, but a number of them. The downtown business center is one nucleus, and dominates financial and trading relations; but there are other nuclei, such as districts of industrial plants, public and governmental services, and entertainment facilities, which exert influence in the life of the city. The multiple nuclei theory is that cities develop a number of such centers, each with its own specialized activity and special kind of influence; physical and social barriers to communication effectively separate these areas into communities which may develop identifying characteristics of language, occupation, recreation, race, or religion.

The figure on page 33 illustrates the concentric zone, sector, and multiple nuclei generalizations about the spatial organization of cities.

Most American cities exhibit in fragmentary form all three kinds of organization at the same time. The specific location of high-rent residences, slums, warehouses, light manufacturing, and business zones depends to some extent upon the particular kinds of communication barriers, natural

[16] Hoyt, Homer, *The Structure and Growth of Residential Neighborhoods in American Cities,* Federal Housing Administration, Washington, D.C., 1939, pp. 112-22.

THE STRUCTURE OF CITIES

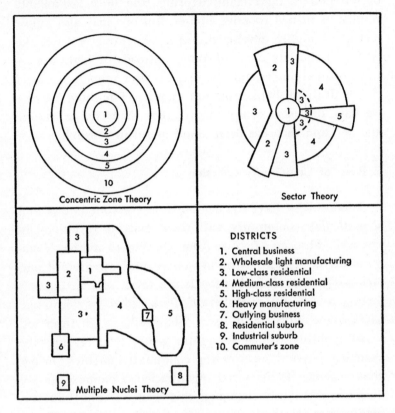

Concentric Zone Theory

Sector Theory

Multiple Nuclei Theory

DISTRICTS

1. Central business
2. Wholesale light manufacturing
3. Low-class residential
4. Medium-class residential
5. High-class residential
6. Heavy manufacturing
7. Outlying business
8. Residential suburb
9. Industrial suburb
10. Commuter's zone

from C. D. Harriss and E. L. Ullman, "The Nature of Cities," Annals
of the American Academy of Political and Social Science, *November,
1945, p. 12.*

or social, which are present as the city grows, and upon terrain features such as the location of hills and water bodies.
These factors, plus those growing out of human choice and
pure happenstance, have served to create individuality in the
spatial organization of cities. However, one may find a cen-

tral business zone by proceeding to the center of nearly any American city, and surrounding it is likely to be a district of warehouses, light manufacturing, and once fashionable residences turned rooming houses. But one may also follow sectors of highly developed, expensive property from the center of the city outward along railroads or highways toward open country; and one may discover numerous nuclei clearly distinguishable from one another. The three theories we have discussed complement rather than contradict one another, and each has been found useful in research.

6. Bases of Community Cohesion

Communities differ tremendously, as everyone knows, and a particular community will show marked variations in physical and social structure from one time to another. Communities, in general, urban as well as rural, are divided into "natural" areas. This division is the result of a sifting and sorting process which Robert E. Park called "segregation." Changing conditions of social life result in physical and social mobility, which segregates group from group; the changing physical form of the community, in turn, brings about changes in its social organization. Communities are dynamic, constantly changing; this change is not, however, random and disorderly, but patterned and predictable. There is enough about communities which is persistent to make it reasonable to say that they have both physical and social structures.

The reasons why community structures persist are many and varied, but all of them are founded in the nature of the social and cultural solidarity of their people. The question is, Why do people "stick together" in communities? or What are the sources of cohesion in communities?

The ultimate answers to these questions lie, quite likely, in the nature of the human organism; that, however, is outside the scope of this discussion. Social cohesion is of two basic kinds. Some communities are held together to a greater extent than others by common tradition and by relationships based on emotion and sentiment. The prototype of such a community is the "folk" society, a construct based upon anthropological descriptions of primitive tribes. As Robert Redfield described the folk society, it is characterized as (1) *small,* (2) *isolated and nonmobile* as to territory and communication, (3) *non-literate,* (4) *homogeneous,* with little division of labor, (5) *strongly patterned as to traditional behavior,* (6) *crescive,* that is, traditionally or not purposively created as to institutions, (7) with *little concern for objective systematization of knowledge, or science,* and (8) *familial* as to relations within the society, even outside the family, highly kinship organized, and composed of families rather than individuals.[17] In America, as elsewhere, such folk societies or communities probably never existed in anything approaching this "pure" form; in the first century of our national existence, however, many communities exhibited a cohesion founded to a considerable extent in tradition, myth, and sentiment which was fostered by the intimate contacts of small numbers of people living together in relative isolation from other groups. These communities, generally rural, or ethnic ones separated from others in a large city by barriers of language and custom, are on the decline in our country as in much of the Western world. For many decades, they have been giving way to a type of community characterized by another kind of cohesion—a "contractual" system based on impersonal, unsentimental, utilitarian arrangements de-

[17] Redfield, Robert, "The Folk Society," *The American Journal of Sociology,* January, 1947, pp. 293-308.

fining rights and responsibilities, privileges and obligations.

The prototype of the contractual community is the "urban" society. As characterized by Louis Wirth, this type exhibits the opposites of the folk society, but with particular emphasis upon: (1) *Size of population.* The greater the size, the wider the potential differentiation among people. This engenders competition and necessitates formal control mechanisms to furnish solidarity rather than solidarity growing out of affectional relations. Segmentalization of human relations, and the utilitarian aspect of such interrelationships is a characteristic of the urban society, as is the necessity of communication through indirect media. (2) *Density of population.* This reinforces numbers in diversifying men and activities; it increases the complexity of the social structure. Density tends to create sensitivity toward the world of artifacts and the removal of men from the world of nature. It fosters the spirit of aggrandizement between people who live and work together but have few or shallow emotional ties. (3) *Heterogeneity.* Class lines are broken down, and the class structure is complicated, as a result of mobility and density. The individual in the urban area has little opportunity to see his city as a whole; he can hardly conceive his own individual place in it.[18]

The old distinction between "urban" and "rural" life continues to be broken down in America by common sys-

---

[18] Wirth, Louis, "Urbanism as a Way of Life," *The American Journal of Sociology,* July, 1938, pp. 1-24. For classic discussions of the bases of social cohesion, see the following: Emile Durkheim, *On the Division of Labor in Society,* translated by George Simpson, The Macmillan Company, New York, 1933, especially pp. 70-229 (*organic* and *mechanical* solidarity); Ferdinand Tönnies, *Gemeinschaft und Gesellschaft,* translated by Charles P. Loomis and published under the title, *Fundamental Concepts of Sociology,* American Book Company, New York, 1940, especially pp. 37-116 (*Gemeinschaft* and *Gesellschaft*); Howard Becker, *Through Values to Social Interpretation,* Duke University Press, Durham, North Carolina, 1950, especially pp. 42-76, 248-80 (*sacred* and *secular* societies).

tems of rapid communication and transportation which create a uniformity not offset by whatever individuality results from the development of "specialized" communities. The evidence points to a broad generalization: American communities tend more and more, as time goes by, to be held together by recognition of functional interrelationships, specialization, division of labor, and the differences among people, while ties of community sentiment, tradition, and myth are slowly forgotten or extinguished. It is too early to know whether new myths are being created to replace the old ones.

SELECTED REFERENCES

Bernard, Jessie, *American Community Behavior,* The Dryden Press, New York, 1949. Chapter Two of this introductory text contains good discussions of factors which determine the location of communities and of community uniqueness.

Chinoy, Ely, *Sociological Perspective,* Studies in Sociology, Random House, Inc., New York, 1954. Chapter Four, "Social Groups," reviews concepts and definitions essential to the study of communities.

Hawley, Amos, *Human Ecology: A Theory of Community Structure,* The Ronald Press Company, New York, 1950. Hawley's volume is an interesting presentation of the general theory of ecology.

Hoyt, Homer, *The Structure and Growth of Residential Neighborhoods in American Cities,* Federal Housing Administration, Washington, D. C., 1939. The sector theory of urban development is fully presented in this book.

Lundberg, George A., Clarence C. Schrag, and Otto N. Larsen, *Sociology,* Harper and Brothers, New York, 1954. This introductory sociology textbook contains a good chapter on human communities.

MacIver, R. M., *Community,* Macmillan and Company, London, 1917. An early study of community which is still valuable, especially for its many definitions of sociological constructs.

MacIver, R. M., and Charles H. Page, *Society,* Rinehart and Company, New York, 1949. Chapter Twelve contains a good discussion of physical and psychological aspects of community, and Chapter Thirteen deals with urban and rural communities and regions.

Park, Robert Ezra, *Human Communities,* The Free Press, Glencoe, Illinois, 1952. This collection of essays and journal articles, posthumously published, presents many of Professor Park's major contributions to ecology and to sociology in general.

Park, Robert E., Ernest W. Burgess, and Roderick D. McKenzie, *The City,* University of Chicago Press, Chicago, 1925. Professor Burgess presents his zonal theory of urban growth in Chapter Two of this collection of ecological studies of Chicago.

Tönnies, Ferdinand, *Gemeinschaft und Gesellschaft,* translated by Charles P. Loomis and published under the title, *Fundamental Concepts of Sociology,* American Book Company, New York, 1940. This welcome English translation of Tönnies' classic essay is good reading for the student interested in the bases of community cohesion.

CHAPTER 3

Community Functions

1. Community Structure and Community Function

Social life is a process of interaction, and its essence is mutual awareness and the attempt of people to predict the behavior of others. When two or more persons become aware of the presence of the other or others and, consciously or unconsciously, predict their behavior, there exists a *social relationship,* one which denotes "the behavior of a plurality of actors in so far as, in its meaningful content, the action of each takes account of that of the others and is oriented in these terms." [1] Social relations are the province of the sociologist and, since they involve individual motivations, actions, and symbolic expressions, it is human behavior, broadly defined, which we study. We are concerned, to be sure, not only with the day-to-day activities of people living in communities, but with their myths, values, and institutions; but these can only be completely known through the study of the dynamic processes of social living.

The social life of any community is dynamic; so, too, is its

[1] Weber, Max, *The Theory of Social and Economic Organization,* translated by A. M. Henderson and Talcott Parsons, Oxford University Press, New York, 1947, p. 118.

structure. The structure of anything is a pattern of organization which persists in time. But all things in this world
change. John Dewey used the analogy of the structure of a
house when he wrote, "It is not something external to which
the changes involved in building and using the house have
to submit. It is rather an arrangement of changing events
such that properties which change slowly, limit and direct
a series of quick changes and give them an order which they
do not otherwise possess. Structure is a constancy of means,
of things used for consequences, not of things taken by themselves or absolutely." [2] Structure, then, can be conceived of
as an ordering of change; and, in scientific analysis, whatever
influences change is itself changed. There is no such thing
as the "unmoved mover." [3]

This does not imply that social change and social structure
are synonymous, for there is, in the structure of social relationships, a tendency to persist. As Georg Simmel put it,
"That destruction is easier than construction, is not un-
qualifiedly true of certain human relations, however indubi-
table it is otherwise." [4] The processes involved in the relationships of people may contribute to the persistence of the
structure—even in instances in which there is a disappearance of conditions without which the relationship would not
have been established in the first place.

An erotic relation, for instance, begun on the basis of physical
beauty, may well survive the decline of this beauty and its change
into ugliness. What has been said of states—that they are maintained only by the means by which they were founded—is only
a very incomplete truth, and anything but an all-pervasive prin-

[2] Dewey, John, *Intelligence in the Modern World*, edited by Joseph Ratner,
The Modern Library, New York, 1939, p. 1053.
[3] *Ibid.*, p. 1054.
[4] Simmel, Georg, *The Sociology of Georg Simmel*, translated and edited
by Kurt H. Wolff, The Free Press, Glencoe, Illinois, 1950, p. 380.

ciple of sociation generally. Sociological connectedness, no matter what its origin, develops a self-preservation and autonomous existence of its form that are independent of its initially connecting motives. Without this inertia of existent sociations, society as a whole would constantly collapse, or change in an unimaginable fashion.[5]

If function is defined as the contribution made by an item to the continuity of a given structure, and if it is agreed that structure may be conceived of as both persistence and an order of change, then it would follow that community function must have something to do with the processes which contribute to persistence and to change in the community or in the larger society of which the community is a part. These functional processes—the social life of the people—are vitally important in the study of a community as of any society. They are the forces which render a community a system of action, which cement groups together, and which bring about the development and operation of those systems of behavior norms which we call institutions.

There are various ways of studying the community. The community may be regarded (1) as merely an aggregate of people living in a geographic area, in which case a census study may be the method of investigation; (2) as a pattern of control mechanisms exerted on the lives of individuals, calling, for example, for a legal study, or (3) as a functional entity, requiring studies based upon the analysis of the interactions of individuals.[6] While we shall not ignore entirely the first two approaches, we shall maintain throughout this book a basic interest in the community as a dynamic, functioning system of the interrelationships of persons. We

[5] *Ibid.*, pp. 380-81.
[6] Park, Robert Ezra, *Human Communities*, The Free Press, Glencoe, Illinois, 1953, p. 118. Park is referring to the study of the city.

shall study patterns of values according to which people, singly and as groups, regulate their behaviors; we shall study institutions and their organization into social systems which have their being in the context of ordinary life interests and everyday affairs. We shall study the arrangements of community members in social structures, and be concerned with patterns of persistence and change in these structures. Finally, the processes of social life, the functional interrelations of people who maintain the structure, will receive our attention.

Community functions may be analyzed from three points of view. The first is focused on the functional contributions of the community to a larger society of which it may be a part. (This cannot be applied to all communities, since not all of them are parts of any larger society.) The second is concerned with the functional interrelations of people within a given community. The third deals with the functions of the community as a whole to the structures of its constituent groups and individual personalities. We proceed to a brief discussion of each of these.

2. Communities and External Functions

Most communities as units have *external* functions, that is, they contribute to the continuity and cohesion of the larger society. These external functions vary from one community to another, although it is possible to classify communities according to the type of function which predominates. Some communities, for example, broadly speaking, contribute primarily *things* and others primarily *services* to the larger society.

Communities whose functional emphasis is things include

factory communities in which are made industrial products of whatever kind and agricultural communities which produce mostly farm commodities. Service communities include, for example, university towns with their educational services and county seats and other governmental centers having control functions. These two general categories can be broken down into several subgroups according to the nature of the product or the service which is contributed. It is difficult to classify some communities in either of these categories, and, it must be emphasized, there is probably no community at all which exclusively contributes things *or* services, but not both. Some communities, however, emphasize one, rather than the other, and categorization is on the basis of this emphasis.

Communities whose basic function is to provide things which find their way into the larger society are clearly making a contribution to the continuity of the larger society. But that contribution is qualitatively different from the functions emphasized by the service community. In the former case, the contribution emphasizes the health, defense, physical comfort, and the socially determined psychological desires of people—in other words, the biological and psychological welfare or what is thought to be the biological and psychological welfare. In the latter case, the contribution is especially related to the maintenance of the social system. Speaking broadly, this is because a larger proportion of the people of service communities tends to be especially concerned with ideas and values, which are the stuff of which the fabric of the social system is woven. The people of communities whose functional emphasis is on things are typically somewhat less involved in their daily lives with value systems, or at least tend to spend less time on them as subjects of thought and discussion; these communities are for this reason less likely to have direct and significant effect upon the social system of the larger society.

No community, as we have noted, contributes solely things or services, for it is difficult if not impossible to separate material things from the ideas which go with them (a basic criticism, by the way, of the old classification of culture items into *material* and *non-material*). But it is clear that in a great many communities, one or another contribution strongly predominates. A town dominated by one large factory making, say, chocolate products, certainly makes external functional contributions which are significantly different qualitatively from those made by another town dominated by a large university. The distinction is useful for the analysis and comparison of external functions of different communities. The situation is somewhat less clear in the case of internal functions.

3. Communities and Internal Functions

The contributions made externally by communities to the larger society are analogous to the contributions made by the institutions, groups, and individuals within it to a specific community. Therefore, what is said here can be referred back on a different plane of analysis to the external functions of communities.

Every community is in itself a society, held together by a social system of rules and values. It must provide, internally, for the maintenance of its population, that is for the satisfaction of the biological necessities of life, sustenance, the protection of its members from crippling or fatal injury, and the replacement of those members who die. There must be some rules for a division of functions among the population, for every community has work which must be done if it is to survive. The people of any community must possess a degree of group solidarity, including some motivation of contact between members and motivation of resistance to strangers within a framework of mutual tolerance of one another. Finally, there must be provided procedures for ensuring the perpetuation of the social system, the normative patterns regulating behavior, the rules and regulations, the values and goals. These procedures include socialization techniques for the transmission of the social heritage from generation to generation.[7]

Later in this book, we shall study status and role, social classes, the family, church, school, economic, and governmental associations, and such processes as conflict and competition. Our fundamental question will continue to be: What functional contribution does the subject of our analysis make to the continuity of structure or its ordered change of the community of which it is a part?

Not every institution, group, or culture item has necessarily a positive community function; some of them result in negative or disruptive contributions. Others produce no significant functional contributions whatever. We shall also note and describe these dysfunctional and nonfunctional aspects of community.

4. Individual and Group Functions

Social groups of smaller size than an entire community or society generally have structures or arrangements of members in terms of institutionalized behavior norms. Personalities, too, can be conceived of as structures of attitudes, habits, and

[7] Based on Kingsley Davis, *Human Society,* The Macmillan Company, New York, 1949, p. 30. (See also Chapter 1 of this book.)

values—in general, tendencies to react to certain stimuli in specific ways. The structures of small groups and individual personalities, as well as of entire communities, are dynamic and *tend* to change in predictable and ordered fashion. Communities, as wholes, make contributions to the structures of their constituent small groups and personalities. These community functions are contributions to sustenance, expression, self-identification and ego-satisfaction, and integration and cooperation.[8]

(1) *Contributions to sustenance.* As our definition indicates (see Chapter 2), no community is self-sufficient, but a person can live his entire life in his community. Human organisms and personalities are "fed" and sustained in communities. Material goods are obtained and consumed there, and education and the satisfactions necessary for the persistence of personality structure are gotten there. People *survive* in communities.

(2) *Contributions to expression.* Most persons receive satisfactions from various kinds of self-expression, and this expression, for the most part, takes place in their own communities. People interact with one another, learn values, inherit or acquire statuses and roles, and, to a large extent, obtain in their communities a sense of purposive living.

(3) *Contributions to self-identification and ego-satisfaction.* People identify themselves with their communities, take pride in them, and develop a sense of belonging with respect to them. One source of ethnocentrism is the individual's identification of himself and his destiny with his community.

(4) *Contributions to integration and cooperation of individuals and groups.* One focus of group life is the community. People develop there a "consciousness of kind" and an

---

[8] This classification of community functions is from Joyce O. Hertzler, *Society in Action*, The Dryden Press, New York, 1954, p. 190.

understanding of the function of human differences (as expressed through division of labor) in the creation and maintenance of social cohesion. The "sense of community" is a factor in orderly social life, and it is in communities that social controls are effected.

5. Structure, Function, and Change

Some writers have pointed out that the positive and identifiable external functions of communities in America seem to be on a decline. "Physical growth and the efficient specialization of functions may be, in terms of community values, disintegrative," Baker Brownell asserts.[9] At the present time, rural communities especially seem to be transferring many of their functions, even agricultural production, to larger centers, or abandoning them altogether. This is due to such factors as new marketing methods, educational concentrations such as school consolidation, rapid communication, the remarkable geographic mobility of the American people, and to their generally expanding horizon of interest and concern. Many American communities are undergoing rapid changes; they are growing larger, both in population and geographic size; their functional contributions to the whole society are becoming more diffuse and difficult of definition; and their people are becoming related to one another more nearly as members of secondary groups than as members of primary groups. This is another way of saying that our communities, broadly speaking, are taking on the urban characteristics we alluded to in the previous chapter and which we shall consider in detail later. (See Chapter 5.) In certain other communities, such as residen-

---

[9] Brownell, Baker, *The Human Community,* Harper and Brothers, New York, 1950, p. 13.

tial suburbs, counter trends toward specialization in external functions can be observed.

While there may be what has been called "functional alienation," the removal of "operational control of a function from the community which it is supposed to serve," [10] this does not necessarily mean that the community is in fact disintegrating. Such movements as school consolidation, the widening of trade, sport, recreation, and public information interests are not sure signs that the community is dissolving. It is true that, as community contacts widen outward in ever growing circles, community functions, both external and internal, may grow beyond the contact of many or most members of the local community. But neither is this development an indication that the community as a system of relationships is being completely disorganized or destroyed. Specialization of function, either by communities as wholes or by groups and individuals, may result in fragmentation and compartmentalization of social life to the extent that a person may interact with others only in specific situations, for example, at work *or* at play *or* at church, but not at work *and* at play *and* at church. But, again, this does not necessarily mean the destruction of community. What it does mean is that the old, isolated *gemeinschaft-like* rural community is being replaced with a newer contract-based urban type of community which, with modifications we will discuss later in this book, appears to be well on the road to becoming the typical American local community.

The American local community, in sum, is dynamic. Its structure should be viewed not only as persistence in the arrangement of people relative to one another, but also as an ordering of change. The processes which make up daily life in the community are the social processes which are

[10] *Ibid.,* p. 15.

functional or dysfunctional to the community structure. And, as the internal functions of institutions, persons, and groups are contributions to a pattern of community persistence and predictable change, so the functions of the community as a whole are contributions to the persistence and ordered change of the structure of the larger society of which it may be a part.

SELECTED REFERENCES

Bernard, Jessie, *American Community Behavior,* The Dryden Press, New York, 1949. Chapter Twenty-six of this basic text on community deals with the relations of community and personality structure.

Chinoy, Ely, *Sociological Perspective,* Studies in Sociology, Random House, Inc., New York, 1954. Chapter Five, "Function and Change," is a good brief analysis of these two concepts.

Hertzler, Joyce O., *Society in Action,* The Dryden Press, New York, 1954. There is a concise discussion of the structure and function of communities on pages 189-90 of this text.

Simmel, Georg, *The Sociology of Georg Simmel,* translated and edited by Kurt Wolff, The Free Press, Glencoe, Illinois, 1950. In the chapter entitled, "Faithfulness and Gratitude," pages 379-95, the famous German sociologist probes the connections of social process and the persistence of social relationships.

PART TWO

The Community Culture

4

Cultural Aspects of Community Life

1. The Culture Concept as an Analytical Tool

Culture is that part of man's environment which he has himself created. As a concept, it is undoubtedly one of the most useful of the analytical tools developed by the social scientist. Culture truly is not more than a concept, for it has reality only in the minds of men. It is a kind of shorthand designation for the conveyance by two simple syllables of a whole host of different ideas. The culture concept has been adopted by all the fields of the social sciences and is used throughout the whole scope of social thinking to the end of thorough understanding of man.

Perhaps we are justified in saying that one of the most precious gifts the social scientist, most especially the anthropologist and the sociologist, can bestow upon his fellow men is this analytical tool, along with its concomitants of tolerant and sympathetic understandings of people unlike themselves and its repudiation of all absolutisms and arbitrarily drawn moral valuations of the social living characteristics of strangers.

Culture, as a concept, has helped take the social sciences from the sterile search for "absolute" truth into the search for relative truths. But culture as a scientific conceptual tool does not deny that there is order in social life; indeed, it is founded in such a proposition. The culture concept can be used to explain and compare one part of nature—including man and his life with other men—with other parts.

Culture is patterned. It consists of interrelated material objects and non-material ideas or values. It shows design; it exhibits repetitive and functionally interrelated connections of its elements or traits. A chair, for example, is more than the pieces of peculiarly shaped wood or iron, glue and nails. It is a patterned relationship of those material things plus a series of ideas concerning its functional connections with man. It is not a chair, but a pile of debris, if torn into its component physical parts and thrown into a corner; no more is it a chair without ideas concerning its appropriate use— it may, instead, be worshipped or used as a weapon by a primitive unacquainted with its potentialities as an object to sit upon.

So, too, a religious creed or the Declaration of Independence or a city ordinance are patterned; they would be meaningless as a jumble of words and syllables, each one in itself denoting an idea. It is only when the separate meanings are placed in a specific relationship one to another that we recognize the particular creed, the Declaration of Independence, or the city ordinance.

Besides the matter of pattern, which involves repetition and understandable interconnections of parts, all human cultures, despite their tremendous diversity, have much in common. Because of this, we can speak of "culture" as well as "cultures." Most social scientists would agree, perhaps, that culture as a concept rests upon the following series of assumptions:[1]

[1] The following paragraphs are based upon George Peter Murdock, "The Cross-Cultural Survey," *American Sociological Review*, June, 1940, pp. 361-70.

In the first place, culture is *learned,* rather than biologically transmitted. It is a plea for tolerance, then, for it bears the assumption that human beings behave *socially* only in ways which they have learned; in fact, this is one of the significant bases for prediction in the social sciences.[2]

Culture, secondly, is *inculcated,* passed on from generation to generation, a feat, it seems safe to say, no creature other than man can accomplish. Different societies use different techniques in accomplishing this inculcation, hence the significance of the comparison of child-rearing techniques and their influence on personality in different societies.

Moreover, people who adhere to a particular culture conceptualize or verbalize their habits into what are termed normative patterns, or social standards, or ideal norms. In this sense, then, culture is *ideational.* The individual's behavior more or less approximates that called for by the various cultural norms he knows about and accepts—or, conversely, he deviates to a greater or lesser degree from them.

Culture, furthermore, *gratifies human biological needs and those needs which are derived from them.* This does not imply that all culture items satisfy certain specific and definable biological needs. We know from modern psychology, however, that people perpetuate habits only so long as *some* gratification is forthcoming from the habitual behavior. Any culture item, therefore, will persist only if it involves satisfactions to all or some members of the society.

The *adaptability* of culture is readily apparent. Cultures change, but not in a random manner; rather, there is a process of adjustment to both the natural environment and the man-made environment which includes other cultures, as well as to the organic demands of humans.

[2] Cf. Douglas G. Haring, "Science and Social Phenomena," *American Scientist,* vol. 35, 1947, pp. 351-63, for a scholarly discussion of this point of view.

Finally, there is a trend in any culture toward *integration,* consistency, and wholeness. This, as Murdock carefully points out, is not a matter of perfect functioning or perfect balance, but, rather, a tendency toward an integration never fully attained, due in part to the fact that man is a choice-making creature and in part to accidents and occurrences outside the possibility of control by members of a society.

Culture, as an analytical concept carrying this load of meaning, is an essential instrument in the analysis of the American community.

2. Culture and Community Sentiment

The people of a society share a common culture, and persistence of a community as a social structure requires a degree of sentimental agreement among its members. There must be present in the minds of the people a system of emotional sentiments strong enough to regulate the individual's behavior so that, to some degree, he conforms to the needs of the group.[3] This means, not that persons are or need be altruistic, but that they *tend* to hold certain attitudes which are cohesive in their influences on the group as a whole. As R. M. MacIver and Charles H. Page observe, the following are the elements of community sentiment: a *we-feeling,* a *role-feeling,* and a *dependency-feeling.* These elements are manifested, respectively, in a person's identification of his own self-interest with the welfare of the community, in the individual's feeling that he has a function and a part to play in his group, and in his sense of dependence upon the community for the fulfillment of physical needs and the provision of the psychological security associated with

[3] Radcliffe-Brown, A. R., *The Andaman Islanders,* Cambridge University Press, London, 1922, pp. 233-34.

"home." [4] The existence of community sentiment is evident in the development of local folkways, customs, and language characteristics, in delight in gossip about neighbors and their activities, and in pride in the products, climate, or institutions of the community.[5] As Caryl Haskins puts it:

Man does not live by bread alone.

Variously phrased by philosopher, poet, and priest, how constantly has this thought been reiterated down the ages! How poignant is the testimony it offers that if we would truly understand the social life of man, we must look far beyond its biological aspects to those mental and spiritual elements which are of controlling importance within it.[6]

These "mental and spiritual elements" hold the society and the community together; moreover, they interest us more than physical forms and biological natures. The people in a community need not understand fully—or at all—the nature of the forces which produce social cohesion in their locality. Indeed, as Kingsley Davis remarks, commonly held sentiments may be more effective if not understood by the mass of citizens. This is most certainly the case with religions, which, it has been observed, tend to stand the more solidly for being scientifically unquestioned.[7] Understood or not, however, any kind of economic, social, or political system is organized under a set of rules. The processes of rule-making and rule-enforcing, furthermore, are the dynamics of organization. In a modern community, organization may be

[4] MacIver, R. M., and Charles H. Page, *Society*, Rinehart and Company, Inc., New York, 1949, pp. 292-94.

[5] *Ibid.*, pp. 294-95.

[6] Haskins, Caryl, *Of Men and Society*, George Allen and Unwin, Ltd., London, 1952, p. 200. Used by permission of W. W. Norton and Company, Inc., and George Allen and Unwin, Ltd.

[7] Davis, Kingsley, *Human Society*, The Macmillan Company, New York, 1949, pp. 518-19.

more or less conscious; in a primitive one, it is likely to be largely unconscious and unplanned.[8] The relative awareness of the functional consequences of social organizations may well be a mark of the modern, complex community.

3. Cultural Complexity and Structural Strains

One of the results of the ordering and patterning of community cultures is the limiting of the possible range of activities of individuals and groups. But this is only one of the effects of patterning. Another is involution, which may be defined as complication within pattern. In both primitive and modern societies, in both tribal communities and American rural and urban communities, there is a tendency to more complicated and elaborate culture configurations. Culture change sometimes takes the form of involution and may result in the elaboration of certain culture traits to a state of complexity which actually threatens the cohesion and very existence of a social group. An example of extreme involution is the elaboration of marriage tabus among certain primitives. It is reported that these tabus were so complex in one tribe that the men had no one at all to marry—a situation which must have been more than mildly dysfunctional for the community.[9]

In modern American communities, such extreme involution is rare, indeed, but the elaboration and overelaboration of such cultural matters as the school Christmas program and women's social club arrangements are phenomena common to everyone's experience. Furthermore, the elaboration of culture *may* be a source of competition and conflict (either

[8] Bernard, Jessie, *American Community Behavior,* The Dryden Press, New York, 1949, pp. 39-43.

[9] Linton, Ralph, *The Study of Man,* D. Appleton-Century Company, Inc., New York, 1936, p. 90.

intrapersonal or interpersonal) with respect to goals and the means for reaching them. This is because the results of cultural elaboration are usually (1) a larger number of socially approved goals which effectively compete with one another for the individual's allegiance and effort; (2) a larger number of socially disapproved goals which are in conflict with approved ends; (3) a larger number of socially approved means to approved goals, which are in effective competition for the individual's loyalty and effort; (4) a larger number of socially disapproved means which are in conflict with approved means; and (5) the consequently enhanced probability of the coupling of socially disapproved means with approved ends, of socially sanctioned means with unsanctioned goals, or even unsanctioned goals with disapproved means.

Increasing cultural complexity does not, however, always result in an increase in amount and intensity of social conflict and competition. One reason for this is that the people of a community typically elaborate their social controls in developing their general culture and pay greater attention to techniques for encouraging and enforcing behavior norms. But even with the provision of more controls, the increase during the last fifty years in size and complexity of many American communities, for example, has resulted in the creation of a larger variety of forms of conflict and competition, of means used, and of parties and objects involved. One manifestation of this change is the much wider use of government as a means of settling and regulating conflict than was the case forty or fifty years ago.

The concept of structural strain is a useful one for the analysis of the cultural system of a community. This construct refers to the destructive tendency which is the result of the play of contradictory forces upon the structure of any social group. There are many structural strains visited upon the community. There are strains which result from contradictions between goals and means in the occupational sphere, from contradictions in family life, and from combinations of the two. For example, Talcott Parsons points out that, historically, there has been an enhancement of the importance of the occupational status of the male as a determinant of family status in America. The increased dependence of family standing on the occupational prestige of the husband has deprived the wife of her place as a partner in what was once a *family* occupational enterprise having significance in status determination. Thus, we have introduced a strain in the "sex role structure of our society." [10]

Structural strains, then, are largely the results of social conflicts growing out of contradictions between goals and goals, and means and means, as held by different individuals and groups in a community. These strains are often stresses in the interrelations of institutions and are manifested in personality conflict, social conflict, or both.[11] We will have occasion to discuss the forms of such conflict later in this book. It suffices to say here that structural strains, as felt by the individual, are the consequences of (1) vagueness or ambiguity in definition of goals, (2) an emphasis on goals and a discrepancy between them and institutionally recognized means of achieving the goals and "technically efficient procedures" involved in the means, (3) an ambivalent attitude on the part of the individual toward a goal or other cultural item, (4) a discrepancy between immediate felt needs or goals and long-term needs or goals, and (5) pressure

[10] Parsons, Talcott, *Essays in Sociological Theory Pure and Applied,* The Free Press, Glencoe, Illinois, 1949, p. 223.

[11] Williams, Robin M., Jr., *American Society,* Alfred A. Knopf, New York, 1951, p. 491.

upon the individual to assume responsibility beyond his capacity.[12] Stresses in the personality structures of individuals may be manifested in personal behavior of a sort which tends to destroy the social arrangements of the community. It is through dysfunctional behavior of individuals that personality disorganization is related to community disorganization.

4. Cultural Uniformities and Variations among Local Communities

Local communities exhibit subcultures which are parts of the total culture of the American society. While there is great diversity of subcultures from region to region and from locality to locality, this diversity exists within a common framework. Uniformities and variations in technologies and material things among communities are fairly readily observed. But similarities and differences in folkways, values, and idea systems are more difficult to observe and, consequently, not easily depicted. Yet, the quest for knowledge of the values of our society and of specific communities is a fascinating and important one.

American local communities are related to one another, and to some degree, bound into an integrated "great" community not only through interdependency with respect to material sustenance, transportation networks, and communication facilities, but through a relatively common adherence of their people to a set of ideas and values. This unity of ideals has been variously called the "American creed," "American dream," and the "American spirit," among other names. The characterizations of the American dream made

[12] The author is indebted to Professor David L. Hatch, Madison College, for this analysis.

by astute observers of our way of life show considerable agreement.[13] An example of these characterizations is Ralph Henry Gabriel's statement that Americans have traditionally shown a pattern of faith which is characterized by (1) nationalism, (2) the idea of a fundamental law above and beyond the meager rules of men, (3) the doctrine of the free individual, and (4) the philosophy of progress. These doctrines are represented by certain symbols, the outstanding of which are the "cult of the Constitution," representing nationalism, the "cult of the Supreme Court," as a substitute for the church to represent stability, and the "Lincoln cult," to represent the mission of America and the doctrine of the free individual, the fundamental law, and even the Constitution. Gabriel adds that attachment to the idea of nationalism has been in our time magnified out of all proportion to the other values, which are now seriously endangered by our apparent willingness to sell our freedom for the sake of security.[14] We shall deal with this problem later in this book. (See Chapter 14.)

There is probably a degree of sentimental attachment on the part of most of the people of every American community to the ideals we have named above, and to some extent, most people probably orient their personal behavior to them. Formal and informal social controls are also used to encourage individuals to conform to behavior patterns im-

[13] For examples of analysis of the "American dream," see Hector St. John de Crevecoeur, *Letters from an American Farmer*, J. M. Dent and Sons, Ltd., London, 1912; Merle Curti, *The Growth of American Thought*, Second Edition, Harper and Brothers, New York, 1943; Harold J. Laski, *The American Democracy*, Viking Press, New York, 1948; Vernon Louis Parrington, *Main Currents in American Thought*, Harcourt, Brace and Company, New York, 1930; Alexis de Tocqueville, *Democracy in America*, Galaxy Edition, Oxford University Press, New York, 1947.

[14] Gabriel, Ralph Henry, *The Course of American Democratic Thought*, The Ronald Press Company, New York, 1940, pp. 414, 417; see Chapter 30 for symbolism and Chapter 31 for tenets of the American democratic faith.

plied in these ideals. In this way, the cultural ethos of America becomes a powerful force in the creation of uniformities in social life among communities. Local variations in social behavior may sometimes profitably be studied as divergences from the American dream, a construct useful, therefore, as a basepoint from which to make comparisons, interpretations, and value judgments regarding specific individual or group actions.

The values and behavior patterns associated with the industrialization of American communities are a further example of cultural elements which create uniformities in the social life of American localities and which help to integrate them into a functioning "American community." One author, Paul Meadows, goes so far as to call industrialism a "cultural system" in its own right. He observes that industrialism, as a system of culture, involves (1) a "technic stage" which is organized around machine production, (2) technology, particularly a core of specialized knowledge, tools and machines, and motivations to exchange activities, and (3) a certain type of organization of people and things; this "relational pattern" includes a factory system, a cooperative organization of the factors involved in production, and community arrangements to provide sustenance and control the behaviors of individuals.[15]

We do not imply that industrialism is exclusively an integrating factor in local communities, for it is obvious that many of the basic conflicts of our time are between owners over such matters as the scale of business enterprise, between owners and non-owners, and between labor and management. Perhaps most community conflicts grow out of the shallowness and segmental nature of personal contacts

[15] Meadows, Paul, *The Culture of Industrial Man,* University of Nebraska Press, Lincoln, 1950, pp. 9-13.

which are the results of industrialism.[16] Certainly the feeling of insecurity of many modern Americans, who are "lost in a crowd," is a basis of personality disorders. Even so, as different local communities are increasingly industrialized and the rural-urban distinction disappears, they tend to take on an even greater cultural uniformity, partly through possession of similar technologies and organizations of men and machines, and partly because they have all had to provide for survival while undergoing the process of being industrialized.

Common systems of transportation and communication and similar patterns of religion and education, for example, are at the same time reflections of likenesses in basic culture among local communities and creators of such similarities. Yet each American community sustains a unique *total* subculture, and, due to its own particular geographic location, population composition, history, and external functions, probably always will. Even so, the industrialization of the nation, with its consequent standardization of consumption and of style, is likely to continue the seemingly inexorable trend to uniformity in cultural patterns and, consequently, in social life from one community to another.

SELECTED REFERENCES

Bernard, Jessie, *American Community Behavior,* The Dryden Press, New York, 1949. Chapter Four, "Rules of Community Behavior: Organization," is a discussion of the normative patterns which regulate behavior in the community.

Gabriel, Ralph Henry, *The Course of American Democratic Thought,* The Ronald Press Company, New York, 1940. A delightfully readable and thoughtful presentation of the history of American democratic thinking. The chapters on the American democratic faith are especially valuable.

[16] *Ibid.,* pp. 25-35.

Kroeber, A. L., and Clyde Kluckhohn, *Culture: A Critical View of Concepts and Definitions,* Papers of the Peabody Museum of American Archaeology and Ethnology, vol. XLVII, no. 1, 1952. Presents and discusses the value of scores of definitions of culture used by anthropologists and sociologists.

Linton, Ralph, *The Study of Man,* D. Appleton-Century Company, Inc., New York, 1936. Contains excellent introductory chapters on the culture concept.

Meadows, Paul, *The Culture of Industrial Man,* University of Nebraska Press, Lincoln, 1950. Industrialism is considered as culture system in this thought-provoking collection of essays.

Miller, Delbert C., and William H. Form, *Industrial Sociology,* Harper and Brothers, New York, 1951. Chapter Twenty-one, pp. 789-828, is an analysis of the interdependence of industry and community.

CHAPTER | 5

Patterns of Community Change

1. Cultural Change and Social Change

As Florian Znaniecki has noted, it took natural scientists centuries to do away with the old idea of the antithesis between stability and change. "They discovered that nothing is changeless in the world of nature; all stability is relative, depending on definite conditions. But they found that change is also relative; it is impossible to investigate changes without defining what is changing." [1] The only way "cultural scientists" can also eliminate this antithesis in their work is to combine the study of ideas with the study of human action, for these two are inseparably related in structural stability and change; ideas and actions mutually affect each other. [2]

The study of the processes of culture change and of social change is one way of approaching this problem, for the first is primarily concerned with changes in ideas and idea systems, and the latter refers especially to changes in the social structure and patterns of human action.

[1] Florian Znaniecki, *Cultural Sciences*, University of Illinois Press, Urbana, Illinois, 1952, p. 280.
[2] *Ibid.*, p. 281.

Culture is both valuation and expression, and it is the nature of values and expressions to change. The values which appeal to one generation do not appeal to another, and there is alteration, also, in the "style," that is, the modes of expression of the culture.[3] Change occurs because individual human beings learn and unlearn the patterns of which cultures are composed. New culture traits are introduced, and, if accepted by the people of a society, may displace old traits or be relatively permanently added to the old culture.

New patterns are originated through inventions and discoveries. An invention is a new application of previous knowledge, and a discovery an addition to knowledge. Discoveries are often unimportant in bringing about culture change until they are put to work through inventions. The *discovery* of atoms, for example, was basic in the long ladder of research, but it was an *invention* which resulted in the atomic bomb.[4]

Culture does not accumulate on the analogy of a snowball rolling down a hill, growing larger and larger with every yard it travels. The people of a society accept an addition to their culture in terms of its meaning in the context of the pre-existing culture. By the same token, they "slough off" culture items which are no longer desired or useful. Furthermore, the adoption of a new trait, however insignificant, generally results in modifications in both the existing culture and in the newly adopted trait. People find it easier to accept additions which are relatively insignificant than to change the very foundation ideas of their culture. Alterations in the basic values and central ideas of a culture are made, but

[3] MacIver, R. M., and Charles H. Page, *Society*, Rinehart and Company, Inc., New York, 1949, p. 517.
[4] Gillin, John, *The Ways of Men*, D. Appleton-Century Company, Inc., New York, 1948, pp. 533-34.

such changes are ordinarily more gradual than is the case with changes in more superficial aspects of the culture.[5]

Culture change involves change in idea systems, in the arts, and philosophy. Culture changes, some sociologists hold, are essentially *trendless,* taking place in spurts and in unpredictable directions.[6] Other sociologists, however, feel that the factors involved in culture change can be described and scientifically predicted.

A somewhat more adequate analysis defines culture change as alterations in any phase of human culture, including technological, artistic, and value systems. Social change, on the other hand, includes only those alterations which take place in the social organization or structure of a society or community. Social change, therefore, is closely related to culture change, but not inevitably tied to it. Some culture changes, such as phonetic changes in language, for example, have little effect on the interrelations of people, that is, on social structure and social function.[7]

One modern sociological approach to the study of societies and social change is to consider a social group an equilibrium, a balance of forces and processes; change, by definition, is a change from a state of equilibrium. If equilibrium is totally destroyed, it is said that social disorganization has taken place. Sociologists undoubtedly borrowed the concept of equilibrium from mechanics and physics. It is, broadly speaking, a useful scientific construct but has a limited value when applied to community. There is little valid evidence that such a balance actually exists; it is impossible to measure the

[5] See John F. Cuber, *Sociology,* D. Appleton-Century Company, Inc., Third Ed., New York, 1955, pp. 147-52, and Ralph Linton, *The Study of Man,* D. Appleton-Century Company, Inc., New York, 1936, pp. 295, 359.

[6] Rudolph Heberle, "A Sociological Interpretation of Social Change in the South," *Social Forces,* October, 1946, pp. 9-15.

[7] Davis, Kingsley, *Human Society,* The Macmillan Company, New York, 1949, p. 622.

forces which, through opposition, maintain a social equilibrium. Indeed, Robert Park quotes Charles Elton to the effect that the so-called "balance of nature" hardly exists at all in the relations of plants and animals in the biotic community. There is, to be sure, always a tendency to this state, but the trend seems generally to be interrupted by unforeseen events or forces.[8] The structural-functional approach to the study of human relations makes use of the construct of social equilibrium, but also pays attention to the "strains and stresses" which appear in any social structure.

Social change is brought about by a complexity of factors in human interrelations. Changes—slow or fast—in one aspect of community life, or in the biophysical setting in which it exists—may produce other alterations—fast or slow—in other aspects of social life. Change can mean shifts in social organization or it can mean social disorganization, that is, it can mean alteration of the structure and the functional process or it can destroy the structure and function. In the past hundred years in America, for example, some communities have been completely disorganized and have disappeared. Other communities have experienced profound structural and functional alteration, but still persist. The most typical change has been, perhaps, away from the emotion-oriented *gemeinschaft-like* community and toward the rational, contract-oriented *gesellschaft-like* society; or, put in different words, a shift from the "communal" to the "associational" society.[9]

[8] Park, Robert Ezra, *Human Communities,* The Free Press, Glencoe, Illinois, 1952, p. 149.
[9] Wilson, Logan, and William L. Kolb, *Sociological Analysis,* Harcourt, Brace and Company, New York, 1949, pp. 766, 847.

2. The Rate of Change

Sociologists have written much about the *rate* of social change. We can say that in our time, social change is rapid, and that many of the social control forms of our earlier communities have been obliterated in recent years.[10] One is hard put, however, to measure or compare rates of change *in general* from one society to another or in one society from time to time. Comparison can be made of rates of change with regard to specific things, such as the proportional increase of auto registrations to population, but measuring units for comparing instances of what is commonly meant by the very general term, "social change," are conspicuous by their continued absence.[11]

All sorts of deterministic theories of social change have been advanced. None of them—whether based on a social factor (such as economic relations) or nonsocial factor (such as geography)—is entirely satisfactory as a scientific explanation. Each of them is partly true, but only partly. Many variables are always present in social change. Perhaps only through the accomplishment of a complete and thorough analysis of the total social situation, the whole complex of human interrelationships in which change is occurring, can anyone have a chance of understanding the process. The local community is a convenient unit for the study of change because it is large enough to provide a sufficiently complex

[10] See Howard W. Odum, *Understanding Society,* The Macmillan Company, New York, 1947, especially pp. 532-33.

[11] Two recent exploratory attempts to effect such measurement are worthy of mention; they indicate that such measurement techniques may be on the way. Both utilize the study of cultural "meanings" and their origination dates. Edward L. Rose, "Innovations in American Culture," *Social Forces,* March, 1948, pp. 255-72, and Robert John Potter, *An Analysis of Culture Growth in Eight American Economic Activities* (unpublished M.A. thesis), University of Colorado, Boulder, 1954.

set of social relations, and yet not so large as to be incomprehensible to the researcher.

Some social philosophers have presented man as the unwitting, helpless, hapless pawn of social forces he cannot understand. The Spenglers and the Sumners to the contrary, there is no monopoly of objective evidence supporting the idea that man is completely at the mercy of unforeseen social forces. There is no need to be fatalistic about change even though it would be the better part of wisdom to admit that we have no evidence either that man can *completely* control the rate and direction of change.[12]

Whether we do, in fact, fully understand at this time the nature and the rate of change in our social structure and processes, we are able to understand, as Ralph Linton points out, that varying conditions of change—insofar as we understand them—do make a difference in the lives of people in society. Societies living under "new or changing conditions" are usually characterized by all sorts of achievable statuses and by opportunities for social mobility. But, as societies become "adjusted to their settings," the social value of individual thought and initiative becomes less and statuses tend to become ascribed, that is, there is a trend toward increasing rigidity of the system of social stratification.[13] This characterization applies to many American communities. Rapidity of social change—whether occasioned by the newness of the community in a frontier wilderness of forest and field or the sudden influx of a new population group or new occupational opportunities occasioned by a new defense plant—brings with it opportunities for individuals to rise in the social scale. Conversely, the adjusted community,

---

[12] See Sidney Hook, *The Hero in History,* The John Day Company, Inc., New York, 1943, pp. 246, and following, for an analysis of these extreme views.

[13] Linton, Ralph, *op. cit.,* pp. 129-30.

existing year after year with little significant change, usually experiences the creation of rigid social barriers between different groups in the population. The ultimate end of the process may possibly be a rigidly stratified system of classes based on economic or other social valuations.

3. Factors in Community Change

Structural alterations are generally more readily observable than changes in ideas and value systems. Because of this, the analysis of community change may logically begin with a study of the dynamics of population, territory, family size and organization, schools, churches, economy, and government. The analysis then proceeds to the study of change in the functions of such associations and of the institutions related to them. Scientific analysis requires, however, study not only of changes in the obvious, recognized and expected manifest functions, but in the concealed latent functions of an association as well. This, admittedly, is difficult with present social science research tools, but, as Merton points out, social "engineering" cannot even exist—there can be little success with social planning for change—unless understanding of latent functions is attained.[14]

Changes in structure and functioning of associations, such as church or school, are often understood or at least felt directly by individuals. Alterations in the structure of institutions, such as religion or education, on the other hand, take on a strongly impersonal quality. In general, social change in the modern, complex community exhibits an impersonal character; it may appear inexorable to the individual. "Vast social forces are continually in operation regardless of the motivation of individuals. Whether individuals or

[14] Merton, Robert K., *Social Theory and Social Structure*, The Free Press, Glencoe, Illinois, 1949, p. 80.

groups meet with success in their actions depends upon how these forces reinforce or thwart their intentions." [15]

The impersonality of social change can be overemphasized, however. As our analysis will show, there are also personal and intended elements in community change. People create change by willing it and by positively creating it.[16] Indeed, people can even bring about change by believing in its coming and acting accordingly; an example is the failure of a bank occasioned by a run on it by depositors who somehow come to believe it is about to fail. A perfectly sound bank may collapse under these conditions. As a matter of fact, the history of American communities is replete with such instances.[17]

The factors involved in community social and culture change are many and varied. The following classification is a useful typology for an analysis of the changes which have occurred and are occurring in American communities.[18]

(1) *Psychological factors.* On the psychological level, a culture is in part a structuring of habits and customs built around a stimulus-reward arrangement. For the individual, then, community change refers to changes in this structuring, and is, accordingly, based on alterations (a) in the stimulus factor leading to acceptance of a particular structuring of culture, (b) in reward conditions with respect to a particular custom or habit, and (c) in biological or psychological drives. In other words, a custom may be changed because the situations which cause an individual to react in a particular way are no longer present or are substantially

---

[15] Bloch, Herbert A., *Disorganization: Personal and Social,* Alfred A. Knopf, New York, 1952, p. 22.

[16] *Ibid.,* pp. 23-24.

[17] Cf. Robert K. Merton, "The Self-Fulfilling Prophecy," *op. cit.,* pp. 179, and following.

[18] This classification is adapted from John Lewis Gillin and John Phillip Gillin, *Cultural Sociology,* The Macmillan Company, New York, 1948, pp. 562-76.

altered; it may be changed because rewards are no longer available for its acceptance; and it may be changed because an acquired drive is altered. Such psychologically oriented analysis as this must be a part of every thorough analysis of community change.

(2) *Environmental factors.* Changes in the environmental factors of a community often profoundly alter the social structure. These changes may be of two types: natural, such as climatic or geographic alteration by wind or rain; and man-made—for example, the creation of new physical features, such as dams, buildings, dry land through swamp drainage, or the destruction of native fauna and flora.

(3) *Population factors.* Size and quality of population is another factor related to community change. Populations change with regard to numbers and density in the space-habitat, sex and age composition, and racial or other genetic composition. Changes in these characteristics affect in turn the stimulus situations mentioned above, the types of response involved in particular social situations, or the motivations and values of a community.

(4) *Sociocultural factors.* A social system is always in somewhat imperfect adjustment and balance; strains and stresses in its structure appear to be a part of every community. These stresses, of course, give rise to all sorts of structural and functional changes in a community. For example, as has been previously noted, the strain between the family values, including broad kin relations, and the demands of our economic system has already resulted in most communities in the creation of the isolated family of husband-wife-children as the usual American type.

(5) *Personality factors.* The researcher, although he ought to be wary of an overemphasis on the "great man" theory of history, cannot afford to ignore the impact of the forceful

and inventive personality as a factor in creating change in the community. No community is ever quite the same after having produced a strongly deviant individual who, by virtue of strong leadership abilities, influences his fellows for good or evil.

(6) *War.* War is a significant element in social change. War disturbs most of the social relationships and adjustments people establish in the peacetime community. Families are broken and their members scattered; schools, churches, and other formal service organizations find themselves confronted by a bewildering variety of new problems and functions; and old patterns of thinking and acting must give way to the new and the expedient. No one who has lived through a major war and seen its effects can doubt its effectiveness as a factor in community change.

4. Patterns of Recent Community Change

Whatever the sources of social change in the community, whatever the variations in its rate, the general outline of its direction to date is clear. These changes have been analyzed in great detail in hundreds of thousands of words of print. But one has only to reflect for a moment upon the comparative differences in the pattern of life of any ordinary person of so short a time as a generation ago and an individual living in today's frenetic world to realize anew the magnitude of community change: in the material base of group life; in the degree of individual mobility; in the expansion of individual contact and experience; and in the increasing superficiality of contact in the urban community.[19]

---

[19] See James H. S. Bossard, "Social Change in the United States," *The Annals* of the American Academy of Political and Social Science, September, 1949, pp. 69-79, for the detailed analysis upon which this section is based.

(1) *Changes in the material base.* These changes are centered about the use of natural power. Labor-saving devices of many sorts have been invented and put to work; the most spectacular of these facilitate human transport and communication. The development of the airplane, radio, motion picture, television, and the automobile, to name a few of the more obvious, has brought remarkable alteration in community life in a very short time. Auto registrations doubled in one generation; the miles flown by planes tripled in a short seven years; television moved from experiment to commonplace in the homes of many millions in a scant half decade.

Such changes in the material base have resulted in significant alteration in the non-material aspects of community life, too: greater geographical mobility—and serious conflict between the patterns of the once-stable community and the new rootlessness of individuals on the move; a magnificent expansion in the scope and breadth of individual contact and interaction; higher productivity of individuals in general and in proportion to time worked; a decrease in self-employment and other phases of individual self-sufficiency, and a corresponding increase in dependence of the individual on centralized business and other formal organizations.

Rapid—sometimes frightening—changes in the material base have placed the community, its work, the activities of its people, the stimuli they experience, and the problems they face in a constant state of revision and alteration. The job of continual adjustment to such change is, in itself, a difficult and often perplexing task for the people of most contemporary American communities.

(2) *Individual mobility.* One of the most obvious characteristics of the modern American is his geographic and social mobility. In part, this mobility is due to the nature of the

material changes we have just discussed, which place a premium upon specialization in the occupational system.

In contrast to the migrations of early man, which typically took place in the movements of whole families, tribes, or clans, the modern American migrates as an individual. Thus, a community is likely to have a constantly shifting, fluid population. The small, isolated family, too, is exceptionally mobile in our day. Of recent years, even homes have come to be bought, sold, and swapped on a short-term basis after the pattern of new and used auto trading; if this does not provide enough mobility, one may even attach his house to the rear of his car and take it with him.

Even before World War II, some four million Americans were each year migrating from one state to another in search of often illusory fortunes. Movements from the country to the city were—and are—proceeding at a rapid rate: from 1920 to 1935, more than forty-six million persons emigrated from rural to urban communities. The dislocations of the last war, many of which are in some respects with us still, further enhanced the mobility of the American people.

Psychologically and sociologically, such extreme mobility, with its rootlessness and restlessness, is of great importance. In general, the severance of old community ties founded in bonds of sympathy and affectional response among relatively small groups of people has a disorganizing influence on both the personality systems of individuals and the systems of social values of communities.

(3) *Expansion of individual experience.* The changes in the material world, most notably in communication and transportation, and the increased social and geographic mobility of the individual, have resulted in a magnificently enlarged scope of social interaction for millions of Americans. Communities themselves have grown as the mental and experien-

tial horizons of their members have grown. The press, radio, television, and the movies have all contributed to making a large world small, or, to put it another way, they have all had a part to play in enlarging the community. The result is that today much more than in earlier generations we think and plan in a generally expansive way, whether in terms of government, social actions, or personal ambition. We sometimes concern ourselves with world situations and ignore aspects of our community or neighborhood life, with the improvement of world government while our local government remains less than wholly admirable, or we worry over world housing conditions while ignoring the slums in our own communities. Whether this expansiveness in current thought is to prove itself good or bad from the point of view of the survival of American community life remains to be seen.

(4) *The trend to urbanization.* More than three-fifths of our people now live in urban communities and another large fraction near enough to feel the influence of city centers. The result is that the contacts made in secondary groups have become more important in the lives of millions than those made in the primary groups in which they spend a steadily decreasing proportion of their time. In the urban society there is a greater degree of individuation and specialization in almost every way, occupationally, recreationally, and even in the development of personality types. Social relationships tend to become contractual, a matter of mutual rights and obligations rather than the matter of sympathy and emotion more nearly characteristic of earlier rural communities. Individualism in the urban community is typically accompanied by a superficiality in personal relations which leaves the person with a sense of rootlessness and frustration. No more significant problem in community study exists than

the problem of how to maintain individuality and at the same time deepen and strengthen the emotional ties people can only develop in small, intimate associations.

5. Cultural Lag in the Community

Few concepts in sociology have had wider general acceptance and use than William Fielding Ogburn's "cultural lag," and few concepts have had more serious misunderstanding and misuse. In his book, *Social Change,* first published in 1922, Ogburn spells out in detail his theory of change. The parts of modern culture, he says, do not change at the same rate, thus requiring constant adjustment.

The most serious source of strains and stresses in a culture system is occasioned by the differences in the rates of change (or the differences in the rates at which the people of a society are willing to accept change) between the material aspects of culture and what Ogburn calls the "adaptive" culture, that is, the mores and techniques by which the material is used. The adaptive culture, due to the reluctance of people to accept rapid changes in it, tends not to be adjusted to the material. The changes in the two aspects are not perfectly synchronized and there is a time lag between the occurrence of material changes and the adjustments in the adaptive culture which caused them.[20]

Adjustment in cultural systems, therefore, is always imperfect. The usual criticisms that the rates of change in material and adaptive culture are impossible of comparison and that the two categories are overlapping and not clearly defined are pertinent ones. However, it is obvious that a great many of the stresses and strains in the structure of any

[20] Ogburn, William Fielding, *Social Change,* Viking Press, Inc., New York, 1950, pp. 200, and following.

American community are due to social change. Sometimes the way to relieve the stress caused by a specific social change is to be found only in a second alteration, and during the time lapse between them, conflict may develop. "Community problems" are, often as not, the product of conflict which arises in this fashion.

6. The Nature of Community Problems

While many citizens are, and ought to be, interested in world affairs and world problems remote from them, it is on those occasions when people are uprooted from their daily routines that they become most completely involved in an emotional way. The crises which affect us most severely are likely to occur in the family, the neighborhood, and the community. Even so great a "world issue" as a war becomes of psychological importance to most people only when their families, their communities, or some other groups of close contact become directly concerned. This is because the abstract "social problem" has become a personal problem for certain individuals and those with whom they have emotional bonds.

A social problem, whether involving nations, one nation, or a community, is whatever a considerable number of the people involved recognize it to be. Sociologists generally apply the concept of *social problem* to groups not smaller than the neighborhood or local community. Furthermore, any social problem—whether Nazi aggression during the nineteen-thirties, housing on a national scale at the end of World War II, or race difficulties in Cicero, Illinois—involves some real or fancied deviation from widely accepted social norms. Thus, our cultural values become involved in every social problem, not only in reaching an agreement as to what is a problem, but, first, in the origin and development of the problem itself, and, last, in the usual conflict over proposals for its solution. Objective conditions alone (for example, poor educational facilities in a rural community or the presence of a few Negroes in a predominantly white residential district) do not in themselves constitute a social problem. There must be conflict of some sort, and the source of conflict is, ultimately, to be found in the simple fact that different people—as individuals and as groups—do not all accept the same values and goals.

Every community problem shows a clearly defined course of development through time.[21] There come to be, in this order, a degree of awareness of the problem, attempts at policy determination, and attempts at reform.

(1) *Awareness of the conditions.* One requisite of a social problem in a community is an agreement by some people that objective conditions are endangering some social value or values which they hold dear. The threat may be to a goal itself or to a means of striving for the goal. Awareness of this threat is usually expressed in statements of concern over existing conditions and the future of the community, and are ordinarily unorganized at first. Gossip and the complaining of neighbors may shortly be reinforced by planned publicity programs, newspaper editorials, and special radio or television appeals. In the later stages of the development of a serious problem, the matter may be, and usually is, taken up and discussed by people holding official position or membership in community government, the schools, churches, and in smaller private organizations, such as social clubs or labor unions. Thus, awareness of conditions which endanger a

---

[21] The following paragraphs are based on the discussion of this subject by Richard C. Fuller and Richard R. Myers, "The Natural History of a Social Problem," *American Sociological Review,* June, 1941, pp. 320-29.

social norm typically follows a pattern of outward expansion from one or a few individuals to many individuals and conscious discussion and action among a constantly growing number of persons acting through formal organizations.

(2) *Attempts at determination of policy.* Once a considerable number of people in a community become aware of the existence of conditions threatening a value they cherish, there soon develop serious differences over the means of ameliorating the situation. Solutions are proposed from every side, by individuals as interested citizens, by persons who draw support from official office, and by organization leaders who present the official policies of those they represent. Serious conflict and much ill will may develop among people whose only important differences are over the means best suited to a goal they agree upon. Such conflict may generate further social problems for a community. Various interest groups typically square off to debate the alternative policies and to attempt to influence the government officials or private citizens who must ultimately make decisions about the problem.

(3) *Attempts at reform.* In the last stage of the development of any social problem in the community, formally organized units or agencies attempt to put in force the policies finally agreed—or partially agreed—upon. Responsibility may be assigned to legal agencies of government, such as a city council or a community health officer, or some specially created public unit; reform may also be attempted by private organizations, such as churches or chambers of commerce.

It is apparent that these three stages in the history of most social problems in the community overlap one another; policy determination on certain aspects of the problem may have taken place before there is complete awareness of the total conditions, and policy decisions are likely to be called for throughout the period of reform.

7. A Case Study of Change in Community and Society

Caliente, Nevada, is a small desert town, built years ago as a stopping place for the servicing of steam locomotives which cross the arid country. The town has always been almost entirely dependent on the railroad, for the other resources of the area are not sufficient to support its population. For many years, Caliente was an ordinarily prosperous and stable American community; since World War II, however, two reasonably simple technological changes—the invention of high tensile steels making possible high pressure boilers and fast steam locomotives, and the even more recent trend toward the use of diesel engines—have brought far-reaching social changes which have threatened the disorganization of the community and have created social problems the people had previously never had to face. W. F. Cottrell describes Caliente and its problems as follows:[22]

Following World War II, the high tensile steels developed to create superior artillery and armor were used for locomotives. As a consequence it was possible to utilize steam at higher temperatures and pressure. Speed, power, and efficiency were increased and the distance between service intervals was increased.

The "ideal distance" between freight divisions became approximately 150 to 200 miles whereas it had formerly been 100 to 150. Wherever possible, freight divisions were increased in length to that formerly used by passenger trains, and passenger

[22] From W. F. Cottrell, "Death by Dieselization: A Case Study in the Reaction to Technological Change," *American Sociological Review*, June, 1951, pp. 358-65. Used by permission of the author.

divisions were lengthened from two old freight divisions to three. Thus towns located at 100 miles from a terminal became obsolescent, those at 200 became freight points only, and those at three hundred miles became passenger division points.

The increase in speed permitted the train crews to make the greater distance in the time previously required for the lesser trip, and roughly a third of the train and engine crews, car inspectors, boilermakers and machinists and other service men were dropped. The towns thus abandoned were crossed off the social record of the nation in the adjustment to these technological changes in the use of the steam locomotive. Caliente, located midway between terminals about six hundred miles apart, survived. In fact it gained, since the less frequent stops caused an increase in the service required of the maintenance crews at those points where it took place. However, the introduction of the change to diesel engines projected a very different future.

In its demands for service the diesel engine differs almost completely from a steam locomotive. It requires infrequent, highly skilled service, carried on within very close limits, in contrast to the frequent, crude adjustments required by the steam locomotive. Diesels operate at about 35 per cent efficiency, in contrast to the approximately 4 per cent efficiency of the steam locomotives in use after World War II in the United States. Hence diesels require much less frequent stops for fuel and water. These facts reduce their operating costs sufficiently to compensate for their much higher initial cost.

In spite of these reductions in operating costs the introduction of diesels ordinarily would have taken a good deal of time. The change-over would have been slowed by the high capital costs of retooling the locomotive works, the long period required to recapture the costs of existing steam locomotives, and the effective resistance of the workers. World War II altered each of these factors. The locomotive works were required to make the change in order to provide marine engines, and the costs of the change were assumed by the government. Steam engines were used up by the tremendous demand placed upon the railroads by war traffic. The costs were recaptured by shipping charges. Labor shortages were such that labor resistance was less formidable and much less acceptable to the public than it would have been in peace time. Hence the shift to diesels was greatly facilitated by the war. In consequence, every third and sometimes every second division point suddenly became technologically obsolescent.

Caliente, like all other towns in similar plight, is supposed to accept its fate in the name of "progress." The general public, as shippers and consumers of shipped goods, reaps the harvest in better, faster service and eventually perhaps in lower charges. A few of the workers in Caliente will also share the gains, as they move to other division points, through higher wages. They will share in the higher pay, though whether this will be adequate to compensate for their costs of moving no one can say. Certain it is that their pay will not be adjusted to compensate for their specific losses . . .

The railroad company can figure its losses at Caliente fairly accurately. It owns 39 private dwellings, a modern clubhouse with 116 single rooms, and a twelve-room hotel with dining-room and lunch-counter facilities. These now become useless, as does much of the fixed physical equipment used for servicing trains. Some of the machinery can be used elsewhere. Some part of the roundhouse can be used to store unused locomotives and standby equipment. The rest will be torn down to save taxes. All of these costs can be entered as capital losses on the statement which the company draws up for its stockholders and for the government. Presumably they will be recovered by use of the more efficient engines.

What are the losses that may not be entered on the company books? The total tax assessment in Caliente was $9,946.80 for the year 1948, of which $6,103.39 represented taxes assessed on the railroad. Thus the railroad valuation was about three-fifths that of the town. This does not take into account tax-free property belonging to the churches, the schools, the hospital, or the municipality itself which included all the public utilities. Some ideas of the losses sustained by the railroad in comparison with the losses of others can be surmised by reflecting on these figures for real estate alone. The story is an old one and often repeated in the economic history of America. It represents the "loss" side of a profit and loss system of adjusting to technological change. Perhaps for sociological purposes we need an answer to the question "just who pays?"

Probably the greatest losses are suffered by the older "non-operating" employees. Seniority among these men extends only within the local shop and craft. A man with twenty-five years' seniority at Caliente has no claim on the job of a similar craftsman at another point who has only twenty-five days' seniority. Moreover, some of the skills formerly valuable are no longer needed. The boilermaker, for example, knows that jobs for his kind are disappearing and he must enter the ranks of the unskilled. The protection and status offered by the union while he was employed have become meaningless now that he is no longer needed. The cost of this is high both in loss of income and in personal demoralization.

Operating employees also pay. Their seniority extends over a division, which in this case includes three division points. The older members can move from Caliente and claim another job at another point, but in many cases they move leaving a good portion of their life savings behind. The younger men must abandon their stake in railroad employment. The loss may mean a new apprenticeship in another occupation, at a time in life when apprenticeship wages are not adequate to meet the obligations of mature men with families. A steam engine hauled 2,000 tons up the hill out of Caliente with the aid of two helpers. The four-unit diesel in command of one crew handles a train of 5,000 tons alone. Thus, to handle the same amount of tonnage required only about a fourth the man-power it formerly took. Three out of four men must start out anew at something else.

The local merchants pay. The boarded windows, half-empty shelves, and abandoned store buildings bear mute evidence of these costs. The older merchants stay, and pay; the younger ones, and those with no stake in the community, will move; but the value of their property will in both cases largely be gone.

The bondholders will pay. They can't foreclose on a dead town. If the town were wiped out altogether, that which would remain for salvage would be too little to satisfy their claims. Should the town continue there is little hope that taxes adequate to carry the overhead of bonds and day-to-day expenses could be secured by taxing the diminished number of property owners or employed persons.

The church will pay. The smaller congregations cannot support services as in the past. As the church men leave, the buildings will be abandoned.

Homeowners will pay. A hundred and thirty-five men owned homes in Caliente. They must accept the available means of support or rent to those who do. In either case the income available will be far less than that on which the houses were built. The least desirable homes will stand unoccupied, their value completely lost. The others must be revalued at a figure far below that at which they were formerly held.

In a word, those pay who are, by traditional American standards, *most moral*. Those who have raised children see friendships broken and neighborhoods disintegrated. The childless more freely shake the dust of Caliente from their feet. Those who built their personalities into the structure of the community watch their work destroyed. Those too wise or too selfish to have entangled themselves in community affairs suffer no such qualms. . . . In short, "good citizens" who assumed family and community responsibility are the greatest losers. Nomads suffer least.

The people of Caliente are asked to accept as "normal" this strange inversion of their expectations. It is assumed that they will, without protest or change in sentiment, accept the dictum of the "law of supply and demand." Certainly they must comply in part with this dictum. While their behavior in part reflects this compliance, there are also other changes perhaps equally important in their attitudes and values.

The first reaction took the form of an effort at community self-preservation. Caliente became visible to its inhabitants as a real entity, as meaningful as the individual personalities which they had hitherto been taught to see as atomistic or nomadic elements. Community survival was seen as prerequisite to many of the individual values that had been given precedence in the past. The organized community made a search for new industry, citing elements of community organization themselves as reasons why industry should move to Caliente. But the conditions that led the railroad to abandon the point made the place even less attractive to new industry than it had hitherto been. Yet the effort to keep the community a going concern persisted.

There was also a change in sentiment. In the past the glib assertion that progress spelled sacrifice could be offered when some distant group was a victim of technological change. There was no such reaction when the event struck home . . .

The people of Caliente continually profess their belief in "The American Way," but . . . they criticize decisions made solely in pursuit of profit, even though these decisions grow out of a clear-cut case of technological "progress." They feel that the company should have based its decision upon consideration for loyalty, citizenship, and community morale. They assume that the company should regard the seniority rights of workers as important considerations, and that it should consider significant the effect of permanent unemployment upon old and faithful employees. They look upon community integrity as an important community asset. Caught between the support of a "rational" system of "economic" forces and laws, and sentiments which they accept as significant values, they seek a solution to their dilemma which will at once permit them to retain their expected rewards for continued adherence to past norms and to defend the social system which they have been taught to revere but which now offers them a stone instead of bread.

The story of social change in Caliente is, fortunately, not the only kind of community story we can read in the history of our country. Some communities, through good fortune, historical accident, or the diligence and planning of their citizens, have had a happier history and can still look to the future with contentment and high expectation. In the story of Caliente, however, one can discern—faintly and dimly, to be sure, for this is the nature of community life—the great complexity of human interactions and the cultural related-ness of men. The people of Caliente find their lives dras-tically altered by a chain of reactions set in motion by tech-nological inventions. The sudden loss of need by a larger society for the external functional contributions of the little town leaves it isolated and alone in its fight for existence. The community problems of which the citizens quickly be-come aware are of such magnitude that their efforts to carry out policies of reform appear to hold but little promise of success.

In the story of Caliente we can observe many of the ele-ments of community change and the developmental sequence of a community problem. We see, too, something of the structural nature of a community and its functional inter-relatedness with a larger society. And Caliente reminds us that the history of a community is also the story of what hap-pens to the human beings who live in it.

SELECTED REFERENCES

Gittler, Joseph B., *Social Dynamics,* McGraw-Hill Book Com-pany, Inc., New York, 1952. Several case studies of social change are included in this introductory sociology textbook. See pp. 226-91.

Linton, Ralph, *The Study of Man,* D. Appleton-Century Company, New York, 1936. The two chapters, "Discovery and Invention" and "Diffusion," are excellent discussions of the mechanics of social change.

MacIver, R. M., and Charles H. Page, *Society,* Rinehart and Company, New York, 1949. The last eight chapters of this book discuss social and cultural change.

Ogburn, William Fielding, *Social Change,* Viking Press, Inc., New York, 1950. This influential book on the nature of change was first published in 1922. The author presents his famous "cultural lag" theory in this volume.

Wilson, Logan, and William L. Kolb, *Sociological Analysis,* Harcourt, Brace and Company, New York, 1949. Includes seven thoughtful articles dealing with social change and disorganization.

PART THREE

*Community
and
Personality*

CHAPTER 6

Personality and Community Life

1. Personality: Uniqueness and Commonality

The study of personality deals with uniqueness within commonality. No person is exactly like any other person, but, at the same time, no person is in every way unlike any other person. The two facts of personality—uniqueness and commonality—make necessary to the thorough study of human beings both the exact and objective methodology of the scientist and the less empirical, but insightful and resourceful, approach of the humanist.

Most men realize their brotherhood with other men and they—partly by functional necessity, but also by choice—join with other men to do the work of the world, to fight their battles, and share the experiences of living. There are few hermits on the earth and even they share certain behavior characteristics with those not hermits. But men are individuals; they recognize this and will do battle to protect their integrity as persons. "Man, all down his history has defended his uniqueness like a point of honour." [1] And the fact is that it is both because of the limitless possible varieties of

[1] Benedict, Ruth, *Patterns of Culture*, Mentor Edition, New American Library, New York, 1949, p. 3.

experience and the truly astronomical number of possible gene combinations—perhaps far beyond the estimated number of electrons and protons in the entire universe—that each human being is a unique individual.[2]

2. The Organic Base of Human Behavior

First of all, the human being is an organism, and, as a class, a very definite and special kind of organism capable of being differentiated from all other classes. What is more, the human organism, like all others, is dynamic, as much a collection of internal processes as it is an observable structure of cells and tissues. Further, the human organism is limited in both its internal processes and its reaction to external stimuli by the restrictions placed upon it by the unique "action system" of the species *Homo sapiens.*

In general, human behavior includes whatever reactions the individual makes to the stimuli emanating both from within his body and from sources outside it. A change in the nature of the reaction is always caused by interference with the processes of the organism. In other words, whenever some changing condition destroys the dynamic balance of the organism, that is, its "homeostasis" or "steady state," the organism will react—a change in behavior will take place. If this change in behavior creates a condition which eliminates or perhaps only relieves the interference with the organic processes, further changes in behavior will not take place as a result of the original imbalance, and the new, relieving condition tends to be maintained. Human behavior is, then, a "readjustment of organic equilibrium" and is al-

---

[2] Cf. L. C. Dunn and Th. Dobzhansky, *Heredity, Race, and Society,* Mentor Edition, Revised, New American Library, New York, 1952, Chapter III, and Clyde Kluckhohn and Henry A. Murray, *Personality in Nature, Society, and Culture,* Second Edition, Alfred A. Knopf, New York, 1953.

ways sequential, that is, it takes place in time-sequented order. It is irreversible and is always based on past acts and behaviors.[3]

It is his organic uniqueness which, in the final analysis, makes man individual. Humans, like other organisms, cannot collectively experience interference in "group organic processes"; such processes themselves do not exist. Groups do not become thirsty, hungry, feel the pain of indigestion or the dulling comfort of a full stomach. Only individuals do these things. Nor do groups "think"; the collective mind concept has been outmoded by deeper understanding and sounder analysis.

Human behavior and human personality, then, have an organic, biological base which makes every person in some way different from every other. At the same time, every person is like all others in the fact of the possession of this collection of biological processes and, thus, in the ultimate well-springs of his behavior.

But the human organism alone is not a person; neither can we conceive of a person without an organism. Therefore, a person must be an organism plus something, and that something, of course, is learning. And he learns, primarily, from other human organisms and what he learns is culture. "Human organic individuals become persons through growth and learning, together compose society, and their activities are social life." [4] Personality can be defined scientifically, as Douglas G. Haring and Mary E. Johnson write, in terms of three factors in its development: the biological organism, the individually modifiable factors in the action system of the human organism, and the total environmental situation in

---

[3] Haring, Douglas G., and Mary E. Johnson, *Order and Possibility in Social Life,* Richard R. Smith, New York, 1940, pp. 285-317.
[4] *Ibid.,* pp. 378-82.

which it exists. To ignore any of these is to be less than complete in one's total analysis of personality. "A person is a human organism who has grown and developed habitual patterns of behavior through participation in social life." [5]

As students of community, we are primarily interested, to be sure, in the third of these factors in personality development, and, even more specifically, in those aspects of social relations which we believe are of especial significance. And, since all people—or nearly all—live in community and experience the greater portion of their social contacts in their own communities, we turn our attentions to the processes of "socialization" in the community. Socialization, at one and the same time, is the process through which a people ensures the transmission of its social heritage from generation to generation and the process through which a squalling little barbarian infant organism becomes an accepted member of a social group, with a collection of patterns of attitudes and behaviors we call a personality.

3. Socio-Psychological Theories of Personality

Recognizing, then, that the biological is a base for human personality development and human behavior, we turn now to our chief interest, the relationship of culture and personality as it can be seen in the community. Following are some of the theories which have been advanced to explain and to describe the nature of this relationship:

(1) *Charles Horton Cooley: primary groups and the "looking-glass" self.* Cooley, the great American "psychological sociologist," held that personality is formed by experiences in primary groups. By "primary," he meant those associations which involve intimate, face-to-face contacts,

[5] *Ibid.*

most notably the family, the play group, and the neighborhood or community. While these groups may be essentially affectional and sympathetic (as the family) or competitive (as the boys' gang), they are universally primary in the formation of the individual's social nature. "Human nature is not something existing separately in the individual, but a *group-nature or primary phase of society,* a relatively simple and general condition of the social mind." Further, because there are essential similarities in these primary groups everywhere, there is an essential similarity of ideas and sentiments in human minds.

There is some evidence for Cooley's belief that individuals and society are inseparable aspects of one whole and that human nature is "a trait of primary groups." [6] For example, the famous cases of "Anna" and "Isabelle," both Americans deprived, almost from birth, of normal experience in what Cooley called primary groups, indicate that, to a large degree, personality is learned. After years of isolation, neither of these children exhibited what might be called a "human personality"; here we have the best observations to date of the results of separation of the two most significant (and, ordinarily, inseparable) factors in human personality, the sociogenic and the biogenic.[7]

Cooley held that, largely as a result of his experience in primary groups, the child *learns* his personality, that is, learns to go through life playing roles in response to the attitudes and reactions of other persons. The individual reacts in terms of his own estimation of the reaction of others to

[6] Cooley, Charles Horton, *Social Organization,* Charles Scribner's Sons, New York, 1909, 1937, pp. 23, and following.

[7] See Kingsley Davis, "Extreme Social Isolation of a Child," *American Journal of Sociology,* January, 1940, pp. 554-65, and also his "Final Note on a Case of Extreme Isolation," *American Journal of Sociology,* March, 1947, pp. 432-37.

him. One imagines his appearance to others, judges this imagination, and then, being sensitive to praise and blame, reacts in terms of pride, mortification, or other feeling toward himself.[8]

(2) *Pitirim Sorokin: the bio-social pluralism of egos.* If a criticism of Cooley's personality theory is to be made, it must include the charge that he to some extent ignored the very biological base we have already had occasion to discuss. Pitirim Sorokin states that every human is composed not only of "social egos," but of "biological egos." The social egos are comparable to the social roles of Cooley, and the biological egos are the dynamic, ever changing physical organizations of the individual. These biological egos undergo change as the human organism grows, with varying speeds or rates, from babyhood to maturity, and ages from infancy to old age. Glandular balance or imbalance, stature, good health or ill, join with other aspects of the physical man to affect him and to become part of his personality structure.

In other words, one's biological ego varies with the state of the total physical organism, just as the social egos vary with the social situation. Thus, one's personality varies with his biological state and the role (in family, at play, or at work) which he is playing at a particular moment.[9]

(3) *Personality-culture theories.* As Herbert Goldhamer has pointed out, anthropological data on factors in personality formation are often contradictory and the methods used "often woefully blunt for the task which they are called upon to perform."[10] Nevertheless, one could hardly deny that the recent contributions of team research by ethnolo-

[8] Cooley, Charles Horton, *Human Nature and the Social Order,* Charles Scribner's Sons, New York, 1902, pp. 152-53.

[9] Cf. Pitirim Sorokin, *Society, Culture, and Personality,* Harper and Brothers, New York, 1947, *passim.*

[10] Goldhamer, Herbert, "Recent Development in Personality Studies," *American Sociological Review,* October, 1948, pp. 555-65.

gists and psychologists have adequately demonstrated the feasibility of making cross-cultural studies and comparisons of the processes of personality formation.[11]

The relation of culture and personality is not completely clear, but that they are related cannot be questioned. The fact that anthropologists and sociologists have not as yet been entirely successful in relating culture patterns and the emergence of specific personality patterns is not strange. The great complexity of social data as well as the complexity of even the individual personality promises to make such relation an exceedingly difficult undertaking.[12] But some important accomplishments have been attained, certain aspects of which we touch upon here.

The assumption behind all culture-personality theories is that personality is a configuration of attitudes, tendencies to respond to particular stimuli in certain ways, and behavior patterns which are learned by one person from others in a social situation. Even the definition of "normality" in personality, accordingly, varies from one society to another. Abnormality in one society may be the personality cornerstone of another, for example the "normality" and great acceptability of the paranoid in Dobu and among the Kwakiutl.[13]

If personality, beyond the limited variations accountable by individual differences in its organic base, is learned, that is, is related to the culture available to be learned, then, as Abram Kardiner and Ralph Linton point out, there ought to be such a thing as "basic personality type." To put it dif-

[11] See the work of Ralph Linton, Abram Kardiner, Clyde Kluckhohn, Margaret Mead, Ruth Benedict, Cora Du Bois, and Erik Erikson, among others.

[12] Sapir, Edward, "Personality," *Encyclopaedia of the Social Sciences,* The Macmillan Company, New York, 1932, vol. 12, p. 87.

[13] Cf. Ruth Benedict, "Anthropology and the Abnormal," *Journal of General Psychology,* 1934, vol. 10, pp. 59-80.

ferently, there ought to be for a particular society a basic personality configuration which is shared by a large proportion of the members of the society because they have shared common experiences, especially in early life. Such a concept has also been called "typical," "modal," and "median" personality by other writers who base their work on the same conceptual framework. Linton describes his and Kardiner's concept in these words:

The concept of basic personality types as developed and used by Dr. Kardiner and myself is in itself a configuration involving several different elements. It rests upon the following postulates:

1. That the individual's early experiences exert a lasting effect upon his personality, especially upon the development of his projective systems.

2. That similar experiences will tend to produce similar personality configurations in the individuals who are subjected to them.

3. That the techniques which the members of any society employ in the care and rearing of children are culturally patterned and will tend to be similar, although never identical, for various families within the society.

4. That the culturally patterned techniques for the care and rearing of children differ from one society to another.

If these postulates are correct, and they seem to be supported by a wealth of evidence, it follows:

1. That the members of any given society will have many elements of early experience in common.

2. That as a result of this they will have many elements of personality in common.

3. That since the early experience of individuals differs from one society to another, the personality norms for various societies will also differ.

The *basic personality type* for any society is that personality configuration which is shared by the bulk of the society's members as a result of the early experiences which they have in common.[14]

Kardiner and Linton support their theories with evidence from the analysis of various primitive tribes, among them the Comanche Indians and the Alorese, and other scholars have made analyses which seem further to support this conception of personality. Among the latter may be cited Cora Du Bois' long study of the character of the Alorese, a Dutch East Indian people, Ruth Benedict's earlier study of the patterning of culture, Margaret Mead's various studies, notably of the relations of sex and personality, and the work of Erik H. Erikson.[15]

Other studies have shown that the dimension of meaning in emotions and gestures is cultural and, therefore, learned. Even the modes of expression of emotions and gestures are culturally conditioned, although they may also have a degree of physiological conditioning.[16]

These brief citations are sufficient to indicate that social scientists at the present time are generally aware of a relationship between culture and the development of personality and that cultural variations from one society to another tend to produce variations in the "basic" or "typical" personality structure of the societies involved. Perhaps this is only an-

[14] From the foreword to Abram Kardiner, Ralph Linton, *et al., The Psychological Frontiers of Society,* Columbia University Press, New York, 1945. Used by permission of the publisher.

[15] See Ruth Benedict, *Patterns of Culture,* Mentor Edition, New American Library, New York, 1949; Cora Du Bois, *The People of Alor,* University of Minnesota Press, Minneapolis, 1944; Erik H. Erikson, *Childhood and Society,* W. W. Norton and Company, New York, 1950; Margaret Mead, *Sex and Temperament in Three Primitive Societies,* William Morrow and Company, Inc., New York, 1935. For a critique, see Alfred R. Lindesmith and Anselm L. Strauss, "A Critique of Culture-Personality Writings," *American Sociological Review,* October, 1950, pp. 587-600.

[16] See Weston LaBarre, "Cultural Basis of Emotions and Gestures," *Journal of Personality,* vol. 16, 1947, pp. 49-68.

other way of saying that, since values are the basis of what is considered "normal" in a society, people tend to "learn" their personalities in accordance with the generally accepted norms of the society in which they live. Since the culture worlds of American communities vary so widely among themselves, such analysis is applicable to the study of community-personality relations.

4. Community Culture and Personality Development: A Case Study

The complexities of the relationships of personality and community culture are indeed difficult to understand; at best, we can still only say that we know *something* of their interconnections. The little we know is, in fact, based on the kind of descriptive case presented in this section.

"Stanley X" is probably the most famous juvenile delinquent who ever lived in America. He is the "Jack-Roller" so well described by Clifford R. Shaw. Stanley, whose record of arrests and convictions is truly of phenomenal length, grew up and learned his delinquency, developed his personality, in three different community culture-worlds of Chicago. There can be no doubt of their effectiveness in influencing the attitudes and behavior patterns of young Stanley.[17]

Stanley, who is at present approximately twenty-two years of age, has lived for comparatively long periods of time in three different areas of the city . . .

Area A

This area, which includes the large packing plants, stock yards, and a portion of the central manufacturing district, is

[17] From Clifford R. Shaw, *The Jack-Roller,* University of Chicago Press, Chicago, 1930. Reprinted by permission of the author.

bounded by Halsted Street on the east, Western Avenue on the west, Thirty-ninth Street on the north, and Forty-seventh Street on the south. During his early childhood Stanley lived in the large Polish neighborhood which occupies the western portion of this area, between Ashland and Western Avenues. It was while he lived in this neighborhood, which is known locally as "Back of the Yards," that his career in delinquency began.

The neighborhood back of the yards is a part of the large industrial community which has developed around the Union Stock Yards and central manufacturing district during the last half-century. It is one of the grimiest and most unattractive neighborhoods in the city, being almost completely surrounded by packing plants, stock yards, railroads, factories, and waste lands. The life in the neighborhood is largely dominated by, and economically dependent upon, the larger industrial community of which it is a part. The population is composed largely of families of unskilled laborers, most of whom depend upon the stock yards and local industries for employment. The air in the neighborhood is smoky and always filled with a disagreeable odor from the stock yards . . .

In the present Polish neighborhood back of the yards, . . . there is a definite break between the foreign-born parents and their native-born children. In many of the families the relation between the child and parent assumes the character of an emotional conflict, which definitely complicates the problem of parental control and greatly interferes with the incorporation of the child into the social milieu of his parents . . .

Although there is comparatively little crime among the adults living in Area A, juvenile delinquency is particularly prevalent . . . During the three-year period between 1924 and 1926, 28 per cent of the young men from seventeen to twenty-one years of age were arrested and arraigned in the Boys' Court on charges of serious crime. No other area in the city had a higher rate during that period . . . It is known also that this area has been characterized by a high rate of delinquency for almost thirty years . . .

In the light of the disorganized community situation back of the yards, the persistence of a high rate of delinquency is not at all surprising. With the marked changes in the composition of population, diffusion of divergent cultural standards, and the rapid disorganization of the alien culture, the continuity of community traditions and cultural institutions is broken. Thus the effectiveness of the community in the control and education of the child is greatly diminished . . .

Area B

Stanley very early became involved in the underworld life of the large rooming-house district west of the Loop, Chicago's central business district . . . According to official records, it was while he lived in this district that his first experiences in "jack-rolling" and burglary occurred. . . .

This district is characterized by physical deterioration, a mobile and transient population composed largely of homeless adult males, and an absence of community organization. Here are to be found also the rescue missions, the flophouses, the cheap hotels, pawnshops and secondhand stores, houses of prostitution, closed dance halls, and the hangout of the criminal. . . .

The freedom and anonymity of the situation offer an environment in which the adult offender may live in relative obscurity and with a minimum of interference from the police. Although most of the criminals living in the district commit their crimes in the more well-to-do sections of the city, cases of "jack-rolling" and homosexual practice are especially common in, or adjacent to, the rooming house district . . .

Area C

This area, which includes portions of the communities of Woodlawn and Hyde Park, stands in marked contrast to the areas described in the foregoing pages. The population is composed chiefly of middle-class native-born Americans, business men, clerks, salesmen, and professional people . . . There is sufficient community tradition, public opinion, and common interest to afford a basis for effective collective action with reference to local and city-wide social problems.

In this area cases of poverty, bad housing, adult crime, physical deterioration, and juvenile delinquency are comparatively infrequent . . .

Stanley's story of his life, written when he was twenty-two years of age, contains many insightful comments on his own personality formation as he viewed it.

To start out in life, everyone has his chances—some good and some very bad. Some are born with fortunes, beautiful homes, good and educated parents; while others are born in ignorance, poverty, and crime. In other words, Fate begins to guide our lives even before we are born and continues to do so throughout life. My start was handicapped by a no-good, ignorant, and selfish stepmother, who thought only of herself and her own children. . . .

I grew old enough to go out on the street. The life in the streets and alleys became fascinating and enticing. I had two close companions that I looked up to with childish admiration and awe. One was William, my stepbrother. The other one was Tony, a dear friend of my stepbrother. They were close friends, four years older than me and well versed in the art of stealing.

To my child-seeing eyes, I visioned Tony as a great leader in the neighborhood, and he directed his gang around with much bravado. He and William were always stealing and talking about stealing and I fell in with them as soon as I began to play around in the neighborhood. . . .

Tony liked his whiskey and in our neighborhood one could find as many as four or five saloons in one block in those days. He would dare me to drink and I would, although it burned my throat. I was what they called "game" and I just swallowed it without a word, to maintain that high distinction which I was openly proud of. . . .

My stepmother sent me out with William (my stepbrother) to

pick rags and bottles in the alleys. She said that would pay for my board and make me more useful than fretting and sulking at home . . . I began to have a great time exploring the whole neighborhood—romping and playing in the alleys and "prairies," gathering rags, bones, and iron, and selling them to the rag peddlers. This romping and roaming became fascinating and appealed to my curiosity, because it was freedom and adventure. We played "Indian" and other games in the alleys, running through the old sheds and vacant houses. Then we gathered cigarette "buttses" along the street and took them to the shed, where we smoked and planned adventure. I was little and young, but I fell in with the older guys. Outside, in the neighborhood, life was full of pleasure and excitement, but at home it was dull and drab and full of nagging, quarreling, and beating, and stuffy and crowded besides. . . .

Stealing in the neighborhood was a common practice among the children and approved by the parents. Whenever the boys got together they talked about robbing and made more plans for stealing. I hardly knew any boys who did not go robbing . . . Fellows who had "done time" were big shots and looked up to and gave the little fellows tips on how to get by and pull off big jobs. . . .

Things became so bad that my brother and sister ran away just to get out of the stepmother's reach. They put them in jail just for running away. That left only me at home, but I was just about ready to go . . . I learned all the meanness of my childhood from my stepbrother William, but never once was he whipped or arrested. Fate was in his favor. I became unhappy, and fear and hatred took possession of me. One day a policeman came to our house and told my stepmother that he saw William and me stealing in a store. After he left, the stepmother accused me of leading William astray, and she proceeded to tie me to a chair for the customary beating. Fear possessed me and gave me added courage and strength. I tore myself loose from her and ran away.

For the first time in my life I was out of the hole I called home, away from my stepmother. But where would I go? A boy of six years and four months. I didn't lose much time, but went back to our old home . . . I met my old chums there and told them I was bumming from home. We played together all day, but at night I got afraid and lonesome. I thought about home and the beating that was waiting for me. Fear kept me from returning home. I roamed the street until late at night, and then found a dry spot under a doorstep, where I curled up and slept till morning. Thus I roamed and begged and stole food until four days later, I was arrested. . . .

Once away from home, the other times were easy. That was the easiest way to get out of my stepmother's reach, and, besides, it made a strong appeal to my young and adventurous spirit. I ran away so many times that my father grew weary of going to the station to get me . . . My feelings were to roam without a care on my mind, to be away from home, where I always got the clouts. And roam I did. I would romp back to our old home and neighborhood, and then on down to West Madison Street and the Loop. I would gaze at the movie houses, restaurants, poolrooms, and at the human wreckage that made its uncertain and guideless way along West Madison Street. Their conversations and carefree personalities appealed to my childish imagination. A score of times or more did I thus roam from home to West Madison when I was eight and nine years old.

In Stanley's story, we see personality as a product of social forces and social experiences, described not in the technical terminology of the psychologist or social psychologist, but in a delinquent's own story of his behavior. Personality, in the final analysis, is analyzable and understandable—for the sociologist at least—primarily in terms of human behavior in group situations. One need not dwell further on this matter than merely to speculate on the possible outcome of Stanley's personality development had he but been born and lived his life in other kinds of communities, of quiet, orderly residential neighborhoods, with stable and more homogeneous populations, higher standards of living and of education, and greater senses of civic responsibility.

5. Community Life and the Structure of Personality[18]

The human personality is a dynamic structure of "value-orientations" and it is in the community that individuals commonly experience most vividly their reciprocal role relationships with others. Out of these interpersonal contacts value-orientations develop.[19] But when one speaks of personality "structure" he is under obligation to spell out in concrete detail just what the pattern of the structure is. We here consider three divisions of personality: (1) the inherent structural elements, (2) those attitudes which are formed early, but which are flexible or elastic, that is, bounce back to their original form, or resist change of a permanent sort, and (3) those aspects which are susceptible to almost daily changes. The third category includes everything in personality not falling into the first two categories but which at the same time falls within the range of restrictive and limiting influences of them.

(1) *The inherent structural elements.* The personality of any particular individual has certain characteristics—perhaps these are truly organic in base, as we have already suggested —which are *relatively* fixed and unchanging. These charac-

---

[18] This section is largely based on Chapter Four of James S. Plant's intriguing book, *Personality and the Cultural Pattern*, The Commonwealth Fund, New York, 1937.

[19] Cf. Talcott Parsons, *The Social System*, The Free Press, Glencoe, Illinois, 1951, especially pp. 226-35, for an irritatingly abstract but insightful discussion of personality and social roles.

teristics, which vary from individual to individual, probably are somehow connected with neural organization. James S. Plant has classified these inherent structural elements in four categories: *alertness, complexity, pliability,* and *temperament,* with a possible fifth, *cadence.*

Some individuals are more *alert* than others, that is, they react more readily to new stimuli than do others who are more nearly "closed" to them. The terms "weathervane" and "stolid" personalities are applied to persons representing the polar types. At least with children, there is evidence that alertness does not change very much in time.

Some personalities are more *complex* than others, that is, some persons are naïve and unable to see themselves objectively while others can describe their own experiences or even project themselves into future experiences in wholly objective terms. Again, there seems to be little change among children as far as this characteristic of personality is concerned. While there may be a close relationship between the complexity of personality and intelligence (higher intelligence correlated with greater complexity) the data available are far from conclusive.

Some personalities have a higher degree of *pliability* than others, that is, some persons more easily adjust to new situations and form new habits. Some learn new pathways of action more easily than others, but some, learning slowly and with apparent difficulty, retain what they have learned with great tenacity. Such evidence as now is available indicates nothing with respect to any possible correlation between pliability and intelligence.

Differences in *temperament* also are at least partially inherent; they are differences primarily in motor expression. Basically temperamental differences involve variation in individual tendencies toward extravertism and introvertism. A child develops a range or band of temperament within which he will live and behave. At adolescence, temperament is often emphasized—the introvert will become more introverted, and the extravert more extraverted; after adolescence, the band of temperament more nearly resembles that of the individual's earlier years.

The category of *cadence* can be less certainly accepted on the evidence available, but it appears that each person has a fairly constant maturational speed, and that this rate of growth or development—partly organic and partly learned —varies from individual to individual. The fact that there are apparent spurts of growth and periods of latency in personality development leaves this category in doubt. Nevertheless, as Plant puts it, it is clear that some persons "stumble their way through life, struggling along through this or that venture always well in the rear. Others run or skip their way."

As a guard against overemphasis upon the influence of community on personality, we must take cognizance of the fact that at least these elements of personality and perhaps many others, too, are basic, inherent, and relatively permanent and vary from individual to individual with little reference to his social and community experiences. As a caution, we cannot emphasize this too strongly, for we feel that current interest in culture-personality studies may all too easily lead to a faddism which would call for explanation of all personality characteristics by cultural factors.

(2) *Flexible and acquired aspects of personality.* There are certain aspects of personality which are acquired in early childhood and which become constantly more resistive to change as a person grows older, but never become structurally constant or permanent as are those characteristics which we have just noted. These aspects include the "mental con-

comitants" of physical habits—that is, the mental patterns associated with sleep and sex-activity, among many others— as well as what we most generally call attitudes. Indeed, a personality is sometimes erroneously defined only in terms of culturally determined attitudes, ignoring those organic bases we have just discussed. To the sociologist, attitudes are the most interesting aspect of personality, but it is clear also that aspects which have their basis in the organic nature of the individual must not be ignored.

There are three categories (at least) of the aspect of personality which we call attitudes. These, as Plant points out, are attitudes toward (1) *security*, (2) *reality*, and (3) *authority*.

Psychologists, social psychologists, and specialists in child education have written much about the child's *need for* security. In reality, it is the child's *attitude toward* security which is most significant in his personality development, and this attitude most likely has its basis in early life experiences. Attitudes toward security in the world of people are learned by children from their parents, teachers, and peer groups, and what they learn founds a generalized attitude toward their own "wantedness," "safety," and "place in the world" which is highly resistive to change in later life. Polar types may be described as "confident—timid" or "certain—uncertain."

Attitudes toward reality are also largely learned in the early years and resist change in later years. These attitudes involve what one does as a result of his perception of the real world in which he lives, and this is connected with the matter of introversion and extraversion, which we discussed above. The development of attitudinal patterns toward the world is closely related to community and cultural matters, for they are developed as a result of experiences in community. One's general acceptance or lack of acceptance of the world in which he must or does live may well be tied in directly with the effect his early environment has upon his behavior, that is, with respect to permissiveness or restrictiveness in behavior.

A person's *attitudes about authority* may be defined as the habitual patterns of behavior which are connected with the understanding that one lives in a world of forces many of which are beyond one's control, and which, indeed, serve to control the individual. Such attitudes toward authority, as Plant points out, are apparent with respect to one's body, other persons, social groups, and extra-human phenomena. The attitudes toward these things are learned in early life, and they tend to persist.

(3) *Rapid change in personality structure.* As Plant says so well, "There is then some sort of structure which arrives in the world—in the making." But a far larger part of the structure of the personality than either of those thus far noted, is that ever-changing aspect which is essentially a result of day-to-day living experiences. It is

. . . the whole mass of mental processes which grows like a rolling snowball—with this extra factor, that each accretion is accepted in the light of the problems which the personality is trying to work out, that it thus has dynamic, problem-provoking qualities of its own, and that of course it finds that each preceding accretion has this same tendency to affect every other part of the mass. Each accretion is loaded with cultural meaning, is loaded with meaning to the individual in the light of the understanding he has arrived at in working out certain problems, and is changed and molded as it enters the personality on the basis of precisely these problems. Thus, for instance, the child in going to school sees the teacher in the light of the whole complex of his relations to his mother and he takes from that teacher (what she means and is to him) that which in one or another way illuminates or works out or confirms what he has at the time arrived at so far as his relationship to his mother is concerned. Each person or each event of life is accepted as it has meaning to the child in the light of "where he has got to today." This is an ever changing, ever adjusting agglomeration out of which emerge patterns of different definition. Some of these reiterate themselves with such frequency as to become attitudes. Others come and go, leaving in each case their mark but never attaining the strength to make them final common pathways to which a great variety of stimuli would lead.[20]

A personality, then, is a growing, dynamic thing, and, with its organic base setting restrictions, it develops according to the kinds of experiences the individual has. The study of personality and its growth, therefore, must include the study, not only of individual experiences with a nonpersonal environment, but of individual experiences with other persons in such associations as family, peer group, school, community, and neighborhood. The case of "Stanley X," jack-roller, presents an illustration of the relationships of community culture-worlds and various aspects of the development of an individual personality.

We have yet much to learn with respect to the processes of personality development through social experience, but the leads from anthropology, psychology, social psychology, and sociology are illuminating and intriguing. One thing is certain: we cannot afford to ignore community culture in our analysis of personality, nor can we afford to ignore personality in the study of community.

[20] Plant, James S., *op. cit.,* pp. 89-90. Reprinted by permission of The Commonwealth Fund and Harvard University Press.

6. Goals, Means, and Personality

Two of the elements in any social structure which are most significant in the development of the learned aspects of personality are the cultural goals accepted by the majority of the people and the institutionalized means provided for reaching them. Goals in any community are more or less integrated, they are placed in an evaluative hierarchy, and there are varying degrees of sentiment and aspiration attached to them. The real problem of any society is how to maintain some reasonable equilibrium between these goals and the institutionalized and approved channels for reaching them. Equilibrium through conformity to both approved goals and approved (or at least not proscribed) means will be maintained only so long as the individuals who conform receive personal satisfactions.[21]

Contemporary American society tends toward "anomie" or normlessness with respect both to goals and means. On the one hand, we have exalted success goals (in terms not only of wealth attainment, but of occupational attainment) without having provided sufficient means of reaching the goals; this is true, at least, to the extent that some of our people have suffered demoralization. Robert K. Merton writes, "The family, the school, and the workplace—the major agencies shaping the personality structure and goal formation of Americans—join to provide the intensive disciplining required if an individual is to retain intact a goal that remains elusively beyond reach, if he is to be motivated by the promise of a gratification which is not redeemed." [22] The fact is that no American community does—or could—provide clear

[21] Merton, Robert K., "Social Structure and Anomie," in his *Social Theory and Social Structure,* The Free Press, Glencoe, Illinois, 1949, pp. 125-49.
[22] *Ibid.,* p. 130.

opportunity for a rags-to-riches climb to occupational success and material wealth for all its people. The result is personality demoralization and deviant behavior on the part of some citizens in nearly every community.

There is, however, another respect in which social goals and means are related to personality. This connection involves the loss of goals in a community, the disappearance of family tradition, local patriotism, or what may be called "community spirit." As a consequence of the deterioration of goals, the once accepted means are also lost, and the behavior of individuals and groups also tends toward anomie, that is, toward a kind of restless, purposeless activism. Activity becomes its own motivation and its own end. Individuals lack purpose, they become seekers after pleasure, and activity is pleasurable. In the final analysis, personality and personal characteristics become unimportant and are replaced in the thinking of people by a kind of restlessness without control and without purpose. This is the case in Hilltown, a small New England community.

The restless activity of the members of the community of Hilltown today is undirected by long-term goals of the family or community. The community itself is, and always has been, inferior in natural endowments and lacking in drive or purpose. Today as never before, the community is unable to provide a stability and purpose for the individuals who compose it. Human beings who grow up in Hilltown today are aware of few definite obligations or privileges associated with their social status, family status, age, or sex. The disparity between goals and means of attaining them gives rise to constant frustration and conflict. No longer is the behavior prescribed for attainment of recognized goals in itself a source of pleasure, satisfaction, and respect. Not only is the activity of the individual of little consequence in the total life activities of the community, but the person himself might drop out at any time without leaving a vacancy long heeded by the family or neighbors. Thus personality tends to become depressingly unimportant, and the activities of the individual tend to resolve themselves into expedient responses to immediate objectives.[23]

Fortunately, not all American communities exhibit the depressing activism of Hilltown. There are many—perhaps the majority—where life is earnest and real, where goals are sought with the same avidity as always, and there is a relative integration of means and ends. The problem of the deteriorating community is a serious one, however, and the Hilltowns are numerous and ranged across the length and breadth of America. The disorganization of some is inevitable, brought about by changing economic and social conditions, like many of those discussed in the preceding chapter. But there are many deteriorating communities which can be and deserve to be preserved. The only solution to their problem lies in the faith, reasonability, and purpose of the people of the communities themselves—but we will come to that in later chapters.

SELECTED REFERENCES

Adams, Donald K., *The Anatomy of Personality,* Papers in Psychology, Random House, Inc., New York, 1954. This forty-four page study presents a field-theory approach to the study of personality. Contains numerous definitions, examples, and concepts.

Du Bois, Cora, *The People of Alor,* University of Minnesota Press, Minneapolis, 1944. This study of personality and culture

---

[23] Hatch, David L., and Mary G. Hatch, *Under the Elms: Yesterday and Today,* Syracuse University Press, Syracuse, New York, 1949, p. 181. Used by permission of the authors.

among a primitive people is always fascinating reading. One of the better analyses of the personality-culture connection.

Erikson, Erik H., *Childhood and Society,* W. W. Norton and Company, New York, 1951. A careful study of variations in child-rearing practices in different societies.

Haring, Douglas G., Editor, *Personal Character and Cultural Milieu,* Revised Edition, Syracuse University Press, Syracuse, New York, 1948. An outstanding collection of readings on cultural aspects of personality formation.

Kluckhohn, Clyde, and Henry A. Murry, Editors, *Personality in Nature, Society, and Culture,* Second Edition, Alfred A. Knopf, New York, 1953. This volume of readings should be read in connection with that edited by Douglas G. Haring, cited above. An informative collection of papers on personality.

Plant, James S., *Personality and the Cultural Pattern,* The Commonwealth Fund, New York, 1937. Plant's book is based on thousands of case histories, and is a provocative and intriguing contribution to our knowledge of personality and its genesis.

PART FOUR

Community
and
Social Status

7

Social Differentiation, Status, and Role in the American Community

1. The Nature of Social Differentiation: Equality and Rank

People quickly discern both their similarities and their differences with respect to other persons. They recognize, in essence, principles of equality and of rank and status, and both are functional parts of every social structure.

The principle of equality is necessary to provide all men with a sense of self-respect and to establish the secular essentials of the Christian belief in brotherhood. It is also necessary to give each citizen the right to participate in making the decisions about the destinies of all.

The principle of rank and status is necessary to provide men with the motives to excel by striving for positions of higher prestige and power for themselves and their families. It is also essential to equip the nation, communities, and their institutions with responsible leadership hierarchies which co-ordinate and regulate the lives of their inhabitants and help maintain an orderly way of life, in which citizens can cultivate the morals and manners of a high civilization.[1]

[1] Reprinted from pp. 104-105, *American Life*, by W. Lloyd Warner, by permission of The University of Chicago Press. Copyright 1953 by The University of Chicago Press.

People in every society take note of individual differences among themselves. Sex, age, ability to learn, and other inherent characteristics, such as skin color, are easily apparent.

There are differences, too, of a subtler sort which are acquired as a result of experience within the social structure, such as variations in education, linguistic facility, manner of deportment, and skills of many kinds. These variations, whether inherent or acquired (which is another way of saying that they are at once cause and effect of the nature of the social structure), of seeming necessity in some cases and the result of apparent human caprice in others, are bases for the allocation of functions and rewards. Social differentiation, whether necessity as some have argued or unnecessary imposition as others have said, is a fact in every society.

Differentiation, with its foundations deep in the inherent and acquired variations among the individuals who make up a society, implies some kind of social prestige ranking system. One aspect of any social relationship between people is mutual placement, done consciously or unconsciously, higher or lower on a scale of social prestige.

Specific and definable traits, such as age, degree or kind of schooling, and sex (and any others which appear to most of the population to be specific and definable) carry different meanings in different societies; this, in part, accounts for the variation of functions or roles assigned to men and women, to the old and young, to the intelligent and stupid, from one society to another. The concept of social differentiation directs one's attention to the inherent and acquired individual differences which have social import. Numbers of people who have actual or supposed traits in common come to be thought of and spoken of as a group; descriptive terms are applied to them and, as a group, they are compared to and contrasted with other groups, the individual members of which are also believed to share characteristics which set them apart. When the traits involved are socioeconomic in nature, when their possession involves a differential in social prestige, and when the groups include persons of both sexes, all ages, and all levels of intelligence, the phenomenon called by the sociologist "social stratification" is present.

2. Social Stratification: A Functional Necessity

Stratification is a term originally borrowed from the field of geology. It is a useful concept if it is understood that it may be somewhat more difficult to classify individuals of a society into "strata" than it is to so categorize rocks. In other words, while it may be relatively easy for the geologist to determine where one stratum of rock ends and another begins, social strata seem, regardless of our most careful definitions, to shade off into one another, and, at best, it must be conceded that the boundaries are dim and indistinct.

The members of a society rate one another in terms of definable traits which carry prestige value. Talcott Parsons lists the following bases for differential evaluation: membership in a kinship unit, personal qualities, achievements, possessions, authority, and power.[2] People are rated according to the degree to which they exhibit "desirable" characteristics with respect to these categories. Placement in a higher "position," rather than a lower one, means that an individual will have greater opportunity to obtain values which are desired by most of the people of his society. Differential opportunity

[2] Parsons, Talcott, *Essays in Sociological Theory Pure and Applied,* The Free Press, Glencoe, Illinois, 1949, Chapter VII. Professor Parsons' revision of this paper presents an analysis of "qualities," "performances," and "possessions." Talcott Parsons, "A Revised Analytical Approach to the Theory of Social Stratification," in Reinhard Bendix and Seymour Martin Lipset, *Class, Status and Power,* The Free Press, 1953, Glencoe, Illinois, pp. 94-100.

to obtain wanted values is the basis of social stratification. Hans Gerth and C. Wright Mills put it this way:

Whatever the value may be that most people seem to want, some people get more of it than others, and some do not share in it at all. The student of stratification is bent on understanding the ranking of people with respect to such values, and in finding out in what respects these ranks differ and why. Each rank or stratum in a society may be viewed as a stratum by virtue of the fact that all of its members have similar opportunities to get the things and experiences that are valued: things like cars, steady and high incomes, toys, or houses; experiences, like being given respect, being educated to certain levels, or being treated kindly. To belong to one stratum or another is to share with the other people in this stratum similar advantages.

If, again, we go behind these strata of people having similar life-chances, and begin to analyze each stratum and the reasons for its formation and persistence, sooner or later we will come upon at least four important keys to the whole phenomenon. We call these "dimensions of stratification." Each provides a way by which we can rank people in accordance with the specific opportunity each has to obtain a given value. And all together, these dimensions, if properly understood, enable us to account for the whole range of these different opportunities. These four dimensions are occupation, class, status, and power:

By an *occupation* we understand a set of activities pursued more or less regularly as a major source of income.

Class situation, in its simplest subjective sense, has to do with the amount and source (property or work) of income as these affect the chances of people to obtain other available values.

Status involves the successful realization of claims to prestige; it refers to the distribution of deference in a society.

Power refers to the realization of one's will, even if this involves the resistance of others . . .[3]

[3] Gerth, Hans, and C. Wright Mills, *Character and Social Structure*, Harcourt, Brace and Company, New York, 1953, pp. 306-307. Reprinted by permission of the publisher.

People in our society most certainly rank one another in terms of such criteria as those listed above. It should be noted, however, that the reasons for the placement of a particular individual in a specific status position can be determined only through special study of his individual case, that is, his position may be the result of evaluation on one only, two, three, or any combination of these bases. Furthermore, the significance of one characteristic, rather than another, may differ from region to region or community to community. For example, the significance of family background and inherited wealth in the status determination of an individual in a traditional New England community is likely to differ considerably from the importance of these same factors in prestige placement in a Montana cattle town. Later in this chapter we shall explore briefly some examples of these variations as they are reported in community studies.

Social stratification is necessary to the functional continuity of any society. The different kinds of work which have to be done are not of equal significance or pleasantness, and not all individuals have equal ability, talent, or training. The two determinants of positional rank, then, are both aspects of the division of labor in society. Positions which have the highest reward and which bestow the highest rank *tend* to be those which are of most importance to a society or which require greatest talent and training for fulfillment.[4]

There can be little doubt that social stratification is related to the functional importance of work-positions and to the scarcity of talent to fill them. However, to say, as Davis and Moore do, that "Any particular system of stratification . . . can be understood as a product of the special conditions affecting the two aforementioned grounds of differential

---

[4] Davis, Kingsley, and Wilbert E. Moore, "Some Principles of Stratification," *American Sociological Review*, April, 1945, pp. 242-49.

reward . . ." leaves no room for consideration of such non-functional bases as kinship membership or personal attractiveness, which might help to explain the high prestige valuation of idle aristocratic groups in America and other societies. To be sure, hereditary aristocracies have been historically less prevalent in America than in some other nations, but even so, it could hardly be said that all positions of high social prestige in this country have their sources in the functional division of labor. Some combination of functional and non-functional considerations is always necessary to a scientific sociological analysis of social stratification in any American community.

3. Status Symbols and the Recognition of Stratification

Ordinary people are very much aware that there is such a thing as social prestige and they form opinions as to its bases. Consciously and unconsciously they seek prestige—or attempt to insure its recognition through verbal or other symbols. While no thorough study of status symbols in the American community has as yet been made, we have at hand some preliminary information. An example is found in the material which follows.

George K. Hundley recorded conversations and impressions on this subject from informal interviews with residents of a Western town of some 20,000. As representative of a large retail dairy concern, Hundley had occasion to interview people of various occupations, ages, incomes, and of both sexes. Statements including references which he could logically interpret as "status" or "prestige" symbols were in all cases volunteered. Income, possessions, "independence," authority, residence, and education—with the references taking various forms, direct and indirect—were the commonest categories into which may be placed the prestige symbols used by these residents of an American community. While the symbols represented in the following excerpts are not necessarily typical for most communities—and most certainly are typical for some—they are interesting and illuminating with regard to the question of the recognition of prestige valuations and prestige criteria by ordinary folk. Words or sentences in italics are interpreted as having significance as status devices or symbols.

Our dairy has certain little souvenirs which we give away, gladly, because they have the name of our dairy on them and are good means of advertisement.

Most people accept these souvenir objects (letter openers, salt and pepper shakers) graciously—but not so Mr. R. He backed off from my extended hand as if I had poison in it. Said no—he didn't care for a letter opener because, *"I don't want to be under obligation to anyone."*

This statement might be interpreted as a status device; it appears that what Mr. R was really trying to do was impress his listener with the fact that he was not under obligation to anyone, a state which few of us enjoy.

During our entire conference, it was obvious that Mrs. N was trying to "impress" me. She used, over and over again, such statements as:

". . . we're not dependent on anyone . . ."

"I have plenty of money."

". . . We don't have any doctor's bills because I feed my family plenty of butter . . . You don't catch us using oleomargarine . . . We use three pounds of real butter every week."

". . . I am a practical nurse—and I could get plenty of work if I wanted it—but I don't have to work."

Mrs. O, a mother of three, says that both she and her daughter became widows within the same year. *She used the word "widow"*

at least twenty times in the first ten minutes of our conversation.
(This might be interpreted as a status device—to show what she
alone had been able to accomplish.)

Mr. P, who, within the first four minutes of our conversation,
informed me that he was *eighty-seven years old,* lives alone in
a small, but well kept, home in the lower section of town. He likes
to boast that, in spite of his years, *he still rides a bicycle* to get
where he wants in town. He remarked, *"People speak to me all
the time*—people I don't know . . . people who don't even
know my name but they say they know me by sight by their
having seen me riding my bicycle."

Mrs. Q, an old woman of perhaps sixty-eight, acts as custodian-
manager for a cheap, run-down-at-the-heels apartment house, one
of the former large private dwellings now converted into six or
eight apartments.

She exhibited every authoritarian device possible to show that,
although Mr. X owns the building, it is she who is "boss." Several weeks ago I had an order from one of the new tenants,
whom I shall call "Zee." When I next saw Mrs. Q, she said:

"I think I should warn you about that Zee couple. I have reason to think they *'drink'* and you know people who *'drink'* don't
usually pay their bills, so if I were you, I wouldn't allow them
much credit.

"Sunday night I was baby-sitting for the lady in the front
apartment, who works nights, and the Zee couple was making so
much noise, *I had to go downstairs and tell them to be quiet.*
I won't say they were exactly fighting, but they were talking
awfully loud . . . so I knocked on their door and told them they
were disturbing the other tenants (although none had com-
plained) and that they had to be quiet. Some young man there,
who I think was Mrs. Zee's brother, shook his fist in my face
and said, 'You are lying . . .'

"I knew this young man was just trying to get me enraged but

I kept calm and said to him, 'This is America where everyone has a right to his opinion—and if your opinion of me is that I am a liar—then that is your opinion and you have a right to it —but I tell you that unless you are quiet, I will put you out, and if I can't do it, *I will get somebody who can.*'

"The young man (I am sure he had been drinking beer) said, 'Oh yeah?'—and I said right back to him 'yeah' . . . but he kept calling me a liar." [5]

Mr. Hundley's interesting (and sometimes hilarious) collection reveals the use of many other status devices—symbols representing wealth (such as television sets, new or newly remodeled homes with picture windows, and new automobiles), family connection, and church membership. The above excerpts, largely unedited, provide examples of these devices, exactly as they are most often used—hidden away in a forest of verbalization. They indicate, nonetheless, the ordinary person's preoccupation with his social status and the seeming desire to verbalize it or otherwise communicate it even to a relative stranger.

With these characteristics of social stratification in American society in mind, we now turn to a brief description of class structure in a specific community.

4. Social Class in an American Community: Hilltown, A Case Study

Hilltown, a New England town of 1022 people, is not representative of all communities in America, but it is probably typical of a large number of towns in its area. Fairly near a city of 200,000, and within a few miles of Chair City and other larger towns of over 10,000, Hilltown presents a combination of farming and industrial occupations, has a

[5] From the collection of George K. Hundley and used with his permission.

majority group (Yankees), a large minority group (Finnish), and, in general, has the marks of an ideal community for the analysis of social stratification. In their excellent study, *Under the Elms: Yesterday and Today,* David and Mary Hatch present the following conclusions based upon a careful analysis of Hilltown's social class structure.

An analysis of the class structure of Hilltown today involves not only a consideration of fundamental interrelationships of the principal aspects of community life, but also reveals the values and goals underlying the activity of the individuals in the community. A comparison of the class structure existing today with that which integrated the community in 1900 provides a crucial point of contrast for the two communities.

Whereas the earlier community included no significant minority group and was comparatively closely integrated within itself, the town today consists in reality of at least two, and possibly three, rather distinct communities. The first generation Finns have not yet developed a system of class differentiation among themselves; the second and third generation Finns and the mixed group are intermediate between Finns and Yankees, while the non-Finns are a community in themselves.

Extensive interaction, which characterized the community in 1900, by virtue of localization of occupation and social life, has given way to limited and sporadic contacts. Trades, farming, and local business transactions, once largely confined to the immediate locality, are placed today by occupational pursuits of a specialized nature outside the community. Organized social activities were formerly an expression of a desire for local contacts, and in turn stimulated social intercourse. The integration of participation and leadership in social organizations, in the churches, and in the political organization of the town with positions of prestige in the class structure created incentive for assuming of obligations and responsibilities. Today occupational activity and recreation are largely centered outside Hilltown. Most important, however, families in Hilltown tend to look upon their residence in town as temporary; few people except Finnish farmers and aged pensioners intend to remain. For mobile families there is little incentive for participation in local affairs, for ultimate attainment of positions of prestige in the social organization, when the town is merely a stopping-off place.

In contrast with the class structure of fifty years ago, the Yankee community in Hilltown today presents relatively little differentiation in social attributes from top to bottom of the scale. The old upper-class Yankee families represent a vestigial evidence of an older class system in which emphasis was upon family and family attributes; with their death an upper class based upon traditional family preeminence will disappear. These families remain in Hilltown because they could not enjoy a comparable position of prestige anywhere else; their present occupations, income, and authority do not set them apart from the middle class in town. The large, relatively undifferentiated Yankee middle class shows little variation of family background, occupation, education, or possessions.

Actually, the class system of Hilltown can be adequately understood only as a part of a widely extended system emanating from Metropolis and Chair City. The Yankee families in Hilltown would fit into the middle-middle or lower-middle groups of Chair City; it is from those groups that many came, and it is there they would return should they choose to live in the city. Although generalizations about the character of various towns in the metropolitan area are beyond the scope of this study, there is little doubt that different suburban areas (once independent towns) attract different occupational and social groups and that Hilltown is developing a reputation for being a lower-middle class area.

The values which underlie the actual placement of families in positions of greater or less prestige in the Yankee community are traditionally family, and to an ever increasing extent, occupational achievement. Except in the placement of the upper group of old Yankee families, a traditional position of prestige in the locality is secondary in the judgment of townspeople of one another; it is part of their general lack of concern for obligation for establishing or carrying on a family.

Personal qualities among both Yankees and Finns are an important factor in placement of individuals in so far as they are manifested in kinds of achievement which the town can evaluate. Education and manners which denote superior social position held outside the town are not easily evaluated by Hilltown people except as these attributes are associated with possession of impressive homes, cars, or clothes.

In the earlier community where social rating tended to be more closely integrated with local activities, personal qualities of neighborliness or leadership were more highly esteemed and were more likely to be developed. Today the consistent occupational emphasis for both men and women has speeded the decline of the local government, the church, and all organized social activities. As there is less need for qualities necessary for the functioning of social organizations, these qualities tend to be less developed. Among the Finns the same process is under way, most conspicuously in the Cooperative, and in the social groups for young women. The lack of a recognized social hierarchy with established modes of expected behavior, with standards of personal conformity, and prescribed obligations and duties results in a kind of anomie.

So strong is the tendency to judge by achievement and possessions that personal qualities become almost inseparable from their overt manifestation. Acquaintance is brief and the areas of contact among Yankee families are so limited that personality tends to be obscured. Judgments are based to a great extent upon what is known about the individual's occupation and his income. With slight modification, the same measures of prestige are applied to young and old, to men and women.

For certain groups, mainly married women with children, and

retired men, there are special impediments to achieving prestige-bearing goals. But for most members of the Yankee community there are strains inherent in the pursuit of ambitions unsuited to their family background, training, and inherent ability. The desire for possession of money and material things is not adjusted to established expectations of particular social classes. Desires and expectation of material rewards tend to be out of keeping with personal qualifications for attainment; for young people disproportionate independent income augments the disparity between expectation and realization. Not only is there lack of accepted integration of goals with the kinship system and social classes, but there is slight definition of legitimate means of achieving. The individual is not under strong compulsion to conform to religious or ethical standards in getting what he wants. Among the Finns, as among the Yankees, the overemphasis upon achievement in terms of money led to an abandonment of any pretence of conformity to government price regulations. Infringements of such laws in no way detracted from respect for the prospering law-breaker. In the same way, individual Finns have been willing to sacrifice loyalty to their group, and specifically to the Cooperative, for the attainment of occupational goals even though the attainment of such goals may mean loneliness and isolation from the group.

With the removal of fields for achievement, other than farming and shopkeeping, from the locality, possessions become an increasingly important measuring rod. The allocation of earnings and expenditures among Yankees tends to be made with less regard for long-term stability and security than for the prestige and immediate satisfaction of the individual. The individual achieves occupational position largely independent of parents and family, and his aims are mainly dissociated from maintaining or raising the position of his parents, or his brothers and sisters. Conspicuous consumption is characteristic of short-term planning. Like the Yankee families of two or three generations ago, the first generation Finns think of achievement as manifested in houses, farms, farm equipment, or education. Their group places great prestige value upon these attributes. The different emphasis of the two groups upon expenditures for immediate prestige increases the difficulty of rating of members of one group by members of the other.

Authority in town organizations was formerly a privilege associated with superior class status, and status at the same time imposed obligations to give time and effort in public service. Today the real spheres of political influence lie outside town, and the offices of town government do not confer important responsibilities. No one thinks of office holding as a way of achieving position. Nor do individuals and families think of participation in community life and the assuming of obligations as a means of establishing status for future generations.

Ambitions for attainment of a superior social position do not include the expectation of establishing a position of respect in the community through the establishment of a family with a stable source of income, with a home and land, and with a tradition of adherence to an approved kind of behavior. Recognized goals are largely those of occupational achievement measured primarily in terms of money. Escape from a town which is identified with lower-middle class existence, and establishing of residence in a more desirable section of Metropolis or Chair City are the desired expression of achievement. Rise in the social scale is dissociated from acceptance into a particular social group or into particular clubs or cliques. Social advancement is visualized by Hilltown people in terms of possession of material things more than in terms of association with particular groups of people. The belief that achievement is possible for anyone, and the fact that certain individuals do achieve precludes the establishment of a permanent community awareness of itself as a lower-middle or middle-middle class group. These people do not at present identify themselves with a rural proletariat because they are convinced that goals of occupational advancement are possible for them or for their children.[6]

The people of Hilltown, like the people of every other American community, live, work, play, enjoy periods of prosperity and suffer adversity, see the young born and the old die within a framework of social differentiation and prestige placement of individuals. Hilltown, furthermore, is typical of many American communities with respect to the criteria used, consciously and unconsciously, in the ranking of citizens by one another. The emphasis on attainment, as represented by possessions, wealth, and expenditures, tied in with family membership, personal qualities, and occupation, represents a typically American value position. Let us turn now to a different set of concepts through which we attempt to translate this value position into meaning for individual motivation and activity.

5. Human Motivation and Human Activity

The motivations of human action are complex, indeed, and it has been the fallacy of many a philosophical system that it failed to take into account this fundamental fact. Perhaps the best known of thought systems based upon a false psychology of a single, determining factor in human behavior is that of the economic doctrines of Adam Smith and his followers. Following the assumption of the rational, self-seeking, economic man, the classical economists built a

[6] Hatch, David, and Mary G. Hatch, *Under the Elms: Yesterday and Today,* Syracuse University Press, Syracuse, New York, 1949, pp. 155-58. Reprinted by permission of the authors. For an interesting analysis of social disorganization based on another version of this community study, see George C. Homans, *The Human Group,* Harcourt, Brace and Company, New York, 1950, Chapter 13.

theoretical structure of human economic life which, most economists would probably now agree, failed to account for a large, but important, area of economic motivation and activity.[7]

Motivations to human action have their sources in various aspects of the environment—natural and man made—as well as in the organic structure and functioning of the individual. Self-interest, economic or otherwise, is one source of human motivation, and an important one, too. But this is not enough completely to explain human activity. As Elton Mayo puts it:

If a number of individuals work together to achieve a common purpose, a harmony of interests will develop among them to which individual self-interest will be subordinated. This is a very different doctrine from the claim that individual self-interest is the solitary human motive.[8]

It is clear that the assumption of self-interest cannot be taken merely as a "given"; a sociological explanation of human action cannot stop with the statement that the individual acted as he did "because it was his interest to do so." We must always take into consideration not only the fact that people are self-interested, but the *content* of the self-interests as well. And the point we wish to emphasize is this: while the *fact* of human self-interest *may* well be a constant, springing from the survival needs of the organism, there are wide variations in the *specific contents* of such self-interests. Furthermore, these *contents* are learned in a social context,

[7] See John S. Gambs, *Man, Money, and Goods,* Columbia University Press, New York, 1951, for an interesting and enlightening presentation of the case for a "new psychology" for the basis of economic theory.

[8] Mayo, Elton, *The Political Problem of Industrial Civilization,* Harvard University Graduate School of Business Administration, Cambridge, Massachusetts, 1947.

that is, through interaction with other people in social groups defined and regulated by institutions.

. . . it is precisely around social institutions that, to a very large extent, the content of self-interest is organized. Indeed, this organization of what are otherwise, within broad limits, almost random potentialities of the self-interest tendencies of human action into a coherent system, may be said, in broad terms, to be one of the most important functions of institutions.[9]

Institutions are normative patterns which define the limits of sanctioned behavior. People participate in institutionalized activities of business, church, family, and government, for example, in terms of their individual *statuses* and *roles*. And, just as there are variations in institutional structure and emphasis from community to community, so there are variations in the contents of various statuses and roles.

Status refers to a "complex of mutual rights, obligations, and functions as defined by the pertinent ideal patterns . . ." of a social group. These rights, obligations, and expected performances spring not from the individual's personality attributes, but from the simple fact of his occupation of a "position" in the prestige hierarchy we discussed in the preceding sections of this chapter.[10]

Translate an individual's *status* or *statuses* (*position* refers to the total of an individual's statuses) into dynamic, psychological terms, and the concept of functional *role* becomes usable. Role is the behavioral aspect of status, that is, one behaves in his various roles, acts the real part of son, father, schoolteacher, doctor, tramp, hero, or coward, in his relations with other people.[11]

[9] Parsons, Talcott, *op. cit.*, pp. 211-12. Reprinted by permission of the publisher.
[10] Parsons, Talcott, *et al.*, "Toward a Common Language for the Area of the Social Sciences," mimeographed, no date, pp. 7-8.
[11] *Ibid.*, pp. 9-10.

A person can only express his view of his own self-interest in terms of the expectations of others and the partaking of his rights in the social group, that is, in the playing of his various roles in his community. Sociological study of the significance of self-interest necessitates analysis of institutional variations; we choose to save this analysis for a later portion of this book, but in the following section we explore certain psychological aspects of role-playing in communities.

6. Individual and Family Status Determinants in the American Community

As we indicated in the preceding sections, the social class systems of communities exhibit much similarity from one geographical region of the United States to another. While it is difficult at times to separate the methodological assumptions of researchers from the actual ways in which people in communities perceive themselves and their neighbors, the evidence is that the range of criteria for the determination of individual status is also quite limited. The following examples, drawn from community surveys and other similar researches, indicate this.

In older, relatively stable communities, as contrasted to newer or more rapidly changing ones, status is quite likely to follow families rather than individuals. This is the case in Elmtown, a Middle Western community, in which August Hollingshead was able to distinguish five separate class levels. Criteria for status placement of families are place of residence, income and material possessions, family background, general reputation, and participation in community affairs. These bases for class affiliation are indicated in the following description of the stratification system of Elmtown.

A Class I (the "upper" stratum) position is acquired in

Elmtown almost exclusively through a combination of wealth and family lineage and the membership of this class is relatively stable from generation to generation. Wealth is the primary characteristic of the class but the continuance of incoming wealth is not important once an individual's position has been established. Leisure time and the modes of using it are of significance. All families of Class I own their own houses and most of them own two or three automobiles. Class I members adhere more strictly to a rigid code of social behavior than do any of the other classes of the town.

Almost half of the families in Class II have achieved their positions through their own efforts; the remainder have inherited them, but a further rise is virtually an impossibility. This is because their origins are too well known and too little time has elapsed between the beginning of their climb up the social ladder and the present to allow them to be accepted in the exclusive circles of Class I. Because these families focus their attentions upon economic and political pursuits, much of the spare time of Class II individuals is spent in civic activities. Security, rather than wealth, is of fundamental importance. Education is recognized as the surest means of getting ahead, and, as a consequence, Class II is the best educated class in Elmtown.

Class III lies at the median level of social prestige in Elmtown, and these people show by far the strongest feelings of class consciousness. They resent the people of Class II because of real or alleged social discrimination. At the same time, they realize that in many cases their lineage could be traced to Class IV and show pride in having risen from the lower ranks. Class III families usually have sufficient income for a comfortable living standard, but not enough for capital investment which might materially improve their economic position. The women of most families work outside the home in order to maintain the existing living standard.

The higher classes characterize Class IV as "poor but honest, hard workers, who pay their taxes, raise their children properly, but never seem to get ahead financially." Most members of this group work for a living day by day in the mills and shops of the town, on the farms, or in the mines of the outlying district. Incomes typically are large enough to provide necessities and some comforts, but any style of living which might by reasonable standards be called luxurious is not in evidence. Family stability, so characteristic of the higher classes, begins to give way to instability; this is probably due in part to the fact that most Class IV women work outside the home. At any rate, exactly a third of the families have been or are broken by divorce, separation, or death. As might be expected, very few if any of the members of Class IV take part in civic or community organizations.

Elmtown families in Class V occupy the lowest ranking positions in the prestige structure. They are often looked upon as "scum" by members of the higher classes. People in Class V know that they are on the bottom of the social scale and rarely attempt to better themselves because they feel it is almost useless to try. Yet they desire money, possessions, education, and social prestige, but they appear unaware of how these are achieved. When an individual of this class attempts to improve his position, he is apt to be discriminated against by many members of his own class who think he is trying to "put on airs." Income from wages usually provides Class V families with sufficient money for meager necessities; in some cases, it is inadequate even for these and private charity or public relief are relied upon.[12]

[12] Hollingshead, August B., *Elmtown's Youth*, John Wiley and Sons, Inc., New York, 1949, pp. 83-120.

Descriptions of the class structures of other American communities indicate similar criteria of social differentiation and status placement. W. Lloyd Warner and Paul S. Lunt, for example, describe six class levels in Yankee City, an Eastern seaboard town of about 17,000 people. The "Upper Upper" is composed of old families, usually among the wealthiest in town, and the "Lower Upper," of families who have recently gained wealth, or who do not have the long history of local residence. The Lower Upper group includes many "high" or especially successful professional people. The "Upper Middle" is composed of families "on the make" and now acquiring wealth. Most professionals and most recent newcomers with wealth are included. The "Lower Middle" class is made up of most merchants and high-level white-collar workers. "Upper Lower" designates a stratum filled mainly by lower-level white-collar employees and skilled laborers, while most unskilled workers, charity families or those on relief, Negroes, many people of Russian or Polish background, and transients fall into the "Lower Lower" class. Warner and Lunt rated individuals and assigned them to one or another class on the basis of such variables as family membership, size and condition of residence, income, and patterns of spending.[13]

James West writes that the people of Plainville, a rural community in the Ozark Mountains, place one another in status positions with reference to such characteristics as their "goodness," honesty, self-respect, occupations, and religious behavior.[14] John Dollard reports that, in a Southern community, people rate one another in terms of "talent, capital,

[13] Warner, W. Lloyd, and Paul S. Lunt, *The Social Life of a Modern Community*, Yale University Press, New Haven, Connecticut, 1941, *passim*, especially pp. 81-91.

[14] West, James, *Plainville, U.S.A.*, Columbia University Press, New York, 1945, especially p. 117.

and ancestry." [15] In the Gold Coast of Chicago (perhaps not truly a community but a transitional area characterized by instability and change) there appeared as early as 1929 to be a shift from an earlier ascription of status on the basis of breeding, family, and aristocratic background to emphasis on clique or "set" membership, wealth, and display.[16] An investigator reports that in Ocean City, New Jersey, criteria were ownership of real property, stability and location of residence, telephones—definitely a luxury in this summer resort town—the hiring of a full-time servant, and educational level.[17] In Hilltown, as we have seen, the bases are kinship, personal qualities, possessions, and authority.[18]

There are definite variations as to relative significance of different status criteria from community to community, but Parsons' six categories, kinship, personal qualities, achievements, possessions, power, and authority, plus religious affiliation, are the ones most widely distributed in our country.

7. Community, Status, and Individual Role Playing

The idea that the human individual has many social roles to play and that he organizes his behavior to accord to a greater or lesser degree with the expectations of other people is one of the important conceptions in sociology. Individuals often play roles which are mutually incompatible, resulting in conflict on the level of personality.[19] Some of these cultural

[15] Dollard, John, *Caste and Class in a Southern Town,* Harper and Brothers, New York, 1937, pp. 62-97.

[16] Zorbaugh, Harvey W., *Gold Coast and Slum,* University of Chicago Press, Chicago, 1929, p. 47.

[17] Voss, J. Ellis, *Summer Resort: An Ecological Analysis of a Satellite Community* (Ph.D. dissertation), University of Pennsylvania, Philadelphia, 1941, *passim,* especially p. 136.

[18] Hatch, David, and Mary G. Hatch, *op. cit.,* pp. 142-47.

[19] Merton, Robert K., *Social Theory and Social Structure,* The Free Press, Glencoe, Illinois, 1949, p. 110.

conflicts, such as discrepancies between role expectations of church and political party (for example, Catholic-Communist or Catholic-Fascist in European communities during the nineteen-thirties and nineteen-forties) are experienced by both men and women. Some conflicts such as those between expectations of religious groups and demands of patriotism and loyalty (for example, Jehovah's Witnesses and military service) are felt almost exclusively by men. Finally, there is a whole series of cultural contradictions affecting sex roles, such as career-role demands versus "home and mother" expectations, or educational accomplishment expectations versus male superiority values which women alone experience.[20]

Such conflicts as these, and those arising out of social class values which include the expectation of attainment of "appropriate" levels of success in occupation, wealth, and social prestige, are dysfunctional for a community. No social group can show integration in its collective life beyond the limits set by the nature of the personality integration of its members. The description of personality and social disorganization in Hilltown makes this clear. Unintegrated, goalless personalities obsessed with a philosophy of activism contribute to the breakdown of orderly, purposeful, and meaningful community life.

Individuals tend to segment the roles they play—to place barriers, real or imagined, between them—in order to minimize such conflicts. For example, a man may convince himself it is possible to work "as a scientist without value judgments" in a scheme which is counter to his values as a man and a citizen.[21] One may separate his role as a church deacon

---

[20] See Mirra Komarovsky, "Cultural Contradictions and Sex Roles," *American Journal of Sociology*, November, 1946, pp. 184-89, and Margaret Mead, "What Women Want," *Fortune*, December, 1946, pp. 172-284.

[21] Merton, Robert K., *op. cit.*, p. 172.

from that of a drunken fun-seeker at the volunteer firemen's convention two hundred miles from home, or as a sentimental husband and father from that of a cynical, calculating business executive.

Furthermore, conflicting social values, such as fertility and celibacy in the Catholic Church, can sometimes be rendered completely compatible through segregating them in different social roles, for example, fertility to the married lay members, celibacy to the priest.[22] Purposeful value segregation by social roles may well be an important but thus far largely unexplored (by sociologists, at least) means of resolving not only personality conflict for the individual, but community group conflict as well.

In sum, human beings live in communities which are organized in terms of a set of generally accepted values and these values are hierarchically arranged in terms of group attachment to them. Individuals are differentiated from one another on the basis of real or imagined possession of qualities and characteristics associated with the value system, and are also placed on a scale of prestige-valuation. There are expectations with respect to behavior and degree of conformity to the value system attached to every position or place on the prestige scale, and the people in a community therefore live under a set of rules which prescribe the means by which the accepted goals are to be sought. When means and goals are not integrated—that is, when goals are absent or when institutional means for reaching goals are not available—such imbalance is expressed in a tendency toward random, purposeless activity or in deviant behavior. Random or highly deviant patterns of behavior may mean a high incidence of personality malintegration as well as community disorganization.

[22] *Ibid.,* p. 258.

8. Caste, Class, and Social Mobility in the Open Society

All societies thus far known to the scholar exhibit the phenomena of social differentiation and social stratification. In all societies there is also *some* possibility that an individual may change his membership from one stratum to another, that is, may enhance or detract from his social prestige according to the degree to which he acquires, retains, or loses those characteristics held valuable by most of the people of his society. The "movement" from one social stratum to another or from lower to higher or higher to lower within one social stratum is what the social scientist means by the term "social mobility."

One of the marks of a democratic society is the relative ease with which an individual can increase his prestige and the degree to which he can do so, that is, the degree to which social mobility is possible on the basis of such characteristics as personal qualities, achievements, self-obtained possessions, authority, and power. In terms of social mobility, the democratic society is the "open" society.[23] Those societies, on the other hand, which place greater significance on the facts of the social ranking of an individual's ancestors than on his own personal qualities and accomplishments in the ultimate determination of his social status are designated as "closed." In the closed society, a person's social position is to a larger extent than in the open society determined by the accidents of birth; social mobility, especially vertical mobility, may be virtually impossible or, more likely, extremely difficult and rare.

[23] See Ralph Linton, *The Study of Man,* D. Appleton-Century Company, New York, 1936, Chapter VIII, for a discussion of "achieved" and "ascribed" status, and Karl Popper's *The Open Society and Its Enemies,* 2 volumes, G. Routledge, London, 1945, for a discussion of democracy and its enemies.

The people of such countries as the United States have prided themselves on having open systems of social stratification. India has long been thought of as having a closed system, although it must be realized that "openness" or "closedness," as the terms are used here, have only relative meaning.

The constructs of *caste* and *class* are related to the concept of social mobility. Class designates strata into and out of which mobility is at least a possibility, while one is born into and remains permanently in a caste. The Brahmins and the pariahs in the Hindu system are castes and there are those who say the American Negro is placed in a caste system.[24] Essentially, from a sociological point of view, the factors which distinguish separate castes and classes from one another are differential social esteem and prestige and differential allocation of functions and rewards.

Most Americans are probably reluctant to admit the presence of social class distinctions. In Plainville, for example, there are three attitudes which got in the way of free recognition of what to an investigator was an obvious class structure: the idea that class distinctions are improper to America, that they exist only in cities, anyway, and that no individual ought to be reminded of his inferiority in any respect.[25] Yet James West, basing his conclusions upon verbalized statements of the people themselves, was able to place all 275 members in the community of Plainville into a rather rigidly defined set of class categories. While disavowing class distinctions as improper, the residents of Plainville apparently saw no contradiction in their references to others in

---

[24] Cf. Gunnar Myrdal, *An American Dilemma*, Harper and Brothers, New York, 1944, especially Part VIII. Note, also, Horace Mann Bond's use of the term "permanent minority" in his "Education as a Social Process: A Case Study of a Higher Institution as an Incident in the Process of Acculturation," *American Journal of Sociology*, May, 1943, pp. 701-709.

[25] West, James, *op. cit.*, p. 115.

colorful terms like "nice refined people," "the people who are all right," "the good, honest, self-respecting average everyday working people," or "people who live like animals." [26]

In America, as W. Lloyd Warner points out, the social class systems of communities are "basically similar" from one region to another; the ease with which people can find their "places" in the class structure when moving from one community to another is evidence of this similarity. There are actually differences in the way people perceive themselves—newer communities tend not to develop superior "old-family" classes and "lower-lower" groups are smaller in proportion to population in Western communities, for example—but the fundamental criteria upon which the ranking of individuals is done remain fairly constant from place to place in our country.[27]

Some scholars feel that, in recent decades, the system of social stratification in the United States has become increasingly rigid. A recent research, for example, reports this tendency and concludes that rigidity is reinforced by our "tight occupational structure and the association of ethnic background with occupational pursuits and by the nature of our educational, religious, marital, and leisure-time institutions." [28] Although not uniform from community to community for the whole nation—and this makes the very practical possibility of attacking blockages in our system of mobility on the community level an interesting one indeed—it is held that there is a growing class consciousness in the nation. Furthermore, although rigidity in the stratification

[26] *Ibid.,* p. 116, and following.
[27] See W. Lloyd Warner, *American Life,* pp. 55-60.
[28] Hollingshead, August B., "Trends in Social Stratification: A Case Study," *American Sociological Review,* December, 1952, pp. 679-86. See also W. Lloyd Warner, *American Life,* p. 107, *passim.*

system is the result of factors of national scope and range, such increasing class consciousness proceeds community by community, manifesting itself in community problems rather than national problems, as we shall see in the next section. People must work through the community and its institutions if a democratic "open" system of mobility in tune with the American tradition of equality of opportunity is to be preserved and passed along to generations yet unborn. If, as these studies indicate, it is now through the educational system rather than the occupational system that people seek and attain vertical mobility, it is, further, the community schools which must assume much of the burden of maintaining the American dream.[29] If the sources just cited are valid, one of the most important problems facing American communities in our day is how to bridge the widening gap between the American heritage of social mobility on the basis of individual worth and the threatening reality of rigid stratification, for conflict between class values and the American idea of individualism generally results in community disorganization.[30] But the situation is by no means as clear as it might appear to be at this point in our discussion, and we must be wary of accepting without question the inevitability of class rigidity and consequent class conflict. Recent innovations in education, such as the G.I. bills, have encouraged to an even greater extent than in the past the use of the educational system as a means of attaining vertical social mobility.

There are other factors, too, as Robin M. Williams, Jr., points out, which tend to *stabilize the existing system* of stratification and, while perhaps not mitigating against its

[29] Warner, W. Lloyd, *American Life,* pp. 110-17, and Elbridge Sibley, "Some Demographic Clues to Stratification," *American Sociological Review,* June, 1942, pp. 322-30.

[30] Cf. August B. Hollingshead, *Elmtown's Youth,* "Summary and Conclusions," pp. 439-53.

effects, serve to counteract tendencies toward greater rigidity. He lists the following: (1) the wide distribution of a high living standard, (2) a relatively high incidence of vertical mobility and the hopes it breeds in the minds of people, (3) a very large middle group with respect to prestige and income, (4) widespread political and legal rights which, at least ideally, are open equally to everyone, (5) the availability of public facilities and services, (6) the presence and persistence of symbols and behavior patterns stressing equality, (7) the heterogeneity within each of the social strata, (8) the barriers between classes themselves, (9) participation in common activities by members of various strata, and (10) the persistence of a large and complex set of ideas and beliefs which support the present stratification system.[31] These characteristics of our society provide valuable clues to means of preserving the open class system in our communities.

Gideon Sjoberg, after examining the redistribution of four objective criteria of class—power, achievements, possessions, and personal attributes—concludes that our class system is less rigid than it was fifty years ago. Since the 1890's and early 1900's businessmen have lost a great deal of their former monopolistic control and power over our economic and political institutions; in other words, there has been a deterioration of a formerly rigid coalescence of social, economic, and political elites. Recent high levels of employment, inflation, our newer progressive tax structure, minimum wage laws, and public relief programs have all contributed to a general modification of class differentials based on achievements and possessions. No longer are the rich getting richer and the poor poorer, but the extremes in the standards of living of various occupational groups are drawing closer to-

[31] Based upon Robin M. Williams, Jr., *American Society*, Alfred A. Knopf, Inc., New York, 1951, pp. 128-29.

gether. For example, with 100 as an index representing the living standard in 1930, it is shown that the index for 1947 is 191 for coal miners, 132 for automobile workers, 109 for teachers, 78 for railway executives, 74 for Congressmen, 38 for bondholders, 31 for wealthy stockholders. Finally, personal attributes have become considerably less significant as criteria of class distinction; mass production of clothing has resulted in a general leveling of style and fashion, both for men and women; the same can be said of hairdo's and beauty treatments, language usages, and social etiquette. Sjoberg reaches four conclusions: (1) that common consumption patterns and other similar forces have created an American system in which classes can only be considered ideal types, (2) even people's ideas about class and class lines have become confused, (3) social mobility includes more than occupational advancement, and many sociological analyses have failed to consider changes in income, personal attributes, and power, and (4) we can go too far in debunking the American dream of a classless society.[32]

While Sjoberg's study is concerned with stratification and mobility of the mass society, it is pointed out that there is some evidence to support the belief that there is a parallel between class structure in local communities and the class system of the mass society.[33] In fact, the contemporary interest of sociologists in stratification and the class system in American society springs to a considerable extent from earlier community studies, especially Warner and Lunt's original Yankee City volume.[34] The six categories of social class used as a research tool in this study have for some persons taken on the character of a rigid system adequately describing

[32] Sjoberg, Gideon, "Are Social Classes in America Becoming More Rigid?" *American Sociological Review*, December, 1951, pp. 775-83.

[33] *Ibid.*, p. 776.

[34] Warner, W. Lloyd, and Paul S. Lunt, *op. cit.*

American society; Max Weber warned against such "reification" many years ago.[35] Reification of any set of categories of social class can hardly be expected to result in anything but the discriminative selection of those factors in our social life which support the contention of increasing rigidity in our system of stratification. The truth at this time would appear to be that the facts are unclear, and that even the concepts of class are not to be taken for granted. Relatively too much attention has been paid to such objective criteria as occupation, income, and wealth, and too little to the more difficult to measure but equally important bases such as power, authority, and a wide variety of talent and other personal attributes. For every factor in community living in America which contributes to a greater rigidity in our stratification system, there can be lined up one which contributes to lesser clarity in class definition. As the work of both Williams and Sjoberg indicates, caution in making sweeping predictions concerning the future of our stratification system is the better part of wisdom.

SELECTED REFERENCES

Bendix, Reinhard, and Seymour Martin Lipset, *Class, Status and Power*, The Free Press, Glencoe, Illinois, 1953. A large and varied collection of readings in social stratification.

Cuber, John F., and William F. Kenkel, *Social Stratification in the United States*, Appleton-Century-Crofts, Inc., New York, 1954. A recent, useful volume on social stratification. Includes discussion of eight community studies.

Gerth, Hans, and C. Wright Mills, *Character and Social Structure*, Harcourt, Brace and Company, New York, 1953. See espe-

---

[35] Weber, Max, *The Theory of Social and Economic Organization*, translated by A. M. Henderson and Talcott Parsons, Oxford University Press, New York, 1947, p. 103.

cially pp. 306-41 for an excellent theoretical analysis of the nature and function of social stratification.

Hatch, David, and Mary G. Hatch, *Under the Elms: Yesterday and Today,* Syracuse University Press, Syracuse, New York, 1949. This careful study of a New England community makes use of the structural-functional mode of analysis in the study of class and social prestige.

Hollingshead, August B., *Elmtown's Youth,* John Wiley and Sons, Inc., New York, 1949. This fascinating community study explores the relationship between class membership and the activities of high-school and out-of-school youth in a midwestern town.

Mayer, Kurt B., *Class and Society,* Studies in Sociology, Random House, Inc., New York, 1955. A competent, brief study of social differentiation and stratification.

Warner, W. Lloyd, and Paul S. Lunt, *The Social Life of a Modern Community,* Yale University Press, New Haven, Connecticut, 1941. In this volume, the first of the famous "Yankee City" series, Professor Warner introduces his famous sixfold system of class membership.

PART FIVE

*The Processes
of Community
Behavior*

CHAPTER **8**

Cooperation and Conflict in the American Community

1. The Social Processes: Cooperation and Conflict

The struggle for survival of animals is an established fact. There is a kind of survival struggle for humans, too; it differs from that among the lower animals in the forms it takes and the greater variety of means used. Any species of lower animal is limited by the relative rigidity of its biological structure to a small collection of means, but man, by nature, is plastic, pliable, and generalized, and a wide range of techniques in conflict is open to him. Brute strength and physical combat may be, and often is, resorted to by man, but, unlike the lower animals, he adds learned response, argument, ridicule, threat, and coercion, to his repertoire, and brings them to bear in conflict.[1]

Conflict is one of the universals of human society; in part, this is because a society, as we have noted a number of times, is always a loose integration of people, things, and ideas, and because even this incomplete integration is on the mental,

[1] Lasswell, Harold D., "Social Conflict," *Encyclopaedia of the Social Sciences*, The Macmillan Company, New York, 1931, Volume IV, p. 195.

rather than the biological, level. The source of conflict is value differences, and disagreement can be over means as well as ends.[2]

It is inconceivable that the people of any society can manage to eliminate all conflict. This is because there always exist, along with common values, goals which are clearly personal and related only to the individual's needs or desires, for example, sex, food, and recreation. People are bound to stand in one another's way while attempting to capture for their individual uses the scarce resources of a niggardly world. While the social group does suppress open conflict— at least as it is expressed in violence—some conflict always persists.

On the other hand, no society can exist without some form of cooperation. People cooperate whenever they deliberately unite either their similar or dissimilar efforts for the purpose of attaining a goal upon which they agree, or which they let fall to some functionary leading them. "Cooperation necessarily implies interdependency. Conversely, interdependency calls for cooperation."[3] Just as it is inconceivable that the people of any society can manage to eliminate conflict, it is also inconceivable that there could be no cooperation in a society.

If any community culture-world is to persist or change along some predictable pattern, there must be a certain, but thus far indefinable, degree of integration or consistency among its cultural elements. Whole societies and communities are capable of holding conflicting attitudes and values, but no community or society can continue to function unless conflicts between its members are generally resolvable. Mem-

[2] Davis, Kingsley, *Human Society,* The Macmillan Company, New York, 1949, p. 157.

[3] Hiller, E. T., *Social Relations and Structure,* Harper and Brothers, New York, 1947, p. 154.

bers cannot be permitted completely uncontrolled behavior which is constantly in opposition, for, if this is the case, the cultural system must eventually suffer some rupture and disorganization and the social group cease to function in some respects at least. This harsh fact is mitigated because of the happy fact that individuals can do one thing while thinking or believing something inconsistent with their actions. Hence, behavior conflicts are not always reflected in culture conflicts.

2. Modes of Cooperation and Conflict

There are a number of different ways of analyzing and categorizing forms of cooperation and conflict. One classification divides conflict into personal, racial, class, political, and international.[4] Another uses "overt" and "covert" as descriptive categories,[5] and yet another presents a long list of types, including "family," "industrial," "national," "personal," "occupational," "ideological," and "sectional." [6] We have chosen to follow the very simple and useful set of four categories outlined years ago by Robert M. MacIver: *direct* and *indirect cooperation* and *direct* and *indirect conflict*.

(1) *Direct and indirect cooperation.*[7] Direct cooperation includes all those activities in which people do like things with one another—such as sing, carry on group worship, and till fields—even though they might effectively do them

[4] Gillin, John Lewis, and John Philip Gillin, *Cultural Sociology,* The Macmillan Company, New York, 1948, pp. 625-32.

[5] LaPiere, Richard T., *Sociology,* The McGraw-Hill Book Company, Inc., New York, 1946, pp. 420-21.

[6] Sutherland, Robert L., Julian L. Woodward, and Milton A. Maxwell, *Introductory Sociology,* J. B. Lippincott Company, New York, 1952, pp. 215-16.

[7] This and the following section are based upon R. M. MacIver and Charles H. Page, *Society,* Rinehart and Company, New York, 1949, pp. 62-64.

separately as individuals. People cooperate for one or both of these reasons: because the grouping stimulates the performance of their tasks, or because they obtain social satisfactions beyond those provided by the tasks in which they are engaged. Direct cooperation is present, for example, when people join together to accomplish something which is impossible for one or all of them working separately, such as the lifting of a heavy weight.

Indirect cooperation includes all activities engaged in by people who do unlike tasks for an agreed-upon end or purpose. Such cooperation requires a division of labor and specialization, and is exemplified by procreation and the rearing of a family.

One of the major problems the members of any community must face is how to maintain direct cooperation (which seems to meet basic human needs for recognition and response) in a time of constantly increasing specialization. The different forms of cooperation, therefore, may generate conflict—for example, specialization may create barriers to communication and understanding between persons of different occupations, resulting in disagreements over values, means, and ends.

(2) *Direct and indirect conflict.* Social conflict, as a general term, refers to any activity in which people are contenders against one another for an object or goal. *Direct conflict* is present whenever persons or groups "thwart or impede or restrain or injure or destroy" each other in their attempts to reach an objective. Examples of direct conflict are war, revolution, propaganda, and litigation.

Indirect conflict is present in those instances when individuals or groups seek goals in such a way as to obstruct the attainment of the same goals by other individuals or groups, but do so without interfering with the efforts of one another.

Competition, as a social process, is one form of indirect conflict.[8] Competition, in the sense we use the term, is a fundamental principle of the organization of the human community; it results in an ordered distribution of people and provides, through the division of labor, for the social differentiation of individuals.[9] The processes of competition can, therefore, be related sociologically to social stratification in the community.

Conflict, whether direct or indirect, and in whatever form it takes, reflects the cultural standards and the general social conditions of the community. For example, conflict not only creates unstable conditions, but reflects them. This is because conflict is itself one means of settling conflict. When a conflict situation results in a victory-and-defeat pattern, issues are usually settled for a time—only to crop up, oftener than not, in new forms of conflict. But victory-and-defeat is not the only result of conflict, for it can be resolved in other ways: through the discovery of like interests of the parties or the changing of hostile to non-hostile attitudes.[10]

Conflict has yet another dimension; it has a meaning in terms of human personality, its development and disorganization. In personal as well as social conflict, values are at stake. Personality disturbance in a conflict situation is centered about the individual and his capability (or lack of it) to win the conflict—that is, to choose between opposing goals

[8] Compare this point of view with the somewhat more elaborate categories and definitions of some sociologists who consider competition a separate process to be compared to and contrasted with conflict, e.g., "We say that when two or more persons want the same thing we have competition, and when they want different but mutually incompatible things we have conflict." Jessie Bernard, *American Community Behavior*, The Dryden Press, New York, 1949, p. 47. Professor Bernard goes on to point out that, in reality, conflict and competition may shade into one another and become difficult to distinguish; in some instances there is overlapping.

[9] Park, Robert Ezra, *Human Communities*, The Free Press, Glencoe, Illinois, 1952, p. 119.

[10] See Section 5 of this chapter.

—or to accept a new value to replace one denied him by the conflict situation.[11]

3. Conflict in the Community: Parties, Issues, Means

The differentiation between direct and indirect conflict is largely between the means used by the contenders rather than between the goals they seek. To recapitulate, direct conflict is present whenever individuals or groups impede, restrain, destroy, or injure one another by the means used in seeking a goal; indirect conflict is present when individuals or groups seek goals in such a manner as to obstruct the attainment of the same goals by others, but do so without interference with the efforts of the others. The goals might be the same in both cases, but the nature of the means used will determine whether direct or indirect conflict is present. We turn now to a brief discussion of parties, issues, and means in direct and indirect conflict in the community.

(1) *Economic conflict.*[12] One way of looking at a community is to divide its population into two general classifications: *buyers* of goods and services and *sellers* of goods and services. Very often, although not always, buyers and sellers are at odds with one another in seeking to satisfy their unlimited wants with limited goods and services and the result is direct or indirect conflict.

The issues between buyers and sellers are mainly concerned with the quality and quantity of goods and services, the truthfulness and reliability of advertising claims, high versus restricted production, high prices against low prices,

[11] Katsoff, Louis O., *The Design of Human Behavior,* Educational Publishers, Inc., Saint Louis, Missouri, 1947, p. 171.

[12] Although recast into a different form, this and immediately following sections draw heavily on Jessie Bernard's excellent discussion of conflict and competition. See her *American Community Behavior,* The Dryden Press, New York, 1949, Chapter 6.

easy versus hard credit, and all the other relationships which determine who gets what, in what quantity, and of what quality. These issues sometimes become so significant to the individuals and groups involved that they engage in direct conflict as a process through which they hope to reconcile their differences. Stealing and the use of violence, deception, embezzlement, fraudulent advertising, and any other technique of either the "blue-collar" or the "white-collar" criminal may be used.

Economic conflict may be indirect, however, and although the parties and issues are the same as in direct conflict, such means as collective bargaining, honest and fair advertising, price cutting, the raising or lowering of salaries offered or held acceptable, and speculating and gambling may be used.

(2) *Political conflict.* Political behavior is concerned with power relationships, and, by its very definition, involves conflict.

The specific issues in political conflict vary widely, but in general they all involve the general power to make policy decisions which have significant social, economic, and political consequences. When the contenders resort to revolution, violence, threats, or bribery, they are engaged in direct conflict; when they use only the lawful and peaceful techniques of electioneering, campaigning, petitioning, and voting, the conflict is indirect. With some exceptions, notably the Civil War, political conflicts have usually been reconciled in America by peaceful and indirect means. As one of the case studies in the next section indicates, however, even in our day an occasional American community suffers an outbreak of violent direct political conflict.

(3) *Social conflict.* The concept of *social conflict* cuts across political and economic conflict. The issues may be political in part, economic in part, or neither, involving in-

stead such cultural patterns as manners. They may concern disagreements over such matters as property relations, the behavior of children, opinions as to what constitutes proper activities for the old or young, the married or unmarried, and the male or female. Aspiration to positions of high social prestige, the search for a mate, and the desire to maintain one's position or keep one's mate, are other important sources of social conflict. The parties involved may be individuals or families living in neighborhoods, cliques, religious groups, races, "high status" or "low status" groups, or persons living in a particular area of a community as over and against those living in another part of the community.

The means used in such conflict may be direct: violence (such as lynching); forcible or intimidating exclusion of one group from places or services; segregation; restriction from residential or business areas by covenants; incarceration; intimidation; and threats. On the other hand, the means used may be indirect: social climbing in all its forms; elaborate or "correct" personal adornment and display of wealth in homes, automobiles, "antiques," or jewelry; attendance at "proper" schools; and, in the case of organizations such as church, school, or lodge groups, elaborate buildings and other facilities. The list of means used in indirect social conflict could be expanded indefinitely and would vary in emphasis according to whether the main interest was in conflict between individuals, families, or organized groups.

4. Case Studies in American Community Conflict

Community conflict sometimes makes an exciting and colorful story; it is often threaded into the folklore of a people and told and retold by the old to the young. But oftener than not community conflict is of a humdrum, routine, colorless, everyday kind. It may burst forth in color and violence from time to time, then ease along through long periods in which people and groups reconcile their differences in quiet and orderly ways. We present in this section some examples of each type: the force and violence of political conflict in Athens, Tennessee, the quiet, but direct, social-political conflict in Triple City, the even quieter racial conflict in Denver, Colorado, and the revealing processes of economic conflict in Yankee City.

(1) *Athens, Tennessee: direct political conflict.* McMinn County, Tennessee, had never been known for its democratic and honest politics. First, the Republican Party held almost uncontested control for many years, and then the Democrats took over for the ten years preceding the outbreak of violence in August, 1946. The Cantrell machine, headed by State Senator Paul Cantrell, was tied in closely with the Crump machine which ran the state. In McMinn County, the machine managed public affairs with a rough hand, using especially the office of county sheriff, filled by one Pat Mansfield with his sixteen regular deputies and any number of "emergency" deputies. It was charged that gambling and bootlegging were tied in with the machine; appeal to the courts was useless and the machine could not be voted out because it controlled the elections, even counting the ballots with no watchers from the opposition—and the machine always won. But McMinn County boys began to think of these things during World War II when they were scattered on the battlefronts of the globe, and when they came back to their community, things changed with a suddenness and violence that startled the entire country.[13]

[13] The quotation which follows is from Theodore H. White, "The Battle of Athens, Tennessee," *Harper's Magazine*, January 1947, pp. 54-61 (copyright 1947 by Theodore H. White), and is used by permission of Ann Watkins, Inc.

By spring of 1946, the GI boys were trickling back to McMinn from France and Germany and Italy and the Pacific. The people of McMinn say there is nothing but what some good doesn't come of it, and what happened afterwards in McMinn came from the war. The boys learned a lot about fighting and more about patriotism in the Army; when they came home they were ready to do something about democracy in Tennessee.

In February they set to planning. They met secretly because the Cantrell forces had the guns, the blackjacks, and the law; and the deputies could make life hell for anyone they could catch. Once in the summer campaign, they seized one boy, locked him up, took his poll-tax receipt from him, and then, threatening his life, made him sign a statement that no such incident had ever taken place. There were five GI's and one civilian in on the first secret meetings. They decided that in the summer election for sheriff and county officials, the GI's would put up a complete slate of their own. Mansfield, Cantrell's sheriff, was going out of office and Cantrell was running for sheriff himself.

The veterans sounded out general feeling and in May they called a mass meeting. To get into the GI meeting you had to show your discharge papers, or your membership card in the American Legion or VFW. The veterans picked a non-partisan slate: three Democrats, two Republicans. Knox Henry, a tall handsome boy who had been hurt in North Africa and ran a filling station, was the man for sheriff. He was Republican, but the county trustee was to be Frank Carmichael, a farmer and a Democrat. Carmichael had been a major in the war and was badly wounded at Saint Lo. The others were GI boys, too, except Charlie Pickel who had been in the first World War and had returned with his wounds to be a carpenter. Jim Buttram, a sturdy, solid chunk of combat infantryman, was to be campaign manager. Jim's family had a grocery store in Athens and Jim was new to politics.

With the slate chosen, the campaign picked up speed. Ralph

Duggan, who had come back from the Navy to his law practice, was legal adviser and they pored over the Tennessee Code to see what the laws allowed them. The business men who feared the Cantrell forces contributed money secretly. They were afraid to give openly because the machine could raise the taxes, or arrest them, or generally make life hard. But eight thousand dollars came into the campaign fund and soon loudspeaker trucks were rolling over the hill roads, the *Daily Athenian* was carrying campaign ads, and the local radio station was putting out fifteen minutes of talk a day. Up and down the pockets and roads went GI's calling meetings in evenings at schoolhouses or homes, begging, urging, pleading with everyone to get out and vote. It wasn't hard to pin scandal on the Cantrell forces; McMinn County had lived with the scandal for almost ten years. Nothing had been done about it for two reasons: first, the only alternative was the old Republicans; and second, it did no good to vote because the Cantrells always counted themselves to victory anyway. So over and over, like the beating of a drum in the darkness, the GI campaign chanted its theme: "Your vote will be counted as cast, your vote will be counted as cast."

"Everybody knew we were trying to do the right thing," said Jim Buttram. "We had twelve public meetings and we knew they were damned good. About three weeks before elections we knew we had won the votes and the hearts of the people of McMinn County. But the hardest thing to do was to build an organization to help us see we got a fair count on election day."

The GI's asked the governor for help; but the governor was elected with Crump backing and was silent. They asked the Attorney General in Washington for help; he did nothing. They made contact with the FBI office in Knoxville; the FBI agent said he couldn't do anything unless Washington told him to, and Washington wasn't telling. The GI's were on their own.

Election day dawned sweet and clear over McMinn County. McMinn numbers twelve voting precincts but the decisive vote is cast in two townships, Etowah and Athens. Etowah is some ten miles in the hills from the main highway, but Athens, the county seat, is dead center. Athens sprawls fragrant and green about the old white courthouse; the Robert E. Lee hotel sits on one side, Woolworth's and a movie house on another, stores and offices on the other two sides. One block up from the courthouse lies the red brick county jail. Maple trees and green lawn surround the courthouse; old people sun themselves on the benches, children romp on the grass, blue-denimed farmers stroll casually about buying supplies for home and land.

Election day saw Athens an armed camp. As the voters came to the polls, they found the Cantrell machine in ominous demonstration of force. Almost two hundred armed deputies strutted about, pistols and blackjacks dangling from their belts, their badges gleaming. The deputies were strangers. Mansfield claims he asked the governor for National Guardsmen to help him, and the governor authorized him to get deputies where he could. The machine had turned up a sodden gang of plug-uglies, most of them from foreign counties, some from as far as Georgia. Fred Puett, the Chamber of Commerce secretary, said that they looked as though they were drugged; their eyes seemed as cold and arrogant and hard as those of a band of Nazis.

By the Tennessee Code of Law, each polling place must be staffed with watchers from both parties, and the GI's had chosen boys of the best families, with the best war records, to stand as their representatives at each place. As the polls opened in Etowah, one of the GI watchers asked to see the ballot box opened and demonstrated empty as required by law. "Hell, no," said one of the deputies; and argument spluttered, a highway patrolman was summoned and Evans, the GI poll watcher, was hauled off to jail.

At 9:30 trouble flickered in Athens; the machine charged Walter Ellis, a GI watcher, with an unspecified federal offense, took him from his appointed place at the polls and put him in jail, too. At three in the afternoon Tom Gillespie, a colored man, appeared at the eleventh precinct complete with poll-tax receipt. "You can't vote here," said the machine watchers.

"He can too," contradicted the GI spokesman.

"Get him," yelled one of the deputies and someone slugged Gillespie. Gillespie broke for the door and ran down the street. As he ran, a deputy at the door drew his pistol and shot him in the back. Gillespie was taken to the hospital. Fifteen minutes later, Bob Hairell, another GI watcher at the twelfth precinct, was in trouble. The machine wanted to vote a nineteen-year-old girl; Hairell objected. One of the deputies settled the argument by pulling his blackjack and laying Hairell's head open. Hairell was off to the hospital. The *Daily Post-Athenian* sent a reporter to get the story on Hairell. He, too, was slugged and told not to ask questions.

. . . It was five now, and following their practice the Cantrell forces removed the ballot boxes of the eleventh and twelfth precincts to the security of the jail for counting.

The GI's had promised to get the vote counted as cast, and they gathered at their campaign headquarters around the corner to confer. As they stood in the street, two Mansfield deputies approached to break up the group . . .

As the deputies stepped into the crowd, the GI's closed about them. They hit hard and high and low. The guns were taken and distributed among the GI's. Three more deputies, then two more walked into the crowd. All were disarmed and the guns handed out. The deputies were loaded on cars, taken to the woods, stripped of their clothes, and left to walk their way out.

The GI's were still indecisive . . . They had struck the first blow; they were vulnerable . . . Dusk was settling and the vets talked. A city policeman walked by to say that Mansfield was coming with tommy-guns and tear gas. Then something happened.

From dusk to dawn, the story of the siege of Athens dissolves into anonymity. The people had voted the GI ticket, trusting to the GI guarantee of a fair count. Five districts which had been fairly tabulated by evening had already given the GI's almost a three-to-one lead. But the ballot boxes of the eleventh and twelfth precincts were being counted in the jail. Tomorrow the Cantrell forces would have victory and no one would be safe. On the one hand, the Common Law says that every citizen has the right to prevent a crime from taking place; on the other hand, to take the jail by storm against the lawfully deputized thugs seemed perilously close to insurrection. A very fine point of law is involved and Crump still runs Tennessee. Therefore, no man knows or tells who played precisely what role in Athens on the night of Thursday, August 1, 1946.

Down the highway from Athens is one of the armories of the National Guard. By eight o'clock rifles and machine guns were held by dozens of the veterans. It was a quiet movement. There was no raving or shouting . . . They collected at their headquarters and gravely, under cover of darkness, walked the two blocks to the jail where the sheriffs had taken the ballot boxes. Behind the jail is a barbed wire enclosure. Facing it, across the street, is a low hill covered with vines and several houses and buildings. The deputies had made a mistake that the battle-wise GI's recognized immediately: they had concentrated forty or fifty of their number in jail and left no reserves in town. The GI's deployed in the darkness in a semicircle above the jail, on the hill behind the cover of vines, on rooftops. A veteran strode into the street and yelled at the silent jail a demand for the ballot boxes and the release of the GI prisoners.

A voice answered, "Are you the law?"

The GI yelled back, "There isn't any law in McMinn County."

A lone shot went off from within the jail. The man that answered from the hill answered with a tommy-gun.

There were several hundred veterans in the semicircle and hundreds of boys and civilians. Some had rifles, a few had tommy-guns, others had bird guns and hunting pieces. The fusillade rose and fell above the night, echoing into the suburbs and hills. Bullets spattered the Chamber of Commerce and the newspaper office a block away . . .

The local radio station had sent a reporter with a microphone to cover the action; up and down the county farmers tuned in to the running account. Some of them put their clothes on, got their guns, came to join in the shoot. Boys too young to cock a rifle came down to see the fun and remained to learn how to shoot in the night.

. . . At midnight a detachment went over to the county farm where a case of dynamite was located. During a lull, the veterans yelled that unless the ballot boxes and prisoners were released in twenty minutes they would blast the jail. An hour went by and the jail made no answer. Somebody fitted a cap to a stick of dynamite and tossed it into the street. A second stick followed. On the third throw, two sticks were tied together and thrown across to the sidewalk of the jail. The fourth throw of two sticks landed on the porch of the jail and tore it wide apart. Somebody had learned about demolition in the war; for the last try they decided to prepare a homemade satchel charge of the rest of the case and place it under the jail wall. But before the charge could be placed, the jail was yelling surrender. It was 3:30 in the morning.

"We're dying in here," came a call. "Don't use any more dynamite, we're giving up."

No one was dying. Four of the deputies were pretty badly hurt and required hospitalization; ten of the GI's were wounded in the day's action but the war was over.

. . . Violence flickered on for several more hours. The GI's had had their fill, but the civilians and boys were carrying on. They smashed in windows of the deputies' automobiles, turned them over, burned cars indiscriminately. It was the GI's now who had to restrain the civilians and protect their prisoners. By ten o'clock, however, the fury had spent itself and the GI's were carefully escorting the prisoners out of town. At three, a giant mass meeting was held in the courthouse, men jamming the assembly hall, overflowing onto the steps and the lawn. The Reverend Bernie Hampton read the twenty-third psalm and asked the body of citizens what their will was. Someone suggested the appointment of a three-man committee to administer the county till things settled down. The three-man committee was elected immediately and from Friday to Monday it conducted the county's affairs on a volunteer basis.

It summoned the county court—the local legislative body—to a meeting on Monday morning. The county court declared vacant the offices held by machine contestants in the elections and declared the GI slate duly elected. Six of the twelve precincts' votes were thrown out entirely, for no fair count had been given there. When the GI's broke into jail they found that some of the tally sheets marked by the machine had been scored fifteen to one for the Cantrell forces. Where the GI's witnessed the count, the margin was three to one GI. Thus it was decided that only in those precincts where both parties had watched should the count be accepted. By Monday afternoon, Knox Henry was sheriff of McMinn County and the law was safe.

(2) *Racial-political conflict in Triple City.* Triple City is a small southwestern town. Of its five hundred people, approximately one third are American Indians, one third Spanish-Americans, and one third Anglo-Americans. Its most significant function is provision of services for the agricultural area which surrounds it; one major source of income to the town is directly related to the income of the Indians. Concern of the population for agricultural and Indian policies reflects itself in political conflict and the question is whether the Indians should be allowed to vote. In contrast to the story of Athens, Tennessee, however, there has been no violence over this issue in Triple City.

. . . Apparently the question of Indian voting has been a very confused issue in the Triple City area for a long time, and has not yet been cleared up. According to an elder of the Bear Tribe, interviewed in 1949, the confusion dates back to 1902. He recalls that in that year some Anglos tried to talk him into voting. At that time he was distrustful and uncertain. Apparently the fear of losing his tax exempt status and his share of government disbursements prompted his feeling that it was not safe to vote. Also, he expressed a bitterness arising from the lack of expected results from Indian voting: "Indians are cheated by the whites . . . we were told if we voted we would be citizens and could buy liquor, but they voted and couldn't buy liquor." His daughter still clung tenaciously in 1949 to the myth about losing tax exemption and other privileges, while his son has tried to influence both his father and his sister into abandoning these groundless fears. In 1948 there were a number of other Indians who also expressed the fear that they would lose their lands and their homes and be made subject to taxation if they voted. Apparently, however, a few Indians have voted regularly for a long time, at least two since 1932. According to one informant ten Indians have voted more or less regularly for many years, claiming that right on the grounds that they were not wards of the Federal Government but taxpaying citizens like anyone else.

Our information indicates that non-Indian Republican politicians threatened to contest the 1946 election if Democrats tried to get many Indians to vote. Some Indians reported that they were not permitted to cast a ballot. A ruling was asked of the County Clerk and County Attorney by telephone and they were reported to have said "no vote." This happened in spite of the fact that the Attorney General had ruled in 1943 that Indians could vote. One Indian reported that he had voted without incident in 1944, but when he tried to vote in 1946, "they told me I did not have the right to vote and would not give me a ballot . . . I was so embarrassed and so mad that I never tried to do it again." In spite of an article in the *Warrior*, August 13, 1948, explaining that Indians had full citizenship rights including the franchise, and citing several legal rulings on the matter, the Indian votes were again challenged in 1948, but, according to the County Clerk, the Indians were allowed to vote in order "to avoid trouble." . . . Most of the Anglo and Spanish citizens questioned on the matter of Indian voting as late as August, 1948, still believed that the Indians did not have the right to vote and some expressed a feeling that they should not be allowed to vote. A few believed that Indians did not have the right to vote prior to 1946, but had this right since that time, attributing their reluctance to ignorance and fear. Only one candidate was known to have actively solicited the Indian votes.

The head of the Indian Agency said that the Indian right to vote was generally recognized after 1946—the County Attorney having ruled affirmatively and the leaders of both parties having agreed that the Indian vote was legal. Local party leaders of both parties admitted, however, that they "have not worked on the Indians." In fact, some actively discouraged the Indians from registering. One Democratic Party worker "blamed" the Republicans for "getting the Indians started." He said that he did not want to encourage the Indians: "I would not trust them . . . if someone gave them whiskey, they would get the vote . . . the Indians don't understand elections." [14]

Here is an example of political-social conflict in which elements of both direct and indirect means are utilized. The resentments here are smoldering but feelings run deep and the situation is always potentially dangerous to order and quiet in the community.

(3) *Denver, Colorado: partial report on racial conflict.* With a relatively small number of Negroes in its population, Denver has never had the violent racial conflicts which characterize some other Northern cities, Detroit for example. But the conflict is present. The following quotation illu-

---

[14] From a report in preparation by the Division of Anthropology, University of Colorado. Used by permission of the Division of Anthropology. Fictitious names are used for the community and Indian tribe.

strates very well the quiet, but direct, conflict that may be present in a community situation without attracting much attention.

This year if you toured city, county, state and federal offices and public utilities firms in Denver you would see many dark faces in responsible positions. And these persons have the titles and pay to go with the job.

Private industry, however, has lagged. The Negro still is welcome only on one side of department store counters—the buying side. Only one store in the downtown area—Cottrell's clothing store—has hired a Negro salesman.

As many as 98 pct. of the jobs advertised in the wanted sections of Denver's newspapers are still closed to Negroes no matter how excellent their qualifications.

. . . On the job front, Jim Crow has developed many tactics designed to deny Negroes equal job opportunities.

Many companies go to a lot of trouble in claiming they do not discriminate, yet when qualified minority persons apply in response to want ads, the job is always "filled." Often the advertisement will run several days after a minority person has applied and been told the position was taken.

Jim Crow also uses another dodge: "We will contact you later if you are selected."

Many employers lay the blame for their hiring practices on their employees who, they claim, "just won't work with Negroes."

A significant step—which race leaders hope is a sign of things to come—was made recently when a Denver employer who for 20 years had firmly stipulated "Caucasian only" in his hiring formula, worked with the Denver Urban League and hired four Negroes.

The Denver public schools added seven new Negro teachers this year, with two of them being placed in schools formerly without Negro teachers. At the University of Denver, Miss Ruby Pernell was appointed to the faculty for the present school term, marking the first full-time Negro teacher at the institution.[15]

(4) *Economic conflict: the strike at Yankee City.* The mid-depression strike in Yankee City, described in the brief quotation below, illustrates many of the characteristics which are common in industrial strife situations in American communities: the concern for strategy and tactics, the inevitable jockeying for public support in the community, the demands and counter-demands, the use of ritual and ceremony in obtaining consensus, the picketing, and the constant argumentation over the conference table.

In the worst year of the depression, all the workers in all the factories of the principal industry of the community walked out. They struck at management with little or no warning; they struck with such impact that all the factories closed and no worker remained at his bench. Management had said they would never strike, for the workers of Yankee City were sensible, dependable, and, by a long peaceful history, had proved that they would always stay on the job. Union men outside the city agreed that Yankee City could not be organized and held that the local shoe workers were obstinate and "always stupid enough to play management's game." Many of the workers had told us that there would be no strike. Most of the townspeople, from the autocrats of Hill Street to the people on city welfare in the clam flats, said Yankee City workers would never strike. But they did—the foreigners and the Yankees of ten generations—the men and the women, the very old and the very young, Jews and Gentiles, Catholics and Protestants—the whole heterogeneous mass of workers left their benches and in a few hours wiped out most of the basic productive system from which Yankee City

[15] "Private Industry Lags in Discrimination Fight," *Denver Post,* March 22, 1954.

earned its living. Not only did they strike and soundly defeat management, but they organized themselves, joined an industrial union, and became strong union members.

The industrial battle was fought between the owners of seven factories and their workers. Four of the factories, "the larger ones," employed the vast majority of the workers and accounted for most of the "34,000-dollar weekly pay roll." This industrial war lasted a month. It began on a bleak and snowy day in early March and lasted well into April. There were three clearly marked periods, each with different objectives and strategy, and in each the industrial workers and the managers were dominated by different feelings.

In the first period, when management and the union fought desperately to gain control over the workers, the union was successful in organizing the workers, and management was prevented from regaining control over them. The second period began when all the workers requested the union to represent them in the struggle with management; then the union began frontal attacks on management. During this time each continued its intense efforts to influence and dominate public opinion in Yankee City. The union also won this fight, since the public identified the union with the workers and most of Yankee City sided with them. The final phase, that of mediation and peace negotiations, began when a government agency entered and started a series of negotiations that ended the strike. Other efforts had been made from the beginning, but none of them had been successful.

The ultimate objective of each side, to which each fashioned its strategy, was, of course, to make the other side capitulate and accept its demands. For management this meant that the workers would return to their benches under approximately the same working conditions and wages as they had left; for the workers it meant that management would agree to their demands and increase wages and improve working conditions; and for the union officials it meant that the union would maintain its control over the workers and keep them members of their organization, and management would be forced to deal directly with the union and not with the unorganized workers.

Each side organized itself and developed its strategies of offense and defense. The workers' defense tactics were centered around maintaining their unity and defeating management's offensive strategy of breaking up the workers' group and of destroying their morale. Accordingly, the workers used ritual and ceremonial procedures in which recognized symbols of solidarity, such as the flag, patriotic hymns, and the American Legion band, played prominent parts. They achieved a defensive organization by means of meetings, speeches, entertainments, and the formation of a large number of committees that gave the mass of the workers opportunities to participate and to become and feel a part of a powerful and aggressive group. They took offensive action against management by making a series of demands for better wages and working conditions, by picketing, by making attacks against management in the newspaper, and by using the speaker's platform to influence public opinion. Management's defense was always to take the offensive. The tactics tried included sending foremen to talk to the workers individually, thereby separating them from the group; insisting on secret balloting by the workers when they voted on the issue of returning to work; and, above all, threatening to move their factories elsewhere, should the workers continue with their demands and join the union. Of course, it must be remembered that each side, throughout the strike, was being deprived of its income—labor of its wages and management of its profits.[16]

Community conflict wears many faces. It may be political, economic, religious, or over a wide range of social issues. It may be over differences of ends, or it may arise from disagreements as to means of reaching agreed upon goals. It may

[16] Reprinted from pp. 125-27, *American Life* by W. Lloyd Warner by permission of The University of Chicago Press. Copyright 1953 by The University of Chicago Press.

be violent or non-violent, blazing furiously in temporary, sporadic outbursts of force and arms, or it may lie smoldering, half hidden below the surface of everyday life, evidenced only by occasional words in the daily press or spoken from the public platform. Such is the complex nature of community conflict. We now turn to the perplexing problem of its relief and reduction.

5. The Reduction of Conflict

"The very fact," writes Reinhold Niebuhr, "that our social life is never pure anarchy proves that we do have some resources for conciliating our conflicts." But, because of the fallibility of man and the limitations of his vision, conflicts will always be a part of human social life. Perhaps man's problem has been as much that he has tried to do too much in the elimination of conflict as that he has done too little. We have attempted to establish Utopias where conflict will not exist, but, like all Utopias, they have escaped us.[17]

Conciliation of conflicts requires the discovery in antagonists of common values which transcend the passions engendered in and engendering conflict. From this standpoint, the problem of the reduction of conflict is a religious one—but this is not to say that it is one which religion and religious institutions are necessarily best equipped to solve.[18]

The "solving" or reduction of conflict takes a number of forms. The term *accommodation* is used to refer to the kinds of adjustments made by people in their attempts to reduce the tensions brought on by conflict. Accommodation mechanisms may be defined as (1) *truce*, a temporary suspension of active conflict, with the issues left unresolved, (2) *compro-*

[17] Niebuhr, Reinhold, "Is Social Conflict Inevitable?" *Scribner's Magazine,* September, 1935, pp. 167-69.
[18] *Ibid.,* pp. 168-69.

mise, in which each side in the conflict situation gives up some of its demands in return for like concessions by the other side, (3) *arbitration,* in which each side accepts the adjudication of the controversy by a third party, and (4) *toleration,* in which the factions decide to accept one another and the situation. Conflict may also be eliminated through the process of *assimilation,* in which groups rid themselves or are rid of their differences to a point where they are no longer significant enough to produce conflict.[19]

Accommodation mechanisms may result in two extreme solutions to conflict. The conflicting parties may be geographically insulated or separated from one another, or their differences may be removed, that is, complete assimilation may occur.[20] Thus, an end product of accommodation efforts may be assimilation.

Conflict is social behavior and social behavior can be reduced, ultimately, to psychological events. To put it another way, all social behavior is, in the final analysis, the behavior of individual people. It follows, therefore, that to understand human social behavior, including that particular pattern we have labeled conflict, necessitates the understanding of individual human behaviors and motivations. The study of individual behaviors and motivations *as such* is primarily the field of the psychologist; it is the configuration or patterning of psychological events which is the subject matter and the interest of the sociologist.

Aggression and aggressive behavior is one such configuration, and conflict is closely associated with aggressiveness on the part of individuals. The study of aggression necessarily entails the study of the situation in which it develops in the

[19] Lundberg, George A., Clarence C. Schrag, and Otto N. Larsen, *Sociology,* Harper and Brothers, New York, 1954, pp. 436-37.
[20] Williams, Robin M., Jr., *The Reduction of Intergroup Tensions,* Social Science Research Council, New York, 1947, p. 61.

individual. And the fact is that there are disruptive, aggression-producing elements in our community life, in our family life, in the mobility and essential rootlessness of individuals required by our occupational structure, and in the rapid and seemingly incomprehensible technological and other social changes. The American community resident often suffers frustration as a result of a general insecurity in a rapidly changing, sometimes mystifying and terrifying, set of social forces and pressures. Frustration, pent up, breeds individual aggression, and this aggression proceeds from the one to the many. It tends to be directed by ethnic groups toward other ethnic groups, toward communities by communities, and even, in the form of war, by nations against nations.[21]

There are, however, mitigating factors in our kinship, occupational, and political structures which operate to prevent the rise of aggressive behavior. These factors could well be more cleverly exploited by community planners in the interest of the reduction of conflict: the separation of roles in the family, the development of the "companionate" family in which aggression is mitigated through democratic relations, the trend toward isolation of occupational acquaintanceships and statuses in the large city from home and social life, which may lessen frustration stemming from job conflict, and the ever-present possibility of the use of peaceful political means to expend aggression—all these are significant factors which can be utilized to restrict the accumulation of aggression in individuals.

The reduction of group conflict in the community may be had through reduction in hostility, the rechanneling of hostility to other subjects, or through the repression of overt conflict.[22] In developing techniques for accomplishing

[21] Parsons, Talcott, "Certain Primary Sources and Patterns of Aggression in the Western World," *Psychiatry*, vol. X, 1947.

[22] Williams, Robin M., Jr., *op. cit.*, pp. 61-62.

these results, however, citizens must take into consideration the fact that an individual's feelings, perceptions, and attitudes develop out of the group or groups to which he belongs,[23] and the reduction of conflict in the community can, for this reason, be successful only when undertaken on a scale larger than that involved in dealing with the single individual. While individual motivations must be considered, groups and their characteristics are also of utmost significance. The social situation, as Lewin says, is "one concrete dynamic whole," and this indicates that community conflict is a community matter, and that the attack on it, to be successful, must be holistic. Basic principles for the reduction of conflict are: (1) Change must be of group atmosphere, not single items. (2) Change of culture of the group must involve change in the power structure. (3) Change in the methods of leadership is the quickest way to change cultural atmosphere.[24] That many people recognize these principles is apparent from everyday examples of community attempts to relieve conflict situations, and most especially from the readiness of people to use political means for this purpose.

The attempts to reduce conflict may in themselves generate new conflicts, as we have already noted in a previous chapter. Such new conflicts may develop from differences over means, goals, techniques, or applications in the attempt to solve what is recognized as a social problem, or they may arise out of dispute over the nature of the conflict situation itself. Indeed, as Sorokin writes, it is sad, but true, that "all altruistic actions and persons have generated social antagonisms and conflicts" themselves.[25] But, in a democracy, the presence of many conflicts is not to be feared or even re-

[23] Allport, Gordon W., in the foreword to Kurt Lewin, *Resolving Social Conflicts,* Harper and Brothers, New York, 1948, p. vii.

[24] Lewin, Kurt, *op. cit.,* p. 49.

[25] Sorokin, Pitirim, *Altruistic Love,* Beacon Press, Boston, 1950.

gretted, for conflict may truly be a part of the democratic process. As Jessie Bernard puts it:

Some students, noting all the conflicts which characterize community life in the United States, may feel depressed. Yet there is nothing to be disturbed about. The presence of many conflicts is, in a way, a more salutary situation than the presence of only one or two. When there are many conflicts they tend, in effect, to cancel one another. People who line up against one another on one issue line up together on another. The presence of many conflicts means that people often have as much in common as they have in conflict.[26]

SELECTED REFERENCES

Bernard, Jessie, *American Community Behavior,* The Dryden Press, New York, 1949. Chapters seven through twenty-one of this study of community life deal with specific forms and processes of cooperation and conflict.

Bonner, Hubert, *Social Psychology,* American Book Company, New York, 1953. Professor Bonner's discussion, "Group Tensions and Conflicts," pp. 351-77, is a good summary of group processes.

Gittler, Joseph B., *Social Dynamics,* McGraw-Hill Book Company, Inc., New York, 1952. Part five of this text and casebook includes varied readings on social processes drawn from the literature of anthropology and sociology. An excellent, short source of illustrative material.

Lewin, Kurt, *Resolving Social Conflicts,* Harper and Brothers, New York, 1948. An influential and widely read volume on the nature of conflict and techniques for its reduction.

MacIver, R. M., and Charles H. Page, *Society,* Rinehart and Company, New York, 1949. Pages 62-70 of this textbook present an excellent theoretical discussion of cooperation and conflict.

Myrdal, Gunnar, *An American Dilemma,* Harper and Broth-

[26] Bernard, Jessie, *American Community Behavior* p. 453. Copyright 1949 by The Dryden Press, Inc. Reprinted by special permission.

ers, New York, 1944. An ambitious study of race and social conflict in America.

Williams, Robin M., Jr., *The Reduction of Intergroup Tensions,* Social Science Research Council, New York, 1947. A well-reasoned and thought-provoking collection of principles for the relief of group conflict.

PART SIX

Basic
Community
Institutions

CHAPTER **9**

Basic Institutions: The Family

1. Institutions and Values

We accept as a usable definition of *value* Ralph Barton Perry's very general "any object of . . . any interest," understanding, to be sure, that "interest" is "a train of events determined by expectation of its outcome" and that it does not necessarily connote awarenes or consciousness.[1] People are not necessarily aware of the values they hold; indeed, it can be maintained that as soon as consciousness intrudes and values are thought about, reasoned upon, they are likely to be weakened and to become less significant than formerly as motivations to behavior. *Institutions* are definable in terms of values; they are "special types of inter-subjective systems, individuals interacting. They are not merely the collection of individuals, but the mode of behavior in which they engage."[2] Institutions are value patterns which govern action in a social system. They define modes of behavior "legiti-

[1] Perry, Ralph Barton, *Realms of Value,* Harvard University Press, Cambridge, Massachusetts, 1954, pp. 2-3. See also Howard Becker, *Through Values to Social Interpretation,* Duke University Press, Durham, North Carolina, 1950, pp. 10, and following.
[2] Kattsoff, Louis O., *The Design of Human Behavior,* Educational Publishers, Inc., Saint Louis, 1947, p. 225.

mately expected" and are, therefore, ideal but not utopian patterns. By this statement we mean simply that institutions exist; people do think and behave at least to some extent according to their understandings of what is required of ·them by the patterns of behavior formalized and generally accepted in the society. Furthermore, institutions are related both to the functional requirements of individuals and to the social system as a whole. No institution will indefinitely be maintained and supported if it calls for behavior which destroys the personalities of people, makes them "sick" in terms of norms and values originating elsewhere in their experience. The institution itself will be scrapped or modified so that one does not have to be mad to live up to it. In addition, there is always some degree of "institutional integration" in any community, that is, different collections of behavior patterns are developed to support one another. In the American community education, for example, complements the family, supporting home values, clinching its teachings, and extending its influence over the personal behavior of the child. A school which taught values counter to those of home and family would hardly be tolerated in any community.

The basic structural principle of institutions is "functional differentiation," and they may be categorized on the basis of three classes of functional patterns. These patterns are: (1) *situational*—those institutional aspects of the total situation over which the individual has no control and about which his roles are organized; kinship membership is an example; (2) *instrumental,* patterns shaped around attainment of a goal or goals, and exemplified by the role of the physician or lawyer; and (3) *integrative*—patterns regulating relations of individuals, such as social differentiation or authority. By structuring his analysis around these categories of functional differentiation, the sociologist can study changes in parts of the institutional system in terms of their interdependence with the entire system.[3]

2. Institutions, Human Behavior, and Community Organization

Institutions, then, are cultural; they are, more specifically, "configurations of functionally related culture traits." [4] Furthermore, the institutions of a society are not simply a random aggregate, or, conversely, a society is not merely "an *array* of institutions; it is the complex *structure* of institutions related to and impinging upon one another which distinguishes one group from another and provides the means whereby men organize their common activities in order to cope with the world around them." [5]

All humans exist in societies which are organized wholes, built upon or within the framework of institutions. And, since every community is a society, the study of institutions is as essential to the student of community as it is to the sociologist analyzing any other aspect of human relations. In functional analysis, the sociologist is necessarily concerned with the contribution of specific institutions to either or both individual and group "needs," and in the articulation and integration of specific institutions and other aspects of the culture system. The final purpose of such analysis is the understanding of the contributions of the separate culture items (institutions in this case) to the survival or ordered change of the society. While it is sometimes justly charged

[3] Parsons, Talcott, *Essays in Sociological Theory Pure and Applied,* The Free Press, Glencoe, Illinois, 1949, pp. 35-36.

[4] Kardiner, Abram, in Ralph Linton (ed.), *The Science of Man in the World Crisis,* Columbia University Press, New York, 1945, p. 107.

[5] Chinoy, Ely, *Sociological Perspective,* Studies in Sociology, Random House, Inc., New York, 1954, p. 22.

that functionalists are not always entirely clear about what they mean by "continuity" or "survival" of a society, it can be answered that this lack of clarity is not an insurmountable barrier to scientific research. It is true that few societies have failed to survive and that, historically, most societies decline before "dying," but the careful specification of the level of "survival" one takes as an assumption makes possible comparative study. A society which has persisted has done more than merely survive. It has changed. By virtue of its survival or failure to "die," a society always creates a constant stream of new conditions (whether alterations in the "natural" environment or new social situations growing out of discovery, invention, or borrowing) which cause it to exist at new levels. Like an organism—but the analogy should go no farther than this—a society exists as an evolutionary and changing, rather than a static, structure.[6]

People, in society and community, are almost constantly involved in institutional behavior, and the old question of self-interest versus group control becomes outmoded and meaningless from the functional point of view. This is because self-interest in the modern society often has meaning in and can only be expressed through institutions and institutionalized behavior. To put it another way, the individual may be able to seek his own self-interest only through some degree of conformance to the expectations of other people. The lack of complete personal self-determination is the price of social life. Institutions define the social situation in which the individual behaves and, therefore, impinge directly upon his behavior; it is the perception of the social

[6] Cf. George C. Homans, *The Human Group*, Harcourt, Brace and Company, New York, 1950, pp. 268-72, for an excellent analysis of the place of institutions in functional theory.

universe which, in the last analysis, motivates individual action.[7]

A community, like all societies, is a structure of integrated institutions defining for individuals the "social situation" (that is, the expectations of others, their statuses, roles, duties, and privileges) and therefore motivating behavior more generally along particular lines or toward some goals than toward others. Certain of these institutions we classify as *primary,* not because they appeared first historically, although this may well be the case, but because they are *dominant* in both their contribution to personality development and to the persistence of the community. Another group of institutions we term *secondary* because they more generally are *influents* or, at any rate, are of lesser significance in either or both the development of personality and the survival or continuity of the community. In the first category, we place *family, school, church, government,* and the *economy;* in the latter we place service and professional, and recreational and "social life" organizations. Our discussion, in this chapter and the three which follow, is limited almost entirely to the primary institutions.

3. The Family in the American Community

It is probably true, as Ruth Nanda Anshen says, that no social institution or custom can survive indefinitely purely as a matter of habit or of conditioned response. Every institution, to survive, must be hallowed by myth.[8] Man once built important myths about family and family life; indeed,

---

[7] Parsons, Talcott, *op. cit.,* p. 170.

[8] Anshen, Ruth Nanda (ed.), *The Family: Its Function and Destiny,* Harper and Brothers, New York, 1949, p. 426.

he once tended to conceptualize the universe in terms of family unity. Recent writers have attempted to demonstrate the possibility of restoring and rebuilding this myth in American life. They claim that: (1) the family is an indispensable entity in human life; (2) the present collapse of family is the "perverted triumph of profound passion . . . divested . . . of . . . ritual"; (3) the dissolution of the family is the same as the profanation of the myth which once bestowed meaning on family life; (4) it is for lack of selfless love that "the world is dying"; (5) morals and politics are identical and are embraced by the same rules, whether in family life or in the state; (6) government as an organizing principle would cease to exist without the family; and (7) government grew out of ordered relations which were first manifested in the institution of family.[9]

The important question, however, is not whether we can restore the American family to the nature it once had, as called for by these seven entreaties for family unity or in the impassioned pleas by Sorokin,[10] but whether we can find for family a *new* kind of unity which is in accord with the larger social structure of which it is a part. In our time, man is greatly occupied with egos; since he is not a product of biological evolution alone, this over-occupation with individuals has caused him to begin to lose identity with life. His very conquest of nature has made him confused as to its inner meaning. We agree with Ruth Anshen that the world is more than man's perception of it: "It is the coexistence of god and man, of eternity and life mirrored in the family

---

[9] *Ibid.*, pp. 426-29.

[10] "Marriage and the family must be restored to their place of dignity among the greatest values in human life, not to be trifled with." Pitirim A. Sorokin, *The Reconstruction of Humanity*, The Beacon Press, Boston, 1948, p. 148.

which is the primal and the universal image of order, of peace, and of salvation." [11]

This is what many adults of sound mind and good conscience hope—and expect—to find in their own families: a key to the locked secrets of life, a selfless expression of self, the meaning and purpose of existence in a world always startling and sometimes frightening. Of no other institution are such extraordinary demands made; it is the history of man that from no other have so many gifts of human joy and satisfaction been forthcoming. By the same token, the failure and disruption of no other institution heaps upon distraught persons such a bitter harvest of grief and despair.

The family is the basic community institution. What happens to family happens to community, for good or evil. A locality with many disrupted families is likely to be a disorganized, disrupted community; one with stable families, the members of which are bound together by familial myths, is likely to be a stable, orderly community.

JIM DeLane = Future Jet Pilot U.S. MARINE CORPS

4. The Structure of the Contemporary American Family

The American family, says Talcott Parsons, can best be characterized as an "open, multilineal, conjugal system" made up of interlocking conjugal families.[12] That is, any individual in what can be considered a normal case, structurally, is a member of two conjugal families, his orientation family, into which he was born, and his family of procreation, which was formed by his marriage.[13] We have an "open" system because it is possible for an individual to form

[11] Anshen, Ruth Nanda, *op. cit.*, pp. 429-35.
[12] Parsons, Talcott, *op. cit.*, p. 234.
[13] *Ibid.*, p. 234. The terms "family of orientation" and "family of procreation" are contributions of W. Lloyd Warner.

a new family of procreation without reference to class distinctions or other arbitrary barriers. It is multilineal because there is little or no bias in favor of one line of descent over the other in any of those aspects in which favor is shown in many other societies, especially in inheritance. There are elements in our society which tend toward the breakdown of the isolated, conjugal, open, multilineal family structure. Some of these are the pressure in rural areas toward the maintenance of the large, extended kinship family, the association of status with ancestry, especially among certain upper class families, and the mother-centering of certain groups having a tendency toward unstable marriages, most notably among some lower class Negro families, but also among some whites.[14] In spite of these limitations, the typical American family is made up of husband, wife, and minor children, living in a separate household. The husband and the wife are each, but separately, members of families of orientation and the children will themselves most likely one day found their own families of procreation.

The typical family in the American community is, then, the isolated, conjugal family; its basis is clearly the marriage relationship. It is founded, most generally, "for love" and when "love" is gone is likely to be broken by divorce or separation. Responsibilities to the larger family—the relatives of the wife and the relatives of the husband included—have largely disappeared, especially with respect to economic support. Consequently, the isolated family is likely to stand or fall as a result of its own functioning, its own production of solidarity, or its generation of conflicts among its members.

There is reason to suppose that our isolated family system, which is something of a rarity among societies, developed as a result of the "strain toward consistency" in the

---

[14] Parsons, Talcott, *op. cit.*, pp. 238-39.

social structure. In many respects, our system is well adapted to our occupation-centered institutional arrangements, which require a degree of individual attainment and geographical and social mobility unknown in most societies. It is well adapted to our occupational structure, which requires considerable mobility and a "breaking away" of young people from their family of orientation at the expected and proper time. Its multilineality, which eliminates sex discrimination in kinship terminology and lines of descent, and the conception of marriage as involving equal duties and rights of spouses, fits well into a democratic pattern.

There are problems related to the kinship structure of the American family, however. The fact that status accrues largely to the family as a result of the husband's occupational achievements sometimes creates conflict between husband and wife; severe strains often develop in child-parent relationships as a result of expectations of the child's occupational accomplishments and the necessity of his separation from his family of orientation; and the sudden disruption of occupational roles at retirement creates problems of many kinds for the aged. Still, one can hardly conceive of a kinship organization more clearly attuned to the functioning of our occupational system, as well as to the functioning of personalities.

It cannot be doubted that a solidary kinship unit has functional significance of the highest order, especially in relation to the socialization of individuals and to the deeper aspects of their psychological security. What would appear to have happened is a process of mutual accommodation between these two fundamental aspects of our social structure. On the one hand our kinship system is of a structural type which, broadly speaking, interferes least with the functional needs of the occupational system, above all in that it exerts *relatively* little pressure for the ascription of an individual's social status—through class affiliation, property, and of course particular "jobs"—by virtue of his kinship status. The conjugal unit can be mobile in status independently of the other kinship ties of its members, that is, those of the spouses to the members of their families of orientation.[15]

5. Situational Aspects of Family

All persons have roles to play which are determined by the "situational" aspects of their membership in a particular family of orientation. We are all born into a family, and, short of denying the truth or making complete separation, we all organize our behavior at some time in our lives and to some extent around the fact that we are sons or daughters of somebody, living or dead, perhaps brothers or sisters, cousins, nephews or nieces, of somebody. Even denial or separation does not eliminate the influence of family, for our kinship is always with us to the extent of denying us membership in a family of orientation not our own.

One's family of orientation is always of significance to his pattern of behavior as a member of a community; sometimes its importance in this respect is particularly irritating because of its situational aspect. Kinship is a "given" in the structure of every known society; one cannot choose his family of orientation, though its influence in his life may be well nigh inestimable. It serves as a determinant of his status in community—although only one among a number of such determinants—it may influence his economic standing, standard of living, his choice of occupation and his success in it, the place he lives, the people he meets, the ideas he learns;

---

[15] *Ibid.*, p. 244.

indeed, it may be primary for some individuals as far as their whole life patterns are concerned.

There are certain situational aspects with respect to one's family of procreation, also. Although one may marry for status—whether this be directly, in terms of selecting a "high status" spouse, or indirectly, in terms of marrying for those things like possessions or authority and deriving prestige from them—once the marriage is a fact and the family established, there are situational aspects which are inherent in it. Short of disruption of the family, its members must live within it, and their lives will reflect its prestige or lack of it. While individuals may work to change the character of the family, enhance its position in the society, or detract from it, in his own community, at least, no one can entirely escape his family of procreation at a given time.

6. Instrumental Aspects of Family

There are such things as family "goals" and the members of individual families play roles patterned around their attainment. In some families there are traditions of high professional attainment, public renown, or of social responsibility. In others there are traditions dictating the choice of particular professions or occupations: some families for generations are "farming" families, some "medical" families, some "business" families, and some "political" families. Every community has its counterparts of these types.

We do not mean to say that families as entities have ends, but merely that, in some families, individual members will have inculcated in them particular goals generation after generation. Furthermore, the functions fulfilled in the community by specific families will be largely determined by these goals and the public acceptance of them. This is especially true of the dominant families in a community, that is, those which are economically powerful, high in status, or in positions of especial political importance. There are many communities in America in which one or a few "important" families appear to dominate the economic, social, and political life of most of the rest of the people.[16]

Families, in this respect, are entities. In older communities there tends to be a strongly developed "upper-class" group which becomes fairly solidified as to goals and values, and which usually develops considerable social distance from the members of those families not considered by the group to have equally high status. Large or ostentatious houses set in spacious grounds, private schools, exclusive churches, and private clubs are typical of the means used to maintain this distance.[17] The behavior of high status individuals appears to be in accord with a generally agreed upon set of family goals and approved means of attaining them. Sometimes the simple maintenance and protection of a status position is the primary goal. Every community has other families which have a tradition of "shiftlessness"—although certain socially minded individuals would deny this—and it is an unusual individual who breaks out of such a learning situation and, setting old goals and traditions aside, strikes off for himself into fields formerly unexplored by his family.[18]

We have been speaking of families as individual entities;

[16] See August B. Hollingshead, *Elmtown's Youth,* John Wiley and Sons, Inc., New York, 1949, for an example.

[17] Warner, W. Lloyd, *American Life,* University of Chicago Press, Chicago, 1953, pp. 94-95.

[18] Erskine Caldwell writes his vivid caricatures about such families, and the "people who live like animals" of James West's *Plainville, U.S.A.* or the "Riverbrookers" of Warner and Lunt's "Yankee City" provide other examples.

the picture becomes somewhat different when family as a community institution is considered. Every community, every society, has certain expectations of family as an institution; family in other words is the "instrumentality" through which the members of the society expect to get certain things done. As R. M. MacIver and Charles H. Page put it, the family, while incapable of fulfilling any social function in itself, combines and harmonizes three basic societal functions: the perpetuation of the race, including procreation and the care and rearing of children, the provision of a stable order for the satisfaction of the sex instinct, and the provision of the home and its satisfactions of material, cultural, and affectional kinds. It is only in the family that the combination of these functions into a harmonious life process can take place.[19]

Other scholars have described the functions of the family in terms of far more elaborate classifications. Ogburn, for example, in a widely quoted treatise, states that family has performed seven basic functions: affectional, economic, educational, protective, recreational, family status, and religious. He goes on to say that the economic, educational, protective, religious, status, and recreational contributions are gradually being taken over by other institutions and that family is, accordingly, becoming increasingly ineffective in fulfilling any but its affectional function.[20] There have been many other analyses of this kind—indeed, almost every textbook

[19] MacIver, R. M., and Charles H. Page, *Society*, Rinehart and Company, Inc., New York, 1949, pp. 263, and following. For different, but not contradictory, treatments of this same subject, see W. Lloyd Warner, *op. cit.*, pp. 82-83, and George A. Lundberg, Clarence C. Schrag, and Otto N. Larsen, *Sociology*, Harper and Brothers, New York, 1954, pp. 519-37.

[20] Ogburn, William F., "The Family and Its Functions," in *Report of the President's Research Committee on Social Trends*, McGraw-Hill Book Company, New York, 1933, Vol. I, pp. 661, and following.

on family will provide an illustration of one—but it is likely that none of them have any particular claim on truth,[21] and the conclusions one reaches are likely to be as much a function of the nature of the classification scheme as of the empirical data supporting them. Such generalizations are based on incomplete evidence or evidence only partly understood, and many of the trends genuinely in evidence when Professor Ogburn made his justly famous study have since been reversed. There is little evidence today that the family is *losing* any of its functions. Affectionally, it is more significant than ever in an increasingly industrial society in which an individual can be "lost in a crowd." Economically, family, while not so important as formerly as a production unit, is the basic earning and spending unit. Protectively, it is in the family that concern for individual welfare is still most effectively expressed. Recreationally, we have recently experienced a revitalization of family activities—witness the rooftop growth of television aerials, the new popularity of family outings, the do-it-yourself fad, and increasing interest in family home-decorating projects. Educationally, the family is expressing its concern for child training through growing membership in P.T.A. and other home-school organizations, through emphasis on the study of child psychology, care in selection of books and recordings; even the recent outcries against unfunny comic books and horror films have come largely from parents and family life organizations.

The relative importance of different family contributions is changing, but in terms of race perpetuation, sex satisfaction, and provision of the home, the basic social functions are being fulfilled as well by the American family today as at any time in the nation's past.[22]

[21] See Francis J. Brown, *Educational Sociology*, Second Edition, Prentice-Hall, Inc., New York, 1954, p. 228, for a brief note on this.

[22] MacIver, R. M., and Charles H. Page, *op. cit.*, p. 264, and following.

7. Integrative Aspects of Family

We call the patterns which regulate the relations of individuals in society "integrative." There are certain aspects of the contemporary American family which fall within this category, whether one considers merely the relations of the members of a particular family themselves, or whether one is concerned with the broader problem of the contribution of the family as an institution to the stability and continuity of the community.

If the ultimate societal organization, as many sociologists hold, is the family,[23] it follows that it must figure substantially as an integrative institution. All institutions have the latent function of stimulating individuals to adhere to non-deviant behavior trends,[24] but the family, along with the other primary institutions, by its very position of importance in the community, is of particular significance in this respect.

Community organization—indeed, all social organization —involves patterns of reciprocal relationships among individuals; privileges, responsibilities, rights, duties, expected behavior, and precluded behavior are all defined by institutional arrangements. Inevitably, these relationships are expressed in sentiments defining dominance-submission relationships of persons. Dominance and submission may be relatively rigidly attached to individuals or offices and remain unchanged through a shifting maze of social situations—although probably no society has established a perfectly rigid pattern of this kind—or they may adhere to social situations rather than to individuals or offices. In the latter case, au-

---

[23] For discussions of this point of view, see Ruth Nanda Anshen, *op. cit.,* p. 3; Carle C. Zimmerman, *The Family and Civilization,* Harper and Brothers, New York, 1947, *passim.*

[24] Parsons, Talcott, *op. cit.,* note, p. 307.

thority may adhere to an individual in a particular situation in which a second individual is expected to submit, and the relationship may be reversed under another set of circumstances. Whatever the case, individuals in community must learn the expected dominance-submission patterns; and, indeed, must learn, in the very first instance, the fact of dominance and submission.

Someone has remarked that the child obtains his first experience in democratic living when the mother says "yes" and the father says "no." This is another way of saying that it is in family that children come first to understand that authority and submission are part of democratic as well as any other kind of living; it is because of this fact that individuals face the necessity of making social choices in the first place. In the final analysis, democratic living places more responsibility upon individuals for the making of choices, but here we have a strange paradox: the making of choices is always hemmed in and restricted by authority-submission patterns generally recognized and followed in day-to-day behavior.

As Max Horkheimer puts it, "The birth of modern civilization emancipated the bourgeois family rather than the individual . . . and thus carried within itself a profound antagonism." Family remains a feudal institution based on "blood"—irrational and kinship-oriented—while a modern, individualistic, industrial society proclaims rationality as a keynote. In early phases of capitalistic development, success in business depended to a very large extent upon family solidarity—thus there was an element of economic dependence of individuals on family—but with the disappearance of this economic dependence in modern times, the power and respect of the head of the family breaks down, and there is always danger that family itself will disintegrate. The right of inheritance, once so important in maintaining solidarity, has less influence in a time when skill and alertness are so highly prized. But in spite of these changes, moral and religious ideas derived from the patriarchal family are still the core of our culture; indeed, our very respect for law and cultural tradition is tied to the respect of children for their elders—and the problem here is how to maintain this respect in the face of declining economic solidarity of the family. Family has become, in America, as everywhere in the Western World, a pragmatic affair, permeated by the spirit of rationality. Even motherhood and fatherhood become a kind of profession. The prevalence of divorce in our country illustrates our rational view of family.

The really serious problem, however, has to do with the personality development of young people. In the past, family taught respect for authority within the framework of sympathy, affection, and general concern for the individual's development. As the family ceases to exercise authority over its members, it becomes a training ground for external authority. The child learns that his parents are not the super-authorities they are pictured to him to be, and he may look for stronger authority; he may replace the father by some collective, as the school class, the club, or the state. Evidence is available that individuals who are susceptible to authoritarian propaganda show uncritical, rigid identification with, family—absolute submission to family authority in early childhood. At the same time, they show no really deep attachments to parents. Rather, they externalize; they combine submissiveness and coldness, and their resistance to parental authority may be displaced and turned against a scapegoat. The authoritarian personality is conventionalized and stereotypical; there is exhibited hatred of the weak, opposition to self-examination, hierarchical thinking, superstition, contempt for mankind in general, overconcern with success and social status, and rejection of "tender-mindedness." If this sounds all too much like some Americans, it may well be because of the failure of many American families to retain the old authority-submission patterns, or—and this is the other alternative and the one toward which most American families appear to be striving with some apparent success—to replace it with a genuinely cooperative, democratic pattern in which every individual takes his rightful place as a person accepting the democratic responsibility for making choices.[25]

The American family has made important adjustments during recent decades. The family, as well as most other institutions, most notably the church and the school, is meeting with definite success in its integrative function in the community. The problem of dominance-submission in an industrial society illustrates the complexity of the functional task required of the family. The amazing thing is not that it has failed where it has failed in the production of cooperative, democratic community citizens, but that, in view of the tremendous integrative responsibilities expected of it, it has fulfilled its task as well as it has.

SELECTED REFERENCES

Anshen, Ruth Nanda, *The Family: Its Function and Destiny*, Harper and Brothers, New York, 1949. A collection of original articles by a number of different scholars; contains some excellent reading for the beginning student of family.

[25] The above paragraphs are based upon Max Horkheimer, "Authoritarianism and the Family Today," in Ruth Nanda Anshen, *op. cit.*, Chapter XVII. See also Erich Fromm, *Escape from Freedom*, Rinehart and Company, New York, 1941, and Bertram Shaffner, *Father Land*, Columbia University Press, New York, 1948.

Arensberg, C. M., and S. T. Kimball, *Family and Community in Ireland,* Harvard University Press, Cambridge, Massachusetts, 1940. An interesting and informative volume on the Irish family and community life.

Burgess, Ernest W., and Harvey J. Locke, *The Family,* Second Edition, American Book Company, New York, 1953. This general study of family contains a wealth of case history material.

Frazier, E. F., *The Negro Family in the United States,* University of Chicago Press, Chicago, 1939. Outstanding as a study of family and as an analysis of a minority group.

Kirkpatrick, Clifford, *The Family as Process and Institution,* The Ronald Press Company, New York, 1955. This recent textbook presents much research data on family.

Queen, S. A., and J. B. Adams, *The Family in Various Cultures,* J. B. Lippincott Co., Philadelphia, 1952. Interesting comparative descriptions of family and family life in a number of different preliterate and modern societies.

Sirjamaki, John, *The American Family in the Twentieth Century,* Harvard University Press, Cambridge, Massachusetts, 1953. This short book is written in rare good humor and provides a useful overview of family life in America in mid-century.

CHAPTER 10

Basic Institutions:
Education and the School

1. The School in the American Community

Americans have an overwhelming faith in education. "Education is good for children; it is good for war veterans; it is good for adults. What it is good for is not always clear."[1]

Some Americans hold the view that education is general, universal, and unchanging, that it has, and has always had, one purpose: to improve men and to make them "good."[2] From this standpoint, anything which does not adhere to absolute standards of value ought not to masquerade under the name of education but should be revealed for what it is, "training." Another view is that education is not general but specific, not universal, but local, and not static, but constantly changing as to goals and purpose.[3]

[1] Brookover, Wilbur B., "Education in American Culture," in Edgar A. Schuler, Duane L. Gibson, Maude L. Fiero, and Wilbur B. Brookover, *Outside Readings in Sociology,* Thomas Y. Crowell Company, New York, 1952, p. 542.

[2] Hutchins, Robert Maynard, *The Conflict in Education in a Democratic Society,* Harper and Brothers, New York, 1953, especially pp. 67-76.

[3] For example, see the Report of the Commission on the Social Studies of the American Historical Association, *Conclusions and Recommendations,* Charles Scribner's Sons, New York, 1934, especially pp. 30-32.

These conflicting views agree, however, that education is a social process and that it always expresses the philosophy of the society and is reflected in it. Education neither takes place in a vacuum nor serves communities which are all alike. Education ought to be understood in terms of the complexities of motivation of many different kinds of people. In fact, many of the critics of contemporary American schools, it seems to us, fail to understand the broad functions of education to the maintenance of a democratic society; they tend to view education as primarily concerned with "cultural" and "artistic" matters. Education as a process of social living, its significance to personality development and self-expression, appears to escape them.[4]

An adequate sociological analysis of education can only be made through a whole series of investigations into the nature of human relations, customs, traditions, and values. The study of education in America, we hold, can combine the analysis of the social scientist with a belief in standards. History can be molded both by the use of our "collective intelligence" and by "good intentions."[5]

Two related, but different, extremes as to the nature and purpose of education are also present in historical and contemporary American thinking. One is that the development of the individual—the child—is its own end and purpose and that the function of the school is to provide facilities in which this growth can take place with the least interference. The opposite view is that the remaking of society is the principal function of education and that, therefore, the school ought to be an instrumentality of social change. These extremes are both based on the fallacious idea that the school exists in a kind of social vacuum, that it is "self-determining"

---

[4] See note 21, below.
[5] Conant, James Bryant, *Education in a Divided World,* Harvard University Press, Cambridge, Mass., 1948, pp. 48-52.

and not really a part of society. The truth of the matter is that such factors as political loyalties, changes in family or other institutions, and nationalism have influenced and wrought change in education and schools.[6]

That education is a social process is not open to doubt, but the relationship between education, the larger process of socialization, and schools as social institutions is a complex matter, indeed.

By "socialization" we mean all those still rather incompletely understood processes through which the human organism becomes a person, that is, develops a personality; or, to put it another way, those processes through which an individual organism is inducted into societal membership through learning the culture patterns which are held important or necessary by the people of the society. Education is the term which is applied to certain formalized, institutionalized aspects of socialization, and the emphasis appears to be —in our society, at least—as much on teaching as on learning. Socialization is, therefore, the more inclusive term and education only one aspect of it.[7] The school is that social institution whose primary function is education of the members of society, although a great many other institutions, such

---

[6] See, for example, I. L. Kandel, "Education and Social Forces," *The Educational Forum*, November, 1949, pp. 5-13, for a masterful critique of these extremes in educational philosophy. For further discussion of the relationship of school and society, see John Dewey, "The Schools in the Social Order," in his *Intelligence in the Modern World* (edited and with an introduction by Joseph Ratner), The Modern Library, New York, 1939, pp. 683-90; Allen Oscar Hansen, *Liberalism and American Education in the Eighteenth Century*, The Macmillan Company, New York, 1926, pp. 44-104; Willis Rudy, "Historical Perspectives and the Contemporary Scene," *Harvard Educational Review*, Summer, 1953, pp. 204-10; and Harold Benjamin, *The Saber-Tooth Curriculum*, McGraw-Hill Book Company, Inc., New York, 1939, *passim*.

[7] For a further elaboration of the relations between the concepts of socialization and education, see Blaine E. Mercer, "Some Notes on the Concepts of Education and Socialization," *The Journal of Teacher Education*, December, 1953, pp. 279-80.

as family, church, and play group are involved in the socialization process; some of these, insofar as teaching is conscious and purposeful, are also engaged to some degree in education.

Some societies have been able to socialize individuals with a minimum of formalized education, others have set up education on a semi-formal basis,[8] and others, like our own, have very highly institutionalized systems of education. Indeed, it appears that, in some instances, our zeal for formal education has led us to create schools which, because they are not in step with the social life and experience of students outside the school, really fail to educate successfully. There are such things as schools without education.[9]

The school as a social institution must operate within the social system of any community. The school exhibits a separate structure, with its own complex of rituals, ceremonies, folkways, mores, laws, and sanctions, its traditions, its innovations and innovators, and its informal groups. In other words, it has, as Willard Waller pointed out so dramatically many years ago, a separate culture.[10] Furthermore, the cultural norms of the school often contradict norms of the community and the larger society. In American colleges, for example, there are sometimes considerable differences between "official" declarations (which accord with community folkways) and "unofficial" interpretations (which do not) made by the officials and by students.[11] Americans, in general, are

[8] See, for example, Robert Redfield, "Culture and Education in the Midwestern Highlands of Guatemala," *The American Journal of Sociology,* May, 1943, pp. 640-48, and Mark Hanna Watkins, "The West African 'Bush' School," *The American Journal of Sociology,* May, 1943, pp. 666-75.

[9] See Horace Mann Bond, "Education as a Social Process: A Case Study of a Higher Institution as an Incident in the Process of Acculturation," *The American Journal of Sociology,* May, 1943, pp. 701-09.

[10] Waller, Willard, *The Sociology of Teaching,* John Wiley and Sons, Inc., New York, 1932, especially pp. 103-19.

[11] Hartshorne, Edward Y., "Undergraduate Society and the College Culture," *American Sociological Review,* June, 1943, pp. 321-32.

probably more tolerant of deviation from the social norms on the part of students than on the part of any other large group in the adult or near-adult population, although deviations, real or imagined, as an official policy (or one believed to be official) are likely to bring a storm of protest and criticism.[12] The people of almost any American community typically take an interest in their schools which is second in intensity only to that of their interest in their families. This is not surprising for, to a greater degree than any other institution, the school is a community concern. Financially, the school is in the main locally supported and (especially on the lower levels) its enrollment, problems, entertainment value, and scholarly and social accomplishments are largely of local interest. On the higher levels, this localism in fact tends to break down, but in the minds of people it may not do so. The citizens of a small community in which is located a large state university drawing its students from every state and a dozen foreign nations, may still think of the university as "theirs," worry over its problems, and take great pride in its accomplishments. Along with family and church the school, through the inculcation of social values, is a significant "integrating" institution in most communities.[13]

[12] For examples of such criticism, see Bernard Iddings Bell, "Know How Vs. Know Why," *Life,* October 16, 1950, pp. 89-90, 92-93, 97-98; and Mrs. W. T. Wood, "How Well Are Our Schools Doing the Job?" *Vital Speeches,* March 1, 1952, pp. 308-11. For answers to the critics, see Jacques Barzun, *Teacher in America,* Little, Brown and Company, Boston, 1945, pp. 6-9; Archibald W. Anderson, "The Charges Against American Education: What Is the Evidence?" *Progressive Education,* January, 1952, pp. 91-104; Blaine E. Mercer, "An Educator Talks Back," *Denver Post,* March 14, 1954 (based on the sources of Professor Anderson's article); Henry Steele Commager, "Our Schools Have Kept Us Free," *Life,* October 16, 1950; and Roper Survey, "What U. S. Thinks About Its Schools," *Life,* October 16, 1950.

[13] For example, see W. E. Baker, "The Mesick Consolidated School," in *Education in Rural Communities,* 51st Yearbook, Part II, National Society for the Study of Education, 1952, pp. 138-44; André Fontaine, "Everybody's Schools," *National Parent-Teacher,* September, 1949, pp. 10-13; Daniel S. Schecter, "A Community Begins to Live," *The Nation's Schools,* October, 1952, pp. 43-47.

2. The Structure of the American School

Perhaps the most significant fact in the structure of American educational institutions is their cultural separateness. The separation of the school from other community activities and institutions, while it is at the same time a part of the community organization, is at once the product and the cause of its further separateness. Teachers, pupils, and any other citizens active in school life create for themselves special attitudes, moralities, and behavior patterns.[14] Since the publication of Waller's *The Sociology of Teaching*, in 1932, sociologists have been well aware of such phenomena as "teacher morality," "pupil culture," and "P.T.A. culture." As a social institution, the school involves a structure of culture patterns by which teachers and pupils are separated from one another. Significant differences in teacher—and pupil—behavior are expected by teachers and pupils themselves, and by parents and the citizenry in general. At the same time, teachers and pupils are together set off in a culture world separate from the larger community. Pupils have a group solidarity of their own with rigidly prescribed behavior standards which include proscription of "telling tales" and of close and affectional relationships with teachers; they have a system of social differentiation and generally definable attitudes toward scholarship and extracurricular activities. Teachers are expected to behave in terms of (and set "professional standards" to ensure such behavior) "fairness" in their dealings with students, parents, and one another, to maintain a significant social distance from pupils and from principals, superintendents, and school board members, to conform to teacher-imposed standards of efficiency and ac-

[14] Williams, Robin M., Jr., *American Society*, Alfred A. Knopf, New York, 1951, pp. 270-72. See also Willard Waller, *The Sociology of Teaching*, John Wiley and Sons, Inc., New York, 1932, *passim*.

complishment, and to the demands of parents and patrons for conformity to moral standards, often of the most personal nature, and to patterns of "politeness" or "manners." In some communities, these standards are so severely imposed upon teachers as to constitute a serious limitation upon what many consider ought to be rightful "spheres of anarchy" in their personal lives.[15]

American faith in education as necessary to a successful democracy has produced an elaborate and large school system, public and private, elementary, secondary, and higher. In its organization and control, the American school is generally state and locally controlled, although there is now some evidence of a shift to greater national control. Public school officials are usually elected directly or appointed by elected officials or boards of education; the board of education has a considerable (although probably decreasing in our time) degree of control over education in the community. In the larger communities, there is a tendency to place greater authority in the hands of professional school administrators. Pupils are not graded out of or into school by selective examinations but may pass from kindergarten through college in terms of year-by-year accomplishments. Elementary education, and to some extent secondary education, is relatively uniform throughout the country (with some significant community variations, of course), some system of grading is used in most schools and the variations in such systems are generally more apparent than real, and there is a conventional set of standards governing teacher-pupil relationships which tends toward uniformity throughout the nation.

Financially, the public schools are supported by public

---

[15] Williams, basing his work heavily on Waller's analysis, has admirably summarized the nature of education as an institution in American society. See Robin M. Williams, Jr., *op. cit.*, pp. 265-72.

taxation levied largely upon the owners of real property. The financial support of the public schools, required even of those who maintain their own private or denominational schools, is a constant source of community and national conflict.

Teachers, pupils, and the community at large typically insist that certain cultural emphases be taught in the school. These include the emphasis upon school education as practically useful, the concern for success in competition, conformity to accepted standards, and especially the values of democracy and patriotism.[16]

Structurally, then, the school is part of the total institutional order of the American community, and yet is a social system in itself, existing in a kind of cultural isolation. At the present time there is a considerable movement among educators and other community leaders to integrate the activities and the goals of the school and the community. We shall turn to this, the "community school" movement, in a subsequent section of this chapter.

3. Situational Aspects of the School as an Institution

In any particular community, the school is only one among many social institutions and must function in accord with its place in the total institutional structure. This may mean that the school is engaged in the preparation of students for college, or vocational training of a particular kind, or, more likely, it may mean that the school must provide a variety of curricula to meet a range of social and individual needs or desires. It may operate within the framework of an integrated, generally agreed upon set of cultural standards or values, or it may be forced constantly to reconcile contradic-

[16] *Ibid.*, pp. 277-79.

tions and conflicts over standards of opposing groups in the community.

This is not to suggest that school officials or community citizens in general must accept these situational aspects of the school and its relation to community structure as something which they cannot alter. At a given time, in any specific community, however, there are situational aspects of educational institutions which must be considered in any program of school or community planning which can achieve success in reaching the goals it seeks to attain.

4. Instrumental Aspects of Education and the School

From a sociological point of view, the school has two major functions: to pass along the cultural heritage from the older to the younger, from one generation to the next, thus assuring social continuity and, indeed, survival; and to serve as an innovator of change. A third function, to contribute to personality development, is sometimes included, although it may logically be subsumed in the other two.

There is probably no universally "primary" function of education. In some societies, the school is, however, expected to serve almost exclusively the function of culture transmission, while in others the function of experiment, innovation, and change is uppermost in the expectations of the people of the society.[17] In the modern society, both functions are invariably recognized, although national or even community variations in emphasis are evident. We have already discussed briefly in this chapter extremes in our educational philosophy which are reflections of and reflect upon these differences in functional emphasis.

The functions of education as stated by educational sociol-

[17] Redfield, Robert, *op. cit., passim.*

ogists and educators are oftener than not a somewhat confusing mixture of societal objectives and psychological and personality development objectives and are likely to be loaded with value orientations. Such a list is that of the Educational Policies Commission, which states educational functions or objectives in terms of "self-realization," "human relationship," "economic efficiency," and "civic responsibility." [18] Discussions of the "all-round man" purpose of education, or the "teach to think," or the "better world" functions also involve such confusion between psychological and sociological orientations.[19] Even such a classification as "transmitting the cultural heritage," "enriching experience for the development of new social patterns," and "providing situations to stimulate creative abilities," [20] reveals such lack of clarity.

To recapitulate: from the viewpoint of the sociologist, the social functions of education are those contributions it makes to the perpetuity or predictable ordered change of a society or a community. From this standpoint, these functions can best be classified simply as cultural transmission and the innovation and instrumentalizing of culture change. The contribution of education to the development of personality along certain desired lines is a psycho-sociological matter; it requires essentially a different, but complementary, approach to the sociological study of education and community.

Specific patterns of the cultural heritage which the people of any particular locality desire—or demand—be passed from the older to the younger generations vary from community

[18] The Educational Policies Commission, *Policies for Education in American Democracy*, Washington, D. C., 1946, pp. 192, 212, 226, 240.

[19] See, for example, Clyde B. Moore and William E. Cole, *Sociology in Educational Practice*, Houghton Mifflin Company, New York, 1952, pp. 13-19.

[20] Brown, Francis J., *Educational Sociology*, Second Edition, Prentice-Hall, Inc., New York, 1954, pp. 202-207.

to community and can only be ascertained in all detail through careful sociological analysis, community by community. The same is true of the degree to which people are willing to accept change and the nature of the changes they will approve.

5. Integrative Aspects of Education and the School

In our time, the public schools have been severely criticized for actual or alleged failure to pass along desired items of the cultural heritage. Some critics make blanket charges that the schools, in the hands of the "educationists," are failing to meet any and all of the traditional American expectations.[21] Others are more specific and make such charges as the one that schools are not teaching the fundamental skills satisfactorily or that they are remiss in their moral or religious obligations.[22]

The important questions here are these: Just what, in specific terms, do the American people expect of their schools and how well are the schools actually meeting these expectations? or, equally important, how well do people feel their expectations are being met?

Wilbur Brookover reports that, on the basis of findings of public opinion polls, the most consistent and significant expectations held by parents with regard to the education of their children are that it will provide vocational training, training in basic skills, transmission of accepted cultural values, means of social adjustment, cures for social problems, and good entertainment. The National Opinion Research

---

[21] See, for example, Albert Lynd, *Quackery in the Public Schools*, Little, Brown and Company, Boston, 1953, and Harl R. Douglass' scathing review of it, "Lynd's Quackery Lacks Intellectual Honesty," *The Nation's Schools*, January, 1954, pp. 74-76.

[22] Bell, Harold Iddings, *op. cit.* This is a thoughtful criticism of this type.

Center in 1944 reported that eighty per cent of parents responding to a poll said they were satisfied with the education their children were obtaining.[23] A Roper Survey poll in 1950 revealed that, while 13.0 per cent of its respondents felt that children are being taught less worthwhile things today than twenty years ago, a full 67.0 per cent believed that more worthwhile things are being taught, while 12.1 per cent saw no difference and 7.9 per cent had no opinion.[24] A famous American historian, declaring that the schools have kept America free, says, "No other people ever demanded so much of education as have the Americans. None other was ever served so well by its schools and education." [25]

The evidence of these polls is that most Americans are fairly consistently agreed upon desirable objectives of education (that is, *specific* objectives within the broader functional definitions of culture transmission and culture change) and that they are reasonably satisfied with the degree to which the schools are meeting these expectations. The criticisms appear to be coming primarily from a small but vociferous group.

American public schools from the kindergarten to the graduate school have always been recognized by the majority of thinking citizens as integrative to their communities. Combined with family and church, the schools form a partnership in the "big three" among the social institutions most important in transmitting those values and standards which retain consistency in a community culture constantly torn by internal dissensions and external pressures.

[23] Brookover, Wilbur B., "Education in American Culture," in Edgar A. Schuler, Duane L. Gibson, Maude L. Fiero, and Wilbur B. Brookover, *Outside Readings in Sociology,* Thomas Y. Crowell Company, New York, 1952, pp. 540-41.

[24] Roper Survey, *op. cit.*

[25] Commager, Henry Steele, *op. cit.*

6. The Schools and Social Class

There is some question whether American public schools are serving the functions of maintaining the "open" society —that is, of serving as avenues of social mobility for the talented and deserving—or whether they are being used as agents to maintain a class system of increasing rigidity. Elbridge Sibley, from an analysis of 5677 Pennsylvania boys who were in the sixth grade in 1926, found that "as a boy passes through the educational sifting process, his parents' status assumes increasing importance, both absolutely and in comparison with his own intelligence, as a factor influencing his chances of continuing his preparation for one of the more advantageous vocations." [26] Various community studies have revealed a relationship between social class membership, educational opportunity, and likelihood of school success.[27] Class membership influences admission to certain private institutions and it is well recognized that class differences are significant to social success of students in many colleges.[28] Furthermore, there is some evidence that the social class of individuals tends to influence their aspirations to higher education and to professional careers.[29]

[26] Sibley, Elbridge, "Some Demographic Clues to Stratification," *American Sociological Review*, June, 1942, pp. 322-30.

[27] See, for example, August B. Hollingshead, *Elmtown's Youth*, John Wiley and Sons, Inc., New York, 1949; W. Lloyd Warner, Robert J. Havighurst, and Martin B. Loeb, *Who Shall Be Educated?* Harper and Brothers, New York, 1944; and Buford H. Junker and Martin B. Loeb, "The School and Social Structure in a Midwestern Community," *School Review*, December, 1942, pp. 686-95.

[28] See Willard Waller, *op. cit.*, Edward Y. Hartshorne, *op. cit.*, and Arnold W. Green, "Young America Takes Over the Colleges: The Two Worlds of the School," *Commentary*, June, 1949, pp. 524-34, for discussions of this relationship.

[29] Consult Joseph A. Kahl, "Educational and Occupational Aspirations of 'Common Man' Boys," *Harvard Educational Review*, Summer, 1953, pp. 186-203.

School curricula, for the most part, are heavily slanted toward the fulfillment of middle class goals and values. Emphasis in high schools on training for "white-collar" occupations is an example of this slant. Textbooks also typically emphasize white-collar occupations—the "father" in the elementary reader nearly always has an office—while "blue-collar" work is almost totally ignored. Most teachers, administrators, and school board members are middle class and influence school policies accordingly.

There has been a trend in recent years toward planned interference with an established connection between class and education. The passing of educational aid legislation for veterans of military service (the so-called "G.I." and "Korean" bills) and the continuing enlargement of public school curricula to include a wider range of training opportunities in other than those leading to professional or pre-professional fields illustrate this trend. It is perhaps too early to judge the effects of these, and other, "democratizing" programs in keeping the school an important agency of social mobility.

7. The Community School

Americans in many communities have recently come to feel that their schools can become more significant than previously in the life of the community (and the rest of the community more important to school life) and have taken steps to accomplish this end. The result is the "community school," an institution designed to improve community and community life.

The concept of the community school has come to be so complex that it is not really possible to define it in brief terms. One attempt at definition differentiates between *basic criteria* (to provide guides for establishment of the community school) and *implementing criteria* (guides to its functioning). The former are: (1) teaching of subject matter for literary and civic competence in the school's social situation, (2) direct concern of the school for the betterment of community living, (3) use of the school for betterment of life by the community, (4) curriculum planning to meet needs of all communities (local to international), (5) use of the school as a center for youth and adults to work in discovery, analysis, and solution of community problems, and (6) the use of the school in direct solution of community problems. The implementing criteria are: (1) organization and administration of the school for the furthering of actions in terms of accepted social goals, (2) school officials and lay citizens cooperatively determining the role of the school in the community and planning the curriculum accordingly, (3) school personnel and lay citizens cooperating in discovering community problems and making the community aware of them, (4) the school coordinated with and participating with other agencies in community affairs, (5) use of the "expertness" of all members of the community in the school's program, and the use of the school by community members in any way it can aid in improving community life, and (6) the seeking of solutions to local problems both in terms of goals and standards of the local community and of the larger society.[30]

Successful schools embodying these criteria have been set up in small rural communities, suburban communities, and in metropolitan centers and, according to reports concerning them, they have brought new meaning to community life.[31]

[30] Hanna, Paul R., and Robert A. Naslund, in *The Community School*, 52nd Yearbook, Part II, National Society for the Study of Education, 1953, pp. 56-61.

[31] See the references cited in footnote 13 above.

The people of a community cannot hope to achieve the ultimate from a community school program, however, unless they develop some organization to provide for the coordination of the school's activities with those of other community institutions. Without such coordination, each institution tends to function separately and conflict over programs and activities is sure to result.[32]

The primary function of a community coordinating council is the coordination of all social institutions in the community in their efforts to reach a consensus as to community life goals and, once this is accomplished, to organize their activities toward these goals. The committee organization of a successful council, in Glencoe, Illinois, illustrates the functions of such an organization: Community Calendar Committee (concerned with collection and publication of dates of community activities and with the resolution of conflicts of dates), Agenda Committee (concerned with preparation of agenda for discussion for council meetings and their publicizing), Resolutions Committee (dealing with preparation of resolutions and recommendations), Community Resources Committee (surveying and recording the nature of and changes in community resources of all kinds), Community Projects Committee (collecting and presenting to the council information on community projects being carried on by various organizations), and a Publicity Committee (concerned with press relations).[33]

Certain sociologists have inquired whether the community school movement is a reasonable one in a society in which the local community as a social unit is of constantly lessening importance in the lives of most citizens. While it is ad-

[32] Hollingshead, August B., *Elmtown's Youth,* John Wiley and Sons, Inc., New York, 1949, 154-55.
[33] Misner, Paul J., "The Work of a Community Coordinating Council," *Teachers College Journal,* November, 1941, pp. 30-32.

mitted that there is no other social unit which can substitute for the community in provision of the cooperation and solidarity so necessary to an integrated society, the fact still remains that it is likely to prove impossible to transform our social life back to an "idyllic communalism." Couple this with the apparent fact that there is a general trend away from the community as the foundation for our political, social, and economic organizations; we are expanding our horizons to include region, nation, and even international "culture areas" as the bases for a constantly increasing proportion of our organizations. If this is true, it follows that the schools ought to emphasize education for living in the larger society: "The school cannot afford to retain a provincial emphasis in an increasingly cosmopolitan world." [34] The real challenge to educators is, of course, to do both: provide a community school without ignoring the importance of the great community. This, however, is embodied in the community school movement in its ideal form.

SELECTED REFERENCES

Barzun, Jacques, *Teacher in America,* Little, Brown and Company, Boston, 1945. This little volume is a delightfully readable criticism of American education and of the critics of education, as well.

Benjamin, Harold, *The Saber-Tooth Curriculum,* McGraw-Hill Book Company, Inc., New York, 1939. A witty and sagacious criticism of American education by one of its leading practitioners.

Brookover, Wilbur B., *A Sociology of Education,* American Book Company, New York, 1955. The author of this textbook draws especially upon sociology and social psychology for his study of human relations in education.

[34] Woodward, Julian L., "Is the Community Emphasis Overdone in the School Program?" *Harvard Educational Review,* October, 1941, pp. 473-80.

Brown, Francis J., *Educational Sociology*, Second Edition, Prentice-Hall, Inc., New York, 1954. One of the leading texts in the sociology of education.

Curti, Merle, *The Social Ideas of American Educators*, Charles Scribner's Sons, New York, 1935. This volume, by a famous historian, traces the conflict of different ideologies for domination and control of American education.

Waller, Willard, *The Sociology of Teaching*, John Wiley and Sons, Inc., New York, 1932. Somewhat out of date, but still a thought-provoking pioneer study of education as a social process.

Warner, W. Lloyd, Robert J. Havighurst, and Martin Loeb, *Who Shall Be Educated?* Harper and Brothers, New York, 1944. An interesting and enlightening enquiry into the relationship of social class and educational opportunity in America.

CHAPTER $\boxed{11}$

Basic Institutions: Religion

1. Religion and Church Structure in America

Religion is probably not, as some people think, on the way to obsolescence in the modern, science-oriented society. "There is no dialectic," as Robin M. Williams, Jr., puts it, "that makes it impossible to understand electronics without being an atheist." [1] The sociology of religion is an important branch of the field of sociology, and religion and religious institutions are fit and proper subjects for analysis by the community researcher.

The simple designation, "church," as applied to religious organization in America is clearly inadequate to describe the important variations in religious groups with regard to the nature of solidarity, means of attaining membership, and degree of integration with other social institutions. Howard Becker's terms, *ecclesia, sect, denomination,* and *cult* provide for such variations. An ecclesia is a large organization, usually combined with the state and dominating the population of a society. One does not join an ecclesia, but is born into it. This kind of religious organization is sometimes of an

[1] Williams, Robin M., Jr., *American Society,* Alfred A. Knopf, New York, 1951, p. 314.

international sort, such as the Roman Catholic Church of Medieval Europe; or it may be national, such as the Lutheran Church or the Anglican Church in certain modern nations. The sect is a smaller group; it is fundamentally exclusive in its membership, appeals to personalities, emphasizes religious experience, and is often in protest against the ecclesia or other aspects of the social organization. A sect becomes a denomination when it has developed to that point at which it becomes adjusted to other sects and to secular institutions. The denomination, accordingly, is less exclusive in its membership than is the sect, and is more readily recognized by secular authorities. A cult is a loosely organized religious group; one does not join it to attain membership, but simply accepts its beliefs. It, therefore, "merges on the abstract crowd," but has a clear enough ideology to be recognizably distinct from other religious groups. It usually provides great emotional satisfaction to its participants, and it can probably exist only in a society which is highly secular and atomistic. Examples of cults from American society are New Thought, Theosophy, and Buchmanism.[2]

American religion embraces these four basic structures; in addition there are certain elements in its organization and functioning which, considered together, reveal the unique nature of our religious life as a whole. Williams has admirably summarized these characteristics in his *American Society*. Religion, as an *institutional system* in America, exhibits the following: separation of church and state; coexistence of many diverse religious groups; a large degree of toleration and religious freedom; tendencies toward emphasis upon the ideas of human perfectibility and progress; "secularization" of religious beliefs rather than literal interpretation

[2] von Wiese, Leopold, and Howard Becker, *Systematic Sociology*, John Wiley and Sons, Inc., New York, 1932, pp. 624-28.

of dogma; a withdrawal from problems considered too strictly religious in nature; the acceptance of religion for reasons of expediency; splits across denominations and within them separately between fundamentalist and liberal or unorthodox dogma and practice; a great deal of indifference to religion, but not much direct opposition to it. Religious *organizations* show strong congregational autonomy; much importance on leadership of lay members; the placing of great emphasis upon evangelizing and missionizing within the society; a large variation among forms of worship and the general scope of activities even among churches of the same denomination; an outward commercialism in church affairs due to the necessity of attaining voluntary financial support. With regard to its *secular orientation,* religion in America exhibits general approval of secular success, but there are always ambivalences in this respect; there is an aloofness from politics and political affairs; a lack of any militant anti-clerical organization or movement; deep inner conflict among religious group members over secular attitudes, for example, whether one should seek for mastery or withdrawal of worldly desires; religious organizations are usually conformist or conservative with respect to the commonly accepted social standards; there is a persistent optimism with respect to human perfectibility, even though religion in America is largely based on a theology stressing natural evil and the sinfulness of man; little unity in religious beliefs and practices among the people, due largely to the great diversity of creeds and organizations.[3]

The church, then, is an organization founded on a set of social norms and behavior patterns in terms of which people are related to one another; it differs from other organizations fundamentally in that the basis for the unity of its

[3] Adapted from Robin M. Williams, Jr., *op. cit.,* pp. 315-18.

members is its relating of the supernatural to the natural—
including people—through rituals. Churches often develop
hierarchies of offices designed to implement the ritualizing;
the specific functions of this hierarchy may undergo—and
ordinarily do undergo—change from time to time, even
though the general functions of the church may remain relatively constant.[4]

Religious institutions in America vary from detailed and
elaborate hierarchical and bureaucratic organizations in
which each participant has a generally prescribed part—as
in the Roman Catholic Church—to an exceedingly loose
arrangement in which every member is an organization unto
himself—as among the Quakers. Integration and concentration of organization and control may proceed to amazing
lengths; witness the example of the Father Divine Peace
Mission Movement, in which it is reported that the sum total
of the organizational scheme is Father Divine. There are
no chairmen, no vice-chairmen, no elders, no deacons—for
Father Divine is God and God needs no lieutenants.[5]

In sum, sectarianism is one of the most important characteristics of the culture of America. And not only do specific
communities to some extent take on the sectarian nature of
the dominant groups, but the separate sects tend also to retain their specific identities in the individual community.
There is a relationship between the American belief in the
separation of Church and state—and, indeed, in the general
separation of Church from all other institutional arrangements—and the sectarian character of religion and its organization. There is, furthermore, a relationship between sectarianism and community conflict which, thus far, has not

[4] Warner, W. Lloyd, and Paul S. Lunt, *The Social Life of a Modern Community*, Yale University Press, New Haven, Connecticut, 1941, p. 33.

[5] Fauset, Arthur H., *Black Gods of the Metropolis*, University of Pennsylvania Press, Philadelphia, 1944, pp. 55, and following.

been deeply explored. It is clear, however, that unity in religious thinking and practice is still not characteristic of most American communities, despite much lip-service to the contrary. Conflict between religious groups—which may vary from simple matters of suspicion and competition for congregations to strong intolerance directed by a community toward a specific religious group—is directly related to the structural nature of religious institutions. The central facts in that structure are separateness and sectarianism.[6]

2. Situational Aspects of Religion and the Church

One is sometimes able to read in the nature of its churches the degree of "ruralness" or "urbanity" which is characteristic of a particular community. In both rural and urban communities the religious institutions, like the schools, are essentially separate social systems, but differentiated, in part, from most of the others by the fact that they serve people of both sexes and all ages.[7] In both rural and urban communities, religious institutions can have potentially integrative as well as potentially disintegrative functions at the same time.[8] But it is the rural church in which recent changes in structure and function are most apparent. Structurally, churches in most rural localities have been for some time and are today in a good deal of difficulty. There is a constant tendency—born of broadening mental horizons of the people, coupled with good transportation facilities which make for a widening of geographical horizons—toward village or city churching. Rural congregations are becoming smaller as individuals

[6] For a useful discussion of the sectarian character of American religious institutions, see John A. Kinneman, *The Community in American Society*, F. S. Crofts and Co., Inc., New York, 1947, pp. 207, 383-84.

[7] Loomis, Charles P., and J. Allan Beegle, *Rural Social Systems*, Prentice-Hall, Inc., New York, 1950, p. 415.

[8] *Ibid.*, pp. 428, and following.

either move to the village or city or at least go there to worship, and as membership decreases, the individual cost of participation in the typical rural church becomes increasingly high.[9] The older chief function of the rural church—Sunday preaching—is shifting in the direction of a constantly more inclusive educational program, especially character-building in a broad, and often secular, sense. This functional shift, even when coupled with structural changes, has not, nevertheless, destroyed the country church. In fact, it still remains the strongest voluntary agency in most rural communities.[10] But the country church does face special problems born of its situational aspects, that is, the fact that it is rural. These problems are the results of the rural church's special collection of attributes in our time: overchurching in some cases, underchurching in others; abandonment or neglect by communities; poorly trained, poorly educated, and poorly paid ministers; inefficient and trivial local organization; sectarian rivalry and conflict; inadequacy of physical plants; a general failure to provide what residents consider to be an adequate social program.[11] There is little evidence, despite recent attempts to revitalize the rural church, that the trends we have described are likely to be reversed in the near future. There is a general tendency toward centralization and "urbanization" of social organizations, including religious ones, which is likely to continue into the reasonably foreseeable future.

Organized religion reaches its most elaborate development, as one might expect, in large cities. But even in our

[9] Sanderson, Dwight, and Robert A. Polson, *Rural Community Organization,* John Wiley and Sons, Inc., New York, 1939, pp. 95, 123, 146, *passim,* and Charles P. Loomis and J. Allan Beegle, *op. cit.,* p. 435.

[10] Burchfield, Laverne, *Our Rural Communities,* Public Administration Service, Chicago, 1947, pp. 49, 51.

[11] Sims, Newell Leroy, *Elements of Rural Sociology,* Third Edition, Thomas Y. Crowell Company, New York, 1940, p. 586.

biggest urban centers, there are still—and perhaps will continue to be for many years—many churches which are small and of an essentially "rural character." There may be found in any city the "store-front" churches, the houses or stores in which some people—generally few in number—gather from time to time for religious purposes. A crudely lettered sign may indicate that, for some small band, a shabby building is the home of "The Only True Church of God," or of the "People's Religion." There are thousands of such places, generally in run-down residential neighborhoods or poor business districts, for, "as goes the neighborhood, so goes the church." Growing neighborhoods tend to have growing churches; deteriorating neighborhoods tend to have deteriorating churches, and there may be successive "invasions" by small sects. Preachers to the "store-front" congregations usually have little education and the services are often of an emotional nature.[12]

Churches in America, in the urban as well as in the rural community, are still typically localized, although they are becoming less so.[13] This is a result—at least in part—of the long tradition of separateness and sectarianism. Multi-sectarian councils and other organizations of cooperation are gradually breaking down this tradition, especially in the large metropolitan centers. It may well be that, in the foreseeable future, churches will base their localism not so much upon a time-honored sectarian tradition as upon their instrumental purposes—that is, upon those functional emphases which vary widely from group to group and which are likely to continue to do so.

[12] Hallenbeck, Wilbur C., American Urban Communities, Harper and Brothers, New York, 1951, pp. 476-79.
[13] Ibid., p. 481.

3. Instrumental Aspects of Religion and the Church

Every social institution in a community is related to all, or some other, institutions. Religion in America is related to our system of stratification, and local denominational groups tend to follow social status differentiations among the population. Religious acceptance or practice is, if not a pre-requisite, at least a significant aid to success in politics. Church groups are sometimes concerned with the "secularization" of the public schools and often engage in formal secular education themselves. The family has a religious sanction —most marriages are still solemnized in a church. Church members generally approve of business activity, although economic matters are an important source of value tensions and conflicts.

American religion, like many other aspects of the American ideology, has been influenced by the philosophy of pragmatism. Many people think religion is good for no other reason than that it helps to get things done—to establish and support social standards and goals they hold important.[14]

The functions expected of religious institutions in America reflect this pragmatism. In general, people who expect anything of churches appear to expect one or more of these functions for themselves or the community as a whole: (1) *Peace of mind for the individual;* this is generally felt to be the first and foremost function of the church, although there is no data to indicate to what extent religious institutions may actually fulfill it. (2) *Social control and guidance;* religion, with its marshaling of emotions and sentiments, tends to support the mores of the community. (3) *Welfare and*

---

[14] Williams, Robin M., Jr., *op. cit.,* pp. 336-37.

recreation, both of which are concerns of the more modern religious institutions.[15] These are the manifest functions; they are obvious and not at all difficult to detect. It is somewhat more difficult to understand the social functions of religion: the provision of values in terms of which social obligations are defined and the reinforcement of these values through sacred sanctions involving otherworldly punishments and rewards.[16] The primary social functions of religion are integrative, as we note later in this chapter, but there are other purposes for which people use their religious institutions.

There can be little doubt that religious institutions play roles in perpetuating class systems; churches themselves may, in a specific community, form a kind of social class hierarchy. West found that in Plainville, for example, people considered the Christian church to rank highest in social prestige, followed by Methodist, Baptist, the Church of God Holiness, and several smaller sects. Relative positions of these churches change in time, but it may be assumed that each group exerts effort toward maintaining its position or reaching a higher one. At one time in Plainville, the Methodists ranked the highest, but the Christian group, through revivalism, a community church movement, and pure good fortune, gained the top place.[17] Churches may play important roles in perpetuating the separate identity of an ethnic group; sects may also be ethnic, or they may tend to split up an ethnic group over some problem of doctrine or practice.[18] Especially in the

[15] Lundberg, George A., Clarence C. Schrag, and Otto N. Larsen, *Sociology,* Harper and Brothers, New York, 1954, pp. 571-76.

[16] For a capable discussion of these functions, see Elizabeth K. Nottingham, *Religion and Society,* Studies in Sociology, Random House, Inc., New York, 1954, Chapter Two.

[17] West, James, *Plainville, U.S.A.,* Columbia University Press, New York, 1945, pp. 142-45.

[18] Warner, W. Lloyd, *American Life,* The University of Chicago Press, Chicago, 1953, pp. 168-69.

South, the support of the class system by churches is an important latent function. Even the colored church sometimes supports the "caste" system in which Negroes are placed; in a Negro church pageant, for example, all the "saints" and "angels" were of light skin shades—this because they were lighter, for, as the people remarked, they were not high in status. The Negro church has served the function of lessening class antagonisms by giving sanction to the class system; caste symbols are taken up by the church and expressed in religious terms or context. For example, the Old Testament God and the white landlord are often considered to be analogous.[19] John Dollard, after studying similar phenomena, reached the same conclusions, remarking that religion, as well as politics and education, is "caste patterned" in the Southern community he analyzed.[20]

Religious institutions, conversely, are instrumentalities of social mobility in most American communities. Warner and his associates found that, in Jonesville, movement from the Gospel Tabernacle to the Baptist or Methodist group, from the Baptist to the Methodist, or from either to the Federated Church, was considered an upward step in the social hierarchy,[21] and many other students of American communities make similar observations.

The religious symbols of a community, like other kinds of symbols, must reflect the social structure if they are to be meaningful in the daily activities of citizens. One of the results of our great diversity of churches is a growing difficulty in reaching common acceptance of symbols.[22] The lack

[19] Davis, Allison, Burleigh B. Gardner, and Mary R. Gardner, *Deep South,* University of Chicago Press, Chicago, 1941, pp. 248, 414-16.

[20] Dollard, John, *Caste and Class in a Southern Town,* Harper and Brothers, New York, 1937, 1949, Chapters 9, 10, 11.

[21] Warner, W. Lloyd, *Democracy in Jonesville,* Harper and Brothers, New York, 1949, p. 167.

[22] Warner, W. Lloyd, *American Life,* p. 23.

of common symbols leads to a further isolation of religious groups from one another and from other institutions, and may account for the fact that churches so often remain aloof from practical social affairs. In the South, for example, where social problems, such as those centering around race, unemployment, and economic difficulty, are so pressing, neither the Negro churches nor the churches of the poorer whites appear to have taken the kind of interest in practical public affairs which might logically have been expected under such circumstances.[23] Indeed, in some communities, there has developed a serious conflict between churches which stress "sociological" sermons and those dealing primarily with "otherworldliness," that is, those concerned with threats to Christian equalitarianism and others which presuppose some class differentiation.[24] In some communities, too, people who belong to the more emotional religious groups consider the churches to be primarily instrumentalities of mutual aid and neighborliness, while among non-church people and some upper-class church members, the church seems to stand in the way of progress.[25] This class difference in attitude toward the church seems strange because it is from among the lower prestige groups that the more hysterical or emotional religious orders which rarely have highly developed social programs recruit their membership.[26]

4. Integrative Aspects of Religion and the Church

A community or a society is integrated if it has a structural and functional congruence of institutions rather than a fun-

---

[23] Myrdal, Gunnar, *An American Dilemma,* Harper and Brothers, New York, 1944, p. 873 and note, p. 1413.
[24] Warner, W. Lloyd, *Democracy in Jonesville,* p. 167.
[25] West, James, *op. cit.,* pp. 163-64.
[26] *Ibid.,* p. 148.

damental pattern of conflict between them, little or no coercion or interference with the survival of institutions, and a large degree of consensus among individual and group definitions of the common situation, that is, goals, purposes, and means.[27] It is clear that, in any community, both integrating and disintegrating forces are always at work at the same time,[28] and, as we have already noted, religious institutions may have either or both influences on the community structure and process.

That there is such a thing as a "religious integration" of life is hardly to be questioned. Such integration is not necessarily supernatural, but lies within human experience and is based on a human desire—we would not say it is universal—for a way of life that is sanctioned by one's fellow men.[29] Industrialization and urbanization, with their consequences of constantly increasing segmentalization and depersonalization of human relationships, move us away from that "holistic" view of life, of nature and man's place in it, which religion can help us maintain.[30]

In their own spheres of influence, religious institutions have been part and parcel of this depersonalization of human relationships. As a reaction to an earlier American revivalism, in which religion was personal and direct, Americans, as one writer puts it, have now "tended to establish an impersonal and institutional pattern of salvation almost as rigid as that represented by the state Churches of Europe

[27] Bloch, Herbert A., *Disorganization: Personal and Social,* Alfred A. Knopf, New York, 1952, p. 72.
[28] For a demonstration of this proposition, see Charles P. Loomis, *Studies of Rural Social Organization in the United States, Latin America, and Germany,* State College Book Store, East Lansing, Michigan, 1945, pp. 50, and following.
[29] Brownell, Baker, *The Human Community,* Harper and Brothers, New York, 1950, pp. 184-85.
[30] *Ibid.,* pp. 178, and following.

in the seventeenth and eighteenth centuries." [31] This depersonalization is directly reflected in the attitudes toward religion of a large proportion of Americans. Many, even "devout" church members, consider membership and participation in religious affairs as a kind of "filial duty." [32] Even in more or less isolated rural communities, a quarter or a third of those not Catholic or Jewish in faith probably no longer even profess to believe fundamental Protestant doctrines and do not accept any literal interpretation of the Bible. This was the situation for Plainville, as James West describes it.[33]

But one should not consider church membership and participation as the sole criterion for the evaluation of the religious character of a community, for it is not always easy to understand the difference between people who are actively engaged in formalized religion and people who are not. The formal member of a church may not actually attend services or be involved in other religious activities as often as his non-member neighbor. Many people are halfway religious and halfway nonreligious. Perhaps a very large proportion of Americans can be thought of as "marginal church participants," [34] but religious, just the same. Furthermore, it would be a mistake to think that the religious community is necessarily the locality full of churches and churchgoers. Rather, it is one whose citizens are aware of the nature of the community as a whole and who coordinate their individual powers with a greater power in working out its destiny.[35] Re-

---

[31] Sweet, William Warren, *Revivalism in America,* Charles Scribner's Sons, New York, 1944.

[32] See, for example, Caroline Ware, *Greenwich Village,* Houghton Mifflin Company, Boston, 1935, p. 199.

[33] West, James, *op. cit.,* p. 142.

[34] Cuber, John F., "Marginal Church Participants," *Sociology and Social Research,* September-October, 1940, pp. 57-62.

[35] Bogardus, Emory S., *Sociology,* Fourth Edition, The Macmillan Company, New York, 1954, p. 302. Bogardus quotes Harry F. Ward's *Social Evangelism,* New York, 1915.

ligion, in other words, is not merely a matter of formal organization and formalized institutions and rituals, but involves a "way of life," of thinking, of looking upon oneself and one's relations with others, with nature, and with a Deity. Religion and churches in the community may, thus, stand in common interest, or they may—and sometimes do —stand at odds.

SELECTED REFERENCES

Brunner, Edmund deS., and Wilbur C. Hallenbeck, *American Society: Urban and Rural Patterns,* Harper and Brothers, New York, 1955. Chapter Twenty-one is an excellent discussion of religious organization in American communities.

Childs, Marquis W., and Douglass Cater, *Ethics in a Business Society,* Mentor Edition, New American Library, New York, 1954. This recent volume deals with Christian ethics and their application to business practice in the American community.

Davis, Kingsley, *Human Society,* The Macmillan Company, New York, 1949. Chapter Nineteen is a thoughtful survey of theories of religion, and a functional analysis of religion in modern society.

Durkheim, Emile, *The Elementary Forms of the Religious Life,* translated by J. W. Swain, The Free Press, Glencoe, Illinois, 1947. A classic study in the sociology of religion.

Nottingham, Elizabeth K., *Religion and Society,* Studies in Sociology, Random House, Inc., New York, 1954. Professor Nottingham's study is a functional analysis of religion, and draws from the fields of anthropology and history, as well as sociology.

Pope, Liston, *Millhands and Preachers,* Yale University Press, New Haven, Connecticut, 1942. This volume is a study of the part played by religious leaders in labor-management relations in Gastonia, North Carolina.

Tawney, R. H., *Religion and the Rise of Capitalism,* Mentor Edition, New American Library, New York, 1948. A readable and thoughtful book dealing with the relationships of religion and economic institutions.

Weber, Max, *The Protestant Ethic and the Spirit of Capitalism*, translated by Talcott Parsons, George Allen and Unwin, London, 1930. Weber's study of the relationship of Protestantism and economic ideas and practice is one of the most famous essays ever written on a social subject.

Yinger, John Milton, *Religion in the Struggle for Power: A Study in the Sociology of Religion*, Duke University Press, Durham, North Carolina, 1946. Yinger's book is a study of the role of religion in human relations.

CHAPTER 12

Basic Institutions: Government and Economy

1. Political Institutions in the American Community

"Ideas," Hegel once remarked, "have hands and feet." And "actual politics," Ernest Barker writes, ". . . are simply actualized philosophies." [1]

Some have concluded that a community deserves its local politics because the politics it gets is merely the actualization of the philosophy the people hold—or that they receive by default as a kind of negative consequence of no positive philosophy. But political life is more complicated than this would indicate. It is too much to hope that even experts in the study of politics, let alone the ordinary lay citizen, can predict with any reasonable accuracy the latent consequences which may be inherent in a particular political structure or behavior pattern. This is in part because there is a vast difference between the motivations of individuals in their own purposes and objectives—in each "potty little person" being his own "potty little self," to paraphrase G. K. Chesterton—and the great flow of social consequences which result from them. Analysis and prediction, if it is to be scientific and

[1] Barker, Ernest, *The Citizen's Choice*, Cambridge University Press, London, 1937, Chapter VI.

accurate, must somehow be on the basis of a combination of individual actions and purposes and the social consequences growing out of them.

One of our major concerns here is the relation of politics and political action to the maintenance of individual freedom in the American community. "From the sociological standpoint," writes Gerard DeGré, "the problem of freedom is primarily a problem of social structure." And social structures range from "atomistic" to "totalitarian" in terms of the degree of concentration of power. Both extremes produce minimal degrees of individual human freedom; there lies between them a medial degree of concentration of political power which produces the greatest freedom.[2] But freedom is a process, too, one which involves and is involved in the political structure. The key to the understanding of the nature of freedom lies as much in the analysis of the processes involved in the attachment of loyalties and their consequences for human behavior as it does in the structural aspects of the power relation.

2. Structure and Function of Government

Nature is wasteful of individuals, human or otherwise, and human culture can be construed as one great attempt at a diversion of this fact. "Culture is engineering, or intervention in nature, for the ultimate purpose of saving individuals as against processes, and that is essentially the purpose of freedom."[3] Those aspects of culture which we call "governmental" or "political" provide a striking example of man's

[2] DeGré, Gerard, "Freedom and Social Structure," *American Sociological Review*, October, 1946, pp. 529-36. For a related discussion, see James L. Busey, "The Forms of Tyranny," *Denver Post*, March 14, 1954.

[3] Bryson, Lyman, *Science and Freedom*, Columbia University Press, New York, 1947, pp. 72-73.

use of learning in an attempt to divert the waste of individuals caused especially by one particularly destructive agent of nature—man himself.

The sociologist's construct of *society* and the political scientist's concept of *state* are closely related terms—it is not the structures which would seem to differ, but the angles from which they are seen. As the sociologist and the political scientist come more and more to recognize this fact, their work will increasingly converge in the interest of understanding man. But like society, state is a concept which is highly abstract and difficult to grasp.

A state is usually defined in some such terms as these: It has, as its *minimum* conditions, a group of persons who (1) are associated for protective purposes, (2) have formalized their protective procedures and processes into an institutional system, (3) have invested a government with a monopoly or near-monopoly on the use of force, and (4) have officials empowered to act in the name of the entire group.[4] The officials, of course, represent the institution of government, which may be defined as the organization which exercises or may exercise the sovereign powers of the state. Under our federal system, political organization in the local community is as much a part of government as is any other political organization, state or national.

"Governments," as Robert Rienow remarks, "are not cut from a pattern; they grow." They do not fit well into molds —they can be understood only through seeing them, one by one, in their geographic and demographic contexts.[5] With this salient observation in mind, we can make some remarks concerning the functions of government in the community,

[4] Lipson, Leslie, *The Great Issues of Politics: An Introduction to Political Science,* Prentice-Hall, Inc., New York, 1954, p. 56.
[5] Rienow, Robert, *Introduction to Government,* Alfred A. Knopf, New York, 1952, p. 41.

whether that community be small and local or as large as the state itself.

The question we wish to discuss is: "If the purpose for which men organize themselves into a state is for *protection,* just what is it that they seek, through the instrumentality of government, to protect *against?*" Is it nature and its waste of individuals, or is it man himself? The answer is that it is both, but most especially, governments deal with men and the problems which they themselves create.

Human beings are driven to associate in groups under the contrary impulses of cooperation and competition. But to reconcile the two and dovetail them within the same structure has always been a problem. Perhaps, however, the answer is found when liberty and equality are synthesized under the master-concept of welfare. It is in the attainment of equality through the mechanisms of the state that men express their altruism, cooperativeness, and sense of solidarity. It is in voicing opposition and responding to incentives of personal advancement that they display their egoism, competitiveness, and individuality. To maintain both principles in equilibrium and guide the two constructively toward the solution of the great issues is the wisdom of statesmanship. When the power of government is directed in the service of that ideal, the good life emerges into the realm of the possible and the art of politics becomes a voyage of ethical discovery.[6]

The functions of government fall into two categories, *internal* and *external.* Internally, the functions are the final enforcement of the social norms, the arbitration of conflict among individuals and groups, and, in general, planning and direction in the community. Externally, governments func-

[6] Lipson, Leslie, *The Great Issues of Politics: An Introduction to Political Science* (copyright, 1954, by Prentice-Hall, Inc., New York), p. 414. Reprinted by permission of the publisher.

tion to handle diplomacy and war.[7] Or, to put it somewhat differently, the great functions of government can be said to be: to maintain public order; to control the violent behavior of the few so as to eliminate fear and establish confidence and cooperation; to control or preside over the struggle for social change, for change breeds conflict; to protect the community from forces which, pressing from without, seek its disruption.[8]

The exercise of political power, which, of course, is necessary to the functions noted above, does not by any means adhere only to formal governmental organization. Pressure groups, sometimes formally structured, and sometimes not, and with little cohesion among the members, exert tremendous political influence in almost every American community. The place of the local pressure group in a community is not entirely a function of the importance of the group on the national level. This is true even in the case of highly organized groups, for local power will depend also on the composition of the membership, especially on the number of important persons on the roster, the importance of services to the community, interrelationships with other groups, either on a cross-membership or interest basis, and the relations with the opposition. The less vigorous the opposition, the greater the public regard for the group is likely to be, and, consequently, the more power it is likely to have.

In addition to formally organized lobbying or pressure groups, there may often be found, especially in larger communities, certain individuals who make themselves heard not only in local political affairs, but those of the state and nation as well. Such persons, ordinarily economically or so-

[7] Davis, Kingsley, *Human Society,* The Macmillan Company, New York, 1949, pp. 481-89.
[8] Corry, J. A., *Elements of Democratic Government,* Oxford University Press, New York, 1951, pp. 5-7.

cially powerful in their communities, may take it upon themselves to represent certain points of view before federal or state government officials, by dollar-a-year government service themselves, or in other ways. The existence of such politically influential figures has been reported many times. One example is Floyd Hunter's recent description of the activities of certain powerful and vocal citizens in Regional City, a busy American finance and industrial center. Hunter reports that one individual, whom he calls James Treat, of the Southern Yarn Mill, for many years was known as a confidant of the governor of the state, and was, in reality, a power behind that official. Although Treat held no official political office, it is reported that the governor "would not go over Treat's head in any matter." Harvey Aiken, another Regional City resident, on one occasion went on his own initiative to Washington to appear before a Congressional committee concerned with a tax change.[9]

Within the community, pressure for conformity with regard to issues economically powerful persons consider settled sometimes takes the form of deliberate manipulation of individuals. The "small" professional—schoolteacher, journalist, and social worker, for example—is especially subject to such power manipulation. Hunter describes in these words the experiences of one such individual in Regional City:

One case which came to the writer's attention in connection with the manipulation of the under-structure professional personnel was that of Joe Cratchett, a professional social worker who ran a locally sponsored neighborhood club for underprivileged boys. Joe may be described as a liberal. His training and associations for several years outside the environs of Regional City made him acutely aware of many of the problems confront-

[9] Hunter, Floyd, Community Power Structure, University of North Carolina Press, Chapel Hill, 1953, pp. 161-69.

ing the constituency which he was hired to serve. The board of his agency was made up of second- and third-rate men in the power structure, and from the beginning of his job Joe found himself in hot water over some of the things he would say. His club put out a little bulletin which he edited, and on two or three occasions he put pieces into the bulletin that involved the larger issues which he felt confronted the community. He was warned to keep the bulletin the "safe" publication which it had been before his arrival in the city.

On one occasion Joe publicly attacked the "clean-up—paint-up" campaign as being sponsored by the power interests to shunt off any vital approach to the housing problem. One of the city politicians took exception to the published material, and quite a furor ensued in Joe's next board meeting. Joe stood his ground and some of his board members stood with him, but he was not to hear the last of the matter. George Delbert was apprised of the situation and called together a few members of the Community Chest board, the agency which underwrote the finances of the Youth Club. He asked them to "look into the matter." The Chest board passed a resolution to "make a study of the agency and to investigate Joe Cratchett's activities in connection with the agency." Joe resisted the efforts to "study" him, and this further aroused the suspicions of the leaders in the Community Chest. The Chest director was told by his board to find ways of "getting rid of Cratchett."

A sub-committee of the Chest board's investigating committee . . . was set up make a "quiet investigation of Cratchett's previous record." This committee was headed by a "little fellow" whom Cratchett described as a hatchet man and who had at one time been the president of the association known locally as "Patriots, Inc.," a veterans' organization. As the investigation proceeded, Joe Cratchett did not cease his agitation on matters of housing. He went further and suggested in a public speech that many of the social ills which were so apparent in the neighborhood in which he worked could be traced to "low wages."

This word spread quickly among the power leaders of the community. The president of Joe's board told him that he wanted to stand by him, but he (Joe) was rapidly becoming a controversial figure in the community and his actions were liable to jeopardize the whole agency program—a program in which the board president had put many years of civic work. . . .

The investigators sent private detectives into the cities in which Joe had worked previously to look up his record, but they evidently did not find anything which they could pin on him, and for a time the situation seemed quiescent. Things went along on a fairly normal basis for about two months until the agency was up for its budget hearings before the Chest. The committee wrangled hard and long with the representatives of Joe's agency over the proposed budget, and finally granted most of it with the exception of a scheduled increase in Joe's salary, an increase that had been agreed upon in his initial contract with the agency. Joe openly attacked George Delbert in the meeting as being the perpetrator of the troubles the agency was having. This was too much for Joe's president, and after the meeting he asked Joe to resign. Joe refused. He had a contract that did not expire for a year, and he proposed to stick to his contract. He based his contention for staying on the fact that his club program was a good one, a point on which most agreed, and that just because he had a different opinion from that of Delbert was no good reason for resignation. He felt that the board "should fight it out along this line."

Some of the members of Joe's board took the position that Joe should leave the agency, but they were lukewarm in the matter in the early stages of controversy. They recognized the program of the agency as being "revitalized" under Joe's direction, and they did not want to become involved in a showdown in the matter.

Joe might have won his fight if matters had remained as they have been described to this point, but he made a fatal mistake. He allowed a meeting of the Progressive party to be held in one of the meeting rooms of his club, and the fact was reported to his board president the following day. A front page story appeared in the press which headlined, "Club Executive Accused of Politics." The story which followed did not openly say that Cratchett was a part of the Progressive party movement, but the innuendoes were there and he was never able to get a straight story into the papers on the matter. He felt that the club rooms should be used for open-forum meetings, regardless of their nature, but this was too much for the power leaders who were very much set against the development of the Progressive party movement.

Eventually Joe Cratchett was fired from his job. He was first offered several months' salary in addition to the amount which he was entitled to by contract "if he would go quietly." He chose to try to carry his fight to his national professional association, but the association did not respond to his appeals until matters had reached a critical stage and it was too late to reverse the trends which had been set in motion for his release from his agency. When the professional association did get around to "looking in on the matter," their field representative "sided with the leaders of Joe's board," who by then were on record as demanding his resignation. The national group felt that Joe had gone beyond the "areas of his competence" in becoming involved in any way in partisan politics. Joe moved to another community, and an editorial in the Regional City Star breathed a sigh of relief and a warning to other men like Joe.

The forces for conformity were greater than the individual in the episode recounted. Most of the under-structure personnel around Joe were privately in sympathy with his fight but publicly they declared that his actions were foolhardy. The actions taken by the community are as described, and we are interested here in those actions rather than in the merits of Joe's case. The point is that the power structure holds the means of coercion in Regional City, and most of the professionals are well aware of the potential force of these elements.[10]

---

[10] *Ibid.*, pp. 190-93. Reprinted by permission of the publisher.

Hunter found Regional City to be a "microcosm of organized power relationships," and the strength of the top power group is clearly evidenced in the case of Joe Cratchett. Positions of leadership and power in the community were based primarily upon wealth and economic strength, two factors increasingly important in social prestige in America as family membership and background becomes more and more difficult to ascertain in our mobile, industrializing communities.

3. Politics, Freedom, and Equalitarianism

There are two kinds of men, Thomas Jefferson once wrote, those who fear and distrust the people and those who identify themselves with the people, cherish and trust them. These groups may form parties—and do—but by whatever name they go, they are either *democratic* or they are *aristocratic*.[11] The study of politics in the American community may well focus on the question of the nature of freedom and the role of formal and informal government in its support or degradation.

It is liberty, not equalitarianism, as de Tocqueville pointed out long ago,[12] which is the essence of human freedom, political or otherwise, but throughout our history, and most especially today, it is equalitarianism, attuned to a deadening conformity, which appears strongest in American thought. And the cruel, harsh fact is that men can be equal and slaves.

There is considerable evidence of the strength of the dogma of equalitarianism. For example, Allison Davis and

[11] Jefferson, Thomas, letter to H. Lee, 1824.
[12] de Tocqueville, Alexis, *Democracy in America*, translated by Henry Reeve, Oxford University Press, New York, 1947, *passim*.

his colleagues report that the idea of political equalitarian-ism is so firmly engrained in the thought patterns of Old County that even among the lower caste, that is, Negroes, it prevents any expression about or recognition of the system of differential social evaluation which is a part of the social structure there. Indeed, while the system permits Negro participation in politics, it is fully recognized that this does not endanger the political supremacy of the white middle class —and yet the dogma persists.[13]

The very essence of community is change, and freedom involves the place of the individual in the forces of change. It is change which produces conflict and the source of conflict is generally in the relations of persons and institutions, and this involves the whole question of loyalty. The democratic community is the community in which institutions and processes serve individuals; the unfree community stands ready to jettison the personality for the institutions. But, one may insist, the basis of community integration and solidarity is deep and abiding loyalty to institutions. And herein lies a basic problem in human freedom. The democratic community is one in which personal loyalties and loyalties to institutions are separable and are generally recognized as separate.[14] It is the primary integrative function of government in a democratic community to promote institutional loyalties (we assume the nature of the institutions to be democratically determined and to be "good") while at the same time leaving the individual free to hold personal loyalties regardless of institutions and institutional memberships. The community which is free is the community which has a diversity of institutions and a large range of oppor-

[13] See Allison Davis, Burleigh B. Gardner, and Mary R. Gardner, *Deep South*, University of Chicago Press, Chicago, 1941, pp. 190, 229-30, 488-90, 496-97.

[14] Bryson, Lyman, *op. cit.*, p. 113.

tunities for the attachment of loyalties to institutions and to individuals, but no *necessary* connection between the two.[15]

In sum, it seems to us that individual freedom and the development of personality ought to be primary goals of political action in any democratic American community. And the reaching of these ends surely requires equality under law and constitutional rights unchallenged by special privilege or power springing from high economic and social position. The American community which in fact meets the challenge to provide human freedom under the rule of law is a democratic community, making an integrative functional contribution to a society which exists within the framework of a democratic ideal; the community which, like Athens, Tennessee, before the "G.I. revolt," or Regional City, with its ascendancy of economic power used to manipulate individuals, violates the principle of freedom under law, is contradictory to the democratic ideal, and surely must be dysfunctional to the American society as a whole. And the sad truth is that, politically as well as otherwise, actual democracy in many localities is a far cry from the ideal democracy of the nation.

4. Economic Institutions in the American Community

It is entirely fitting that we turn now from our discussion of government to one of the economy, for it is through their political institutions that a people in fact sustain and support their economic system. The control and use of property is the goal of most economic activity, and property rights, as MacIver points out so clearly, are *legal* rights. "A particular government may do little more than uphold an already established system of rights but in the longer perspective *it is gov-*

---

[15] *Ibid.,* p. 176.

ernment that creates property."[16] Ultimate property rights are retained in government, as illustrated by the power to tax and exercise the "right of eminent domain" in our own nation, and a large proportion of laws and regulations at any time is concerned with property and economic activity. But there are also other dimensions to the economy.

Economic institutions, like all other institutions, are definable sociologically as integrated patterns of expected or normative behavior; because they have meaning on the psychological as well as the social level, not only the structure of the norms, but the motivations of individuals behaving in institutionally defined roles ought to be studied. To be a banker, business executive, craftsman, or farmer in an American community is to play a role; since occupation is a major status criterion in American communities, to become a banker or farmer is almost automatically to attain a definable status position.

It is evident from comparative study of primitives that there is no such thing as a universally human economic motivation, but that non-economic institutional patterns in a social system are important as motivations for economic activities. Only for analytical purposes are we justified in selecting a particular set of institutions—as we have done in this and the preceding chapters—for study in comfortable isolation. The motivation of individuals and groups to economic behavior is, therefore, inextricably related to the structure of the whole community system; human self-interest is not the sole motivation to economic activities. Motivation to economic behavior lies not only in the personality and emotional make-up of the individual, but in the integrated institutional structure of the whole community, most

[16] MacIver, R. M., *The Web of Government*, The Macmillan Company, New York, 1947, p. 126.

especially, economic norms themselves. In one sense, then, economic institutions, like all institutions, are self-energizing and self-perpetuating.[17] In the study of any particular American community, it is therefore necessary to analyze the interrelationships of the economic and other institutions in the social system.

5. Economic Organization and Community Harmony

As R. M. MacIver and Charles H. Page point out, there is no necessary harmony between economic associations and social welfare; an association with the manifest function of acquiring wealth for its members may be in direct contradiction to social harmony in a community. For this reason, the people of societies and communities have found it necessary to regulate and check the business interests and motivations of persons in such associations.[18] The use of government as an instrumentality of business regulation and control as well as a creator and protector of property rights is a manifestation of the structural strain between economic associations and the community as a whole.

Economic organizations are themselves breeders of strain and tension in the community. Contention between rival associations and between individuals in business relationships engenders the processes of competition and bargaining in the community[19] and can always erupt into direct or indirect community conflict. Almost any industrial strike provides an example of this process.

The key issue we wish to discuss here, however, is the

[17] For a careful analysis of economic motivation, see Talcott Parsons, *Essays in Sociological Theory Pure and Applied*, The Free Press, Glencoe, Illinois, 1949, pp. 200-17.

[18] MacIver, R. M., and Charles H. Page, *Society*, Rinehart and Company, Inc., New York, 1949, pp. 473-74.

[19] *Ibid.*, p. 474.

matter of the relationship of our specialized, impersonal, corporate, and tremendously pervasive economic system and individual freedom for people living in communities.

6. Economic Structure and Human Freedom

Freedom and unfreedom can be economic as well as political. The structure of the economy in the human community is as important to personal freedom as is the organization of government. Indeed, as we have already pointed out, the two structures are in fact inseparable.

In the Western World man has taken a great deal of economic freedom for himself and may set his economic behavior apart from his religious and ethical life. This compartmentalization is reflected in the fact that only rarely does an economist discuss the relationships of religion and ethics to economic life; for such discussion, one must go to theologians or other specialists in ethics. Business actions and value structures exist in separate and distinct compartments for many of our citizens. Many Americans are probably able to separate their economic behavior to some degree from the system of values and ethics which they honestly believe they hold sacred. For example, a "clever" financial manipulation to someone else's loss is "part of the game," but "stealing" is immoral.

Beyond the usually discussed characteristics of business organizational patterns (corporate, partnership, individual enterprise, and cooperative) and the matters of size and technological organization, perhaps the two most important characteristics of the contemporary American economy, from the sociological point of view, are its impersonality and its pervasiveness in community life.

Pervasiveness and impersonality may well characterize

industrialism as a culture system as well as capitalism as an economic system. There are, doubtless, different kinds of "capitalism" in the world. Eric Johnston, a vigorous supporter of the capitalistic economy, says there are three: (1) capitalism of the bureaucrats; in extreme forms it is state capitalism and totalitarianism; (2) capitalism of monopoly and private privilege; even at its worst, because it is private, governmental power is usable against it; and (3) "people's capitalism," which requires a population with capital; it puts the *total* people first, it is adaptable and flexible, rather than monopolistic, and it takes diverse forms and undertakings.[20] Sociological criticisms, if they are to be made, must center about the wastefulness of resources, limitations on freedom resulting from concentration of economic power which spills over into other aspects of social life in the American community, and certain other latent manifestations of our economic organization and behavior.

America is known as a wasteful country. And the view seems borne out by the history of our squandering of mineral, forest, and land resources, most especially during the age of the "robber barons" after the Civil War. But the waste of natural resources stems not only from deliberate exploitation by ruthless, ignorant, or careless men; it stems as well from idleness of men or machinery and the failure to use the most effective known technology.[21]

The concentration of economic power in our society has been of concern to many social scientists as well as to public officials. Franklin Delano Roosevelt, basing his statements on figures from government agencies and committees, had this to say to the American people in 1936:

[20] Johnston, Eric, *America Unlimited,* Doubleday and Company, Inc., New York, 1944, pp. 87-98.
[21] National Resources Committee, *The Structure of the American Economy,* Part I, Washington, Government Printing Office, 1939, pp. 1-3.

Of all corporations reporting from every part of the Nation, one-tenth of 1 percent of them owned 52 percent of the assets of all of them. And to clinch the point: Of all corporations reporting, less than 5 percent of them owned 87 percent of all the assets of all of them. . . .

Of all the corporations reporting from every part of the country, one-tenth of 1 percent of them earned 50 percent of the net income of all of them. And to clinch the point: Of all the manufacturing corporations reporting, less than 4 percent of them earned 84 percent of all the net profits of all of them.

He went on to point out that this concentration is reflected in income distribution among Americans. Quoting the National Resources Committee for 1935-36, he said:

Forty-seven percent of all American families and single individuals living alone had incomes of less than $1,000 for the year; and at the other end of the ladder a little less than 1½ percent of the Nation's families received incomes which in dollars and cents reached the same total as the incomes of the 47 percent at the bottom.[22]

While the figures and the proportions have, of course, changed in the past fifteen or so years, there can still be little doubt of the great concentration of wealth and its resulting inequality of income right up to the present. And that such disparity in economic power and control among American citizens has its effects upon social relations in general can hardly be questioned. Organization for industrial production is significant, too. Peter F. Drucker writes that the modern corporation is not an *economic* institution at all, for it serves no economic function which could not be served by a partnership or some other form of business structure. It is really a

[22] Roosevelt, Franklin Delano, *Statement on Economic Concentration*, S. Doc. 173, 75 Cong., 3 Sess.

political institution, for it has as its purpose the creation of power. This power, however, is no longer necessarily associated with economic ownership, for we have effectively divorced management and ownership in America. Power in the modern corporation derives from management itself. It knows little control and it owes responsibility to nobody; such power, Drucker holds, is illegitimate. The result is that the worker is lost in the industrial machine; he lacks social status; he lacks function as an individual person. This is especially true of the craftsman, who has been replaced, functionally, by the unskilled machine operator, a worker who "is not a human being in society, but a freely replaceable cog in an inhumanly efficient machine." [23]

To the American to whom freedom means personal dignity, Drucker paints a nightmare. But fortunately the nightmare is not entirely real, or at least not in all American communities. To some extent the people of most localities organize to control the power of corporations and to mitigate the painful conformity required by modern industrial production; through labor unions, through government, and through informal group action they seek to insure greater recognition of the individuality of the worker. Increased leisure, higher living standards, and pleasant working conditions all contribute to human individuality and human dignity.

But a basic social problem in America is still essentially economic: how to provide equality of opportunity. The policies presently under debate among our citizens are these: (1) initiating a broad anti-trust program to eliminate artificial discriminations upon entry into fields of economic endeavor, (2) encouragement of voluntary recognition of social respon-

---

[23] Drucker, Peter F., *The Future of Industrial Man,* The John Day Company, New York, 1942, pp. 74-112, *passim.*

sibility by large corporations—the establishment of philanthropic foundations in the public interest, such as the Ford Foundation, is evidence of the fruit of this policy, (3) removing of employment discriminations as to sex, race, and creed, (4) broadening of educational opportunities, (5) promotion of collective bargaining, (6) increasing the mobility of labor, and (7) modification of income inequalities. The trend appears to be in the direction of an increased use of government to effect these policies.

7. Planning and the Economy

The planless economy is no more for Americans, although many of them cling with tenacity to the myth and only give it up with reluctance and anguish.

Man is a community creature. The future of industrial man lies in the philosophy and culture of the human community. The new liberal State must seek and must establish ways and means of "communalizing" this search for significance. This road is sure to be a new road, and probably a revolutionary one, and it may quite possibly lead to a neo-industrial age. But along its way free men will pass, pursuing the ends of their being in a community of human values which has given them the power to act and which thereby helps them to make of themselves significant human beings.[24]

The industrial economy will be planned; it will be planned by government, on every level from local to federal; it will be planned by citizen groups and pressure groups; it will be planned by business enterprises and organizations themselves. The only real question is the relative significance in the

[24] Meadows, Paul, *The Culture of Industrial Man*, University of Nebraska Press, Lincoln, 1950, pp. 204-05. Reprinted by permission of the publisher.

planning process to be attached to the roles of each of these groups. Most Americans realize that one of the major problems facing them today is how to organize life in the machine age. As planless competitive capitalism fades into the realm of the mythical, and as we come to face "the portent of an industrial civilization, with its paralyzing division of labor, standardization of life, supremacy of mechanism over organism, and organization over spontaneity," [25] its segmentalization of human contacts, and its separation of man from the nature of which he in fact is a part, Americans everywhere will recognize even more surely than today the need for planning and for thinking together in the sphere of the economic as well as in other areas of social living.

8. Institutions and Associations

In this chapter and the previous three, we have discussed the basic institutions in every American community: family, educational, religious, political, and economic. We have seen that these institutions, defined as patterns of expected behavior, are inextricably interrelated to such an extent that even separation and distinction for discussion purposes is difficult. The matter is further complicated by the fact that people in any social group of size, such as the community, form associations designed to promote the interests of special subgroups.

An association is an organization of a group; in this sense, family, the state, school, church, government, and business firm are all associations. The organization itself is the association; the procedures and behavior patterns connected with it may be an institution (as in the case of the family) or

[25] Polanyi, Karl, "Our Obsolete Market Mentality," *Commentary*, February, 1947, pp. 109-17.

include a proportion, out of context, of an institution (as in the case of a criminal gang which accepts the institutionalized approval of economic wealth-getting.) [26]

All sorts of associations exist in the typical American community, interlacing the great institutions, implementing institutional control over individuals, and serving to create changes in institutional structures. "Social" and recreational, professional, health, labor, businessmen's, boosters', children's, and lodge organizations, and a hundred other types, appear in any urban community, and many of them in even the smallest rural community. They differ widely in membership attributes, purposes, and activities, but they all have in common the fact that they exist and function within the influence of the great associations, family, school, church, government, and economy, and are dominated by the institutions connected with them. The small associations in the community are essentially influents of the larger, dominant five, and, while conflicts may result in change in the dominants, it, thus far at least, has never resulted in their outright destruction as institutions. But the influents, as recognizable structures, come and go, sometimes not to come again.

Functionally, influent associations contribute to the community in that they make articulate specific fragments of the basic institutions. They may be dysfunctional as well. As an example, a Parent-Teacher Association group may, and usually does, serve to articulate family values for school authorities, thus serving to mitigate conflict (through truce, arbitration, or concession, perhaps) between the two basic institutions. A criminal association or a narrowly specific interest group may seek to destroy one institution or cause

---

[26] See R. M. MacIver and Charles H. Page, *op. cit.*, pp. 11-17, for an excellent discussion of associations and institutions.

conflict between people of different associations. A business association seeking to subvert institutionalized business ethics and a political association seeking to "buy" votes are examples of dysfunctional associations.

Smaller associations in the American community can be studied sociologically from the point of view of their functional and dysfunctional contributions to the basic institutions and associations and to the community as a whole.

SELECTED REFERENCES

Davis, Kingsley, *Human Society,* The Macmillan Company, New York, 1949. Chapters Seventeen and Eighteen of this introductory textbook present excellent discussions of the structure and function of the economy and government.

Hunter, Floyd, *Community Power Structure,* The University of North Carolina Press, Chapel Hill, 1953. A revealing study of power and its exercise in an American financial and industrial city. Contains a useful appendix on the methods used in the research.

Lipson, Leslie, *The Great Issues of Politics,* Prentice-Hall, Inc., New York, 1954. This recent volume presents the major problems and issues in politics and political behavior.

MacIver, R. M., *The Web of Government,* The Macmillan Company, New York, 1947. An enlightening sociological study of the nature of government.

Moore, Wilbert E., *Economy and Society,* Studies in Sociology, Random House, Inc., New York, 1955. An excellent brief discussion of the relationships of society and the economy. Illustrates the fruitful results of cross-disciplinary research in sociology and economics.

Moore, Wilbert E., *Industrial Relations and the Social Order,* Revised Edition, The Macmillan Company, New York, 1951. A sociological study of industry, its organization, and its relationships to other institutions.

de Tocqueville, Alexis, *Democracy in America,* translated by

Henry Reeve, Oxford University Press, New York, 1947. A classic essay on the American political system.

Veblen, Thorstein, *The Theory of Business Enterprise,* Huebsch, New York, 1923. This critical discussion of business and business institutions by a founder of institutionalism in economics is a stimulating source of ideas on the American economy.

Warner, W. Lloyd, and J. O. Low, *The Social System of the Modern Factory,* Yale University Press, New Haven, Connecticut, 1947. An interesting volume on industrial organization and the social aspects of the factory.

PART SEVEN

The Community and the Future

CHAPTER 13

The Possibility of Planning

1. Order and Possibility in Community Life

We have studied the ordering and patterning of communities in many of their varied aspects: geographical, institutional, and psychological. We have analyzed their functioning processes, and discovered order there. But now the question arises: What is the relationship between the fact of order in the community and the possibility of planning in the interest of accepted goals?

No one has better answered that question than Franklin H. Giddings:

To the scientific mind the universe is order; to the practical mind it is possibility. Both minds, however, know that order and possibility are compatible; it is only the mind that is neither practical nor scientific which imagines that they are not.[1]

The purpose of science, Giddings held, is description, but *"scientific description discovers the possibilities of interchangeability between perceptions and conceptions."*[2]

[1] Giddings, Franklin H., *Studies in the Theory of Human Society*, The Macmillan Company, New York, 1922, p. 127.

[2] *Ibid.*, pp. 128-30.

Possibility and planning in social life are dependent upon scientific description, which is the process of discovery and communication of the order of the social structure. American communities have been largely unplanned; citizens have made little use of scientific description, although professing allegiance to it, and the result has too often been ugliness and chaos instead of beauty and order.

There are many ugly communities in America: a Pennsylvania mill town with its dirt and grime and hopelessness, the squalid sameness of a prairie village, the slum district of almost any large city. The hideousness of such communities is sometimes deeper than surface appearances, too; it may be a cancer which is bored deep into the moral life of the citizens. Witness what may well be considered a monumental display of man's ability to create ugliness where beauty might have reigned: Butte, the sprawling, brawling, lusty copper city of Montana. Here, in part, is what Joseph Kinsey Howard, who loved Butte as only a few Montanans do, had to say about the town:

You round a corner on a highway clinging to the Continental Divide and there, suddenly, is Butte. It is sprawling and slovenly, a bully of a city, stridently male, profane and blustering and boastful: "The biggest mining camp in the world!" "A mile high and a mile deep!" "The richest hill on earth!"

Butte is no longer any of these; certainly it is no longer what its police chief once called it, "an island of easy money entirely surrounded by whisky"—though it still behaves like that. There was a time when the mine pay rolls of Butte averaged $50 monthly for every man, woman, and child, when miners made $10 to $20 a day on contract. Now money is not so easily come by, but it is still easily spent: the habit persists.

This city remains what Joseph Pennell called it in his *Wonders of Work*—"the most pictorial place in America." It could be one of those selected centers of sin which columnist Heywood Broun once facetiously suggested America might establish as places in which the ordinarily virtuous citizen might occasionally blow off steam, for Butte is notorious the nation over as a "good time" town. Indeed, its chamber of commerce has hinted delicately but nonetheless frankly in its literature: "Here they [visitors] may relax in the tradition handed down from the days of wayfaring prospectors, mining and cattle men, laugh and play in the red-blooded manner that is peculiarly Butte's. . . . Doors are wide open, nothing is hidden."

Butte is the black heart of Montana, feared and distrusted. From the sixth floor of one of its office buildings go forth the corporate commands to politicians, preachers, and press, all the pensioners and servile penny-a-liners of corporate capitalism. Butte is a sooty memorial to personal heroism, to courage and vigor even in rascality; and it is a monument to a wasted land.

It is a mile high, even a little more; but it is not a mile deep —the deepest mine is still a thousand feet short of that. If it is no longer "the richest hill on earth," probably it was: above the city, denuded of grass or tree, gray-tan and dirty, squats the mountain of copper which has yielded up metal worth $2,500,-000,000 in half a century. Black triangles crowned with circles, like children's classroom compasses slightly askew, thrust up through the crust of this hill to stamp fantastic abstractions on the limitless Montana sky. Under the city twist 2,700 miles of tunnels, and in their dim hot depths thousands of men have worked and fought and died; thousands of feet in the earth, at the bidding of their masters, they have thrown up barricades, fashioned crude grenades of mine powder, and prepared to blow each other up—while their masters, securely above-ground, fought in corrupted courts for possession of a disputed vein.

Bullets have raked the tired streets hung awkwardly on this mountainside as these men have fought one another or have been fought by their bosses; and the battles have helped build vast fortunes—for other men. The miners have risen in wrath and smitten the Lords of the Hill, and struck, and fought again; and they have been betrayed and defeated and driven back into their holes. But sometimes they have won and wrested away a little more of their Hill's riches for themselves. Then the surface has rocked with Rabelaisian mirth, the drinks have been on the house, the girls on "the line" have bought new dresses, the effigies of the scab have been cut down from telephone poles, and everyone has gone cheerily back to work.

Butte was born in violence, bred in it, and lives it. Back in the boom days the mines killed or injured a man a day; there were sales on crutches in drug stores . . .

Business has been tolerant, too, of the big gambling establishments which, though closed in intermittent reform waves, have given the city a nationwide reputation. They resent bitterly much of the sensational publicity, insisting "other towns are just the same, but not so honest about it." There is a measure of truth in this, but Butte's gambling has certainly been on a scale one would be unlikely to find in other cities of 50,000 . . .

The restricted district is in a narrow alley-courtyard just two and a half blocks from Butte's new modern high school and on the same street. When the school was built there was some reckless talk of closing the line, but it had been there for many years, it was accepted, and Butte decided it was necessary. So a compromise was reached: the three entrances were closed off with fences built somewhat like a maze, painted green and bearing the words "Men under 21 Keep Out . . ."

Butte has behind it three quarters of a century of haphazard mining-camp development, decades of municipal mismanagement, and a community psychology born of miners' tradition—generous but heedless. Here are people oddly different from their nearest neighbors, even in other Montana cities. A spontaneous gesture of good-fellowship, perhaps a benefit dance to provide a "seeing eye" dog for a blind musician, can find wholehearted, immediate support; but Butte's patience is short and its vision dim, so a long-term program of community planning is more apt to run up against the phrase, "Oh, the hell with it!" [3]

The picture of boisterous, planless Butte is exciting, to be sure, but the picture of ordinary American citizens banding together to plan their communities is exciting, too. Indeed, it can be one of the most stirring pictures of democracy in action one is likely to see.[4]

2. The Hyde Park–Kenwood Story: A Case Study of the Planning Process

As we have pointed out many times in this book, a case can be made that the single unchanging fact of community life is the fact of change. And it is only in the context of social change that community planning as a concept makes sense. A part of the order of community is the order of its change and planning is, as Himes puts it, "the dynamic nexus joining continuous social change and conscious human values." [5] Community planning is a process of deliberate social change; it is directed by the value context in which the planners work and it involves four related activities: investigation, discussion, agreement, and action.[6] These four steps in the technique of planning are discernible in the Hyde Park-Kenwood story.

[3] Howard, Joseph Kinsey, *Montana High, Wide, and Handsome*, Yale University Press, New Haven, 1943, *passim*, pp. 85-96. Used by permission of the publisher.

[4] For expressions of this view, see Baker Brownell, *The Human Community*, Harper and Brothers, New York, 1950, *passim*, and Richard Waverly Poston, *Small Town Renaissance*, Harper and Brothers, New York, 1950, and *Democracy Is You*, Harper and Brothers, New York, 1953, *passim*.

[5] Himes, Joseph H., *Social Planning in America*, Studies in Sociology, Random House, Inc., New York, 1954, p. 18.

[6] *Ibid.*, Chapter Three.

By 1949 the Hyde Park-Kenwood area of Chicago was a deteriorating community; experts predicted that within a few years it would be a slum, and the fact that Negroes were moving into the area seemed to indicate to its residents that if anything were to be done to halt the process it must be done at once and on a massive scale. Accordingly, in early 1950, a first block meeting was held.

As it turned out, this block meeting was planned at a strategic time—when rumors were sweeping the block that a house was about to be sold to exploiters who would pack a Negro family into each room. People were concerned; there was something to discuss, no question of that! As soon as the rumors swept the block, four people put up their houses for sale.

Everybody in a row of fifteen owner-occupied houses was invited to the meeting by a small planning group of four. These four personally visited the families with whom they were already acquainted—it was easier that way. As the people came into the house, it was clear that they had different expectations, ranging from the notion that we were met to consider strategies to keep the Negroes out to the feeling that we ought to invite Negroes in and turn the neighborhood into an interracial paradise. These attitudes were discussed fairly readily by people in small discussion groups which had formed before the meeting started.

After about twenty minutes, the feeling arose that we should get started, and there were many glances toward the chairman and host. An old man about eighty climbed up on the stair landing and opened the meeting with this gem: "What do you want me to tell you about those damn niggers?" There was a decidedly awkward pause. The leader replied that while listening to the informal conversations before the meeting opened he had discovered that we had a wide range of feelings about Negroes among us, and he suggested that we might as well accept this as a fact about ourselves about which we could do nothing. He pointed out, however, that Negroes had bought the apartment building across the street and he felt that the block faced certain objective possibilities:

1. It could form a pitchfork mob to try to drive the Negroes out.

2. It could attempt to ignore them.

3. It could attempt to establish communication with them with the idea of explaining the block's determination to prevent physical deterioration and to make the block a pleasant place in which to live.

Posed in this way, looking toward alternative possibilities for action growing out of a real situation, the group quickly decided to begin talking to people. A committee, combining the features of investigating team and friendship group, was appointed to go calling on the new neighbors. The Negroes, fortunately, could see the committee's embarrassment and were mature enough to help them establish communication. The fact that members of the committee did not have strong feelings either way about Negroes undoubtedly made matters easier.

Three other actions were taken at the first meeting; and the second meeting started with a report of these actions, the introduction of new people, and the setting-up of an agenda consisting of the things people on the block thought were problems to be looked into.

As the neighbors left the first meeting they felt considerable relief from anxiety. The meeting had not yet done anything very important by way of taking action but the neighbors had found out something that they knew intellectually but could never have really felt if they had not been called together to enter into action. They had found out that there were a lot of people just as concerned and just as frustrated as they were. Instead of feeling that "everybody else is perfectly able to cope with the situation, but I am not," the individual found that everybody was equally unable to cope with the situation, so that the feeling of inadequacy dissolved and was replaced by the much more objective perception that the group as a whole had problems. Thus the feeling of being out of the group, of being a helpless spectator on the sidelines—feelings which had led individuals to turn inwardly on themselves and feel lonely— these were replaced by a complete reversal of the relationship to the group. The group of neighbors was felt now to be supportive; one was no longer alone. Under these conditions of establishment of communication and support the individual could feel free to act intelligently rather than out of anxiety.

The restoration of communication thus grew around the need for reducing anxiety, but it continued as a new pattern on the block. The neighbors had become acquainted at the block meeting, and each day, as they passed up and down the block, they would greet each other. The network of communication on the block was reinforced and grew because it became a part of the way of life on the block.

The reduction of anxiety freed the group for active problem-solving efforts. To feel better was nice—and the neighbors openly acknowledged it. But they also saw that improvement of the neighborhood requires people to take action; feeling good makes action possible, but does not, by itself, rebuild the block.

Thus there arose spontaneously from the meeting a demand for subcommittees to get busy. The group identified a wide range of practical problems: the moving of abandoned cars, the installing of porch lights to dispel darkness, the prompt reporting of movements of materials into houses so that the plans for conversions could be checked, the development of tot-lot and recreational space, the collective buying and sharing of garden implements. Working committees arose from volunteers who felt strongly about one or another of these problems. And committee action, supported, encouraged, and supervised by the block group, resulted in positive acts of neighborhood improvement.

The actions resulting from working together had their effect on the physical community. In addition, during the processes of co-operation, neighbors began to make some highly significant personal discoveries about themselves and each other. They learned that the things they used to worry about don't need to matter. A Negro worker or a low-income renter can have just as useful ideas, make as many phone calls, dig out just as valuable facts, and be just as helpful as anyone else. Through these discoveries, the neighborhood as a community of people became stabilized. The block began to feel like home; life on the block acquired new richness of meaning and satisfaction. The neighbors learned that the physical and social communities are inextricably linked: actions are taken to maintain and improve the physical community, but it is the way in which neighbors participate to take action that maintains and improves the social community.

With the first successful actions, the neighbors began to think of themselves as a group. They gave their group a name, an identity. They developed loyalty to the group, and standards of upkeep which strengthened their individual desires to keep their own houses in order. The group found the language in which to state its goals, and it began to take a long look outside itself at the city government. As time went on and other neighborhood groups developed under the leadership of the Conference, loyalty spread from the block to the community, and, through the central Conference organization, community feelings and pressures began to be felt in many offices of the city hall. The local organizations, which had not been ready for action in the beginning, began, one by one, to respond to the new attitudes of the citizens, and to add their efforts to the program. At the end of four years, it is literally true that practically every major institution of the community is actively participating in the total program.

Events in the Hyde Park-Kenwood community have amply demonstrated the importance for community betterment of massive, creative participation by the citizenry.[7]

---

[7] Reprinted from *Dynamics of Groups at Work* by Herbert A. Thelen, by permission of The University of Chicago Press. Copyright 1954 by The University of Chicago Press.

Community planning is a social process, and like all social organizations, planning groups have their latent functions. In the Hyde Park-Kenwood community, one of the major functions probably little expected or predicted by organizational leaders was the creation of a new social solidarity and the reduction of individual anxiety and tension. Investigation of the problem, discussion of common interests in it, the reaching of agreement, and the taking of group action served to bring the members of the community together in a more solidary unit within which the individual personality, because of the very fact that he no longer stood alone in a world of relentless forces, could retain his feeling of importance and his dignity.

The reliance on facts, scientifically obtained and objectively utilized, is a characteristic of all successful community planning operating within the democratic context. Indeed, as Herbert A. Thelen concludes from a study of the block program just described, democracy and the method of science are closely related. Scientific objectivity requires the evaluation of evidence, the testing of hypotheses, and the acceptance or rejection of ideas and individual services on the basis of factual evidence instead of status position. In a planning program, such objectivity requires the acceptance and evaluation of individuals on the basis of their contributions to group ends rather than on racial, religious, educational, or other status-bearing characteristics.

3. Organization and Dynamics of Community Planning

Community planning and group action require organization; the story of the Hyde Park-Kenwood community illustrates something of the nature of organizational structure as well as certain of the dynamic human interaction processes which are involved. In this brief section, we shall interweave our discussion of organization and dynamics of community planning under the topics of community councils, community centers, leadership and planning, and citizen participation and group action.

(1) *Community councils.* The community council is a body of volunteers, ordinarily representative of organizations of the community and possibly having provision for individual participation, as well. Smaller communities undertaking serious planning programs may function effectively with only one council, but larger cities usually have more than one, each covering a "district," "neighborhood," or "area." [8]

Councils are ordinarily formed for general purposes, such as "to work for a better community"; sometimes they restrict themselves simply to planning, leaving active reforms or service operations to separate agencies. Oftener than not, they are concerned with such matters as: (1) coordination of existing community activities, especially those affecting recreation facilities, youth organizations, community health and safety, physical planning, and the planning of new services, (2) establishment of new social relations patterns through bringing together for discussion and planning individuals and representatives of local groups who would not otherwise be in contact, and (3) representation of local interests in larger planning programs of city or region and, in turn, serving to decentralize such large scale programming.[9]

Arthur Hillman states that the following list of organizations *should be considered* for membership (but, presumably, not necessarily all made members) in the community council:

[8] Hillman, Arthur, *Community Organization and Planning*, The Macmillan Company, New York, 1950, p. 157.
[9] *Ibid.*, pp. 160-62.

Governmental agencies, including
   Health Department
   Juvenile Court
   Library
   Public Schools
   Welfare Departments
   Recreation Departments
Social agencies, including
   Youth serving agencies
   Family welfare societies
   Settlements
Parent-teacher association
Women's clubs
Service clubs
Fraternal organizations
Veterans' groups
Churches and religious organizations
Labor unions
Chamber of commerce
Business and professional organizations.[10]

However inclusively a coordinating council brings together in a voluntary organization all groups devoted to the common welfare, it is still unlikely to function well unless different status, sex, and age groups are included. "Indeed, its success depends upon a rounded approach to the community's problems, and this means bringing pharisees, publicans, and sinners together." [11]

(2) *Community centers.* There is a community center—or more than one—in every locality, a place where people gather to discuss their problems and their interests. It may be only a drugstore or the general store of historic America,

---

[10] *Ibid.*, p. 163.
[11] Hayes, Wayland J., *The Small Community Looks Ahead,* Harcourt, Brace and Company, New York, 1947, p. 109.

or it may be, and quite likely is today, a formal center for all sorts of community activities. With adequate building, it can provide space and facilities for such activities as photographic developing and printing, various kinds of recreation, study facilities, meeting places to increase and encourage social interaction among community residents, and a whole host of other facilities not readily available in today's compact, often crowded home. The community school can serve as a center, and, as we have indicated in Chapter 10, often does. Social settlements, especially in disorganized communities, sometimes serve as vital centers; such agencies as the United Service Organizations during the last war, churches, libraries, lodges, and labor union halls are also possibilities.[12] Few generalizations can be made concerning the "best" type of community center, for there is great variation in needs and facilities from locality to locality. We cannot even say whether the center, for the sake of efficiency, ought to be consciously planned, or permitted indirectly and perhaps accidentally to evolve out of some private facility. Size, wealth, proximity to outside recreation sources, and many other factors are involved, and the people of each community must answer the question in the light of their unique characteristics and wishes. But every locality needs some center for the provision of services not readily available in the usual home and for increasing social interaction which may lead to more intense social consciousness and hence to participation in planning and the execution of the plans.

(3) *Leadership and community planning.* The organization of working groups such as community coordinating councils, the processes of planning, and the execution of plans all require leadership. Councils and other planning groups do not just happen; they do not come out of the

---

[12] Hillman, Arthur, *op. cit.*, pp. 138-52.

nowhere into the here. In addition to his role in the initial organization of a planning body, the leader serves four major functions: (1) creating conditions under which members can experiment in planning, (2) setting criteria for individual participation—for example, limiting the range of discussion and action in planning, (3) obtaining group consensus on the order of steps in planning, and (4) steering the group, that is, marshaling and utilizing individual abilities and resources so as to ensure progress toward the agreed-upon goal.[13]

The questions, what is a leader? and how do we find him?, are of utmost significance to social planning in the community. Arthur Hillman analyzed a number of studies on leadership in planning situations and concludes that leadership involves personal attributes and skills, but emphasizes the relation of the leader to the group situation. Under democratic conditions, this means that "the essential test of effectiveness becomes the extent and voluntary character of group participation induced by leaders." One implication of this newer concept of leadership as a role rather than as a product of innate "strength" is the important idea that leaders can be trained.[14] The professional worker in a social agency or the executive secretary of a community council, as examples, are not necessarily efficient leaders of a planning body, for leaders must be recognized as such by the members of the group. In some instances, while a lay member is the ostensible group leader, conducting meetings and settling disputes, a professional worker may be an "indirect leader." He may work skillfully behind the scenes, a task which requires a high degree of moral responsibility or it becomes Machia-

[13] Thelen, Herbert A., *op. cit,* pp. 302-10.
[14] Hillman, Arthur, *op. cit.,* p. 187.

vellian.[15] Conversely, there often appears in the community council or other agency a strong "informal" leader—a "lay" member who works quietly behind the "formal" leader.

(4) *Citizen participation and group action.* Group action of any kind in a democratic community requires citizen participation; obtaining such participation is the most difficult of the tasks of leadership. Citizens refuse to engage in planning activities for a variety of reasons: lack of time, energy, or money, fear of loss of job or other reprisal, a sense of futility in the face of community problems, reluctance to be considered "reformers," lack of knowledge of organization for planning, leader failure in interpretation of programs, and lack of definiteness or concreteness of opportunity for service. Conversely, citizens do participate for other reasons: civic pride, social consciousness, enjoyment of fellowship and power through association with others, for the expression of resentment and grievances, as an energy outlet, for prestige, to keep up with family or peer groups, and for business and professional contacts.[16] This wide variety of motives suggests that appeals for participation can be—and perhaps *must be* for success—varied in content and tone according to information on the nature of interests of the individuals or groups to which they are being slanted.

But citizen participation in planning in a democratic community places certain responsibilities on leaders. After a study of community groups in action, Herbert A. Thelen concludes that the following principles or assumptions of group action are basic to effective operation in the democratic context: (1) Organizational power is subordinated to problem-solving for the community. (2) Services of persons

---

[15] *Ibid.*, p. 188.
[16] *Ibid.*, pp. 199-200.

who can aid in problem-solving are welcomed, regardless of beliefs about their personalities. (3) Attempts are made to reach working agreements with other groups interested in the same problem. (4) The planning body serves to reduce conflict among other groups to which loyalty is owed by individual members. (5) The experimental method is used. (6) The training of its membership is a concern of the group, especially with regard to leadership, the provision of realistic goals, and the formulation of practical solutions to problems. (7) Objective data are collected. (8) Professional aid is obtained if needed and self-appraisal is part of the program. (9) "Enemies" are thought of as objective conditions in need of change, rather than as individuals.[17] The successful leader in community planning is one whose group lives up to these principles.

4. The Scope of Planning: The Urban-Rural Unit

Community planning in the United States must embrace the country as well as the town and the city, or, as Hallenbeck puts it, "a fundamentally significant planning unit will be the integral urban-rural community." [18] The classification of rural and urban as applied to American communities has always had a certain spuriousness, anyway, and most especially it rings falsely in our time of rapid communication and transportation. A very large proportion of our people now play roles and lead lives which are neither wholly urban nor wholly rural, nor yet exactly a blend of the two. Living in suburbs and working in cities, working in the country and

[17] Thelen, Herbert A., *op. cit.*, pp. 365-66.
[18] Hallenbeck, Wilbur C., *American Urban Communities*, Harper and Brothers, New York, 1951, p. 104.

seeking recreation in the city, or living in the city and spending leisure time in the country, a great many Americans segmentalize their lives and the old distinction between the urban and the rural is breaking down. The words of Thomas Sharp apply to our society as well as to England, about which they were written:

A new balance between town and country must be struck. These two parts of the national scene are now inseparably interrelated. They are linked by far closer bonds than they have ever been in the past. The new means of communication have broken down all the old barriers. Now, though, the success of the whole which they together make demands their being welded in a firm social as well as economic relationship. The country can supply certain essential deep needs for the townsman. The town can supply essential needs of the country-man. Town and country are not two organisms but parts of one organism. They are two related utilities making the one great synthesis of national life. The new means of communication now make possible the perfect development of that synthesis, and in any planning for living the attainment of the full synthesis must be regarded as the prime object of activity.[19]

Sharp goes on to say that the future townsman's requirements of the country will be of two kinds: facilities for leisure activities in the country and residence facilities for full-time living.[20] And, of course, the city will need country products and the country will require city products. But the role of the city in ministering to the leisure-time requirements of the country dweller who is no longer tied by time and the

[19] Sharp, Thomas, *Town Planning*, Penguin Books, Harmondsworth, Middlesex, England, Further Revised Edition, 1945, p. 92. Reprinted by permission of the publisher.

[20] *Ibid.*, p. 92, and following.

slowness of transportation to his rural habitat is not clearly understood—in itself a testimonial that the barriers between rural and urban life are breaking down in America.

5. The Role of the Social Scientist in Community Planning

The role of the social scientist in community planning is the same role the scientist plays everywhere: his purpose is to describe and to predict. Strictly as a scientist, he need not be concerned with application of his description and with the use made of his techniques for prediction. In other words, arriving at valid knowledge is the business of the social scientist (or any other kind of scientist); its application and the deciding of the goals to be pursued are, in a democratic society, the province of the citizen.[21] The scientist, as a scientist, therefore, plays altogether a different role from the man as a citizen. In the latter role he may very well—and as a citizen with specialized knowledge and skills has, we believe, a moral duty to—take active part in goal-determination and planning in his community.

The scientist's unique contribution to social planning is made through research. The functions of research in planning are, as Joseph H. Himes puts it, the following: (1) problem definition, (2) learning the limits of possible accomplishment (in a "practical" sense), (3) provision of knowledge of experiences of other groups where useful or significant, (4) resource assessment, and (5) delimitation of planning units and planning areas.[22] The unique contribution of the social scientist is, therefore, description and prediction as an outgrowth of empirical research in his special field of compe-

[21] For a recent elaboration of this point of view, see George A. Lundberg, Clarence C. Schrag, and Otto N. Larsen, *Sociology*, Harper and Brothers, New York, 1954, p. 11.

[22] Himes, Joseph H., *op. cit.*, pp. 28-31.

tence. One of the more significant practical applications of scientific knowledge is the discovery of the various alternative courses of action open to planners in a specific situation and indication of the probabilities of success (in terms of desired goals) of each alternative. Planning for the "integral urban-rural community" requires the knowledge and techniques of social science. Wilbur C. Hallenbeck sums up the role of the scientist as follows:

> The development of such communities would seem to require the coordinated findings of diverse scientific investigators, natural and social, and the refinement of comprehensive planning procedures. Such procedures include: the survey and appraisal of biological, mineral, technical, and human resources; the survey and appraisal of community performance as evident both in the flow chart of energy and material transformations and, ultimately, in the quality of living of individuals; the location of problem areas by comparing community performance; the projection of a comprehensive, time-scheduled, yet flexible plan for closing the gap between performance and possibility; the education and organization of people for participation in planning and in carrying plans into effect; the provision for democratic processes in the making of social policy—in the making of value choices among the predicted consequences of alternate proposals.[23]

SELECTED REFERENCES

Hillman, Arthur, *Community Organization and Planning*, The Macmillan Company, New York, 1950. A standard text on the subject of community organization.

Himes, Joseph S., *Social Planning in America*, Studies in Sociology, Random House, Inc., New York, 1954. A short mono-

[23] Hallenbeck, Wilbur C., *op. cit.*, p. 104. Reprinted by permission of the publisher.

graph on planning as social change and the nature and method of planning, with illustrations drawn from American society. Interesting and well written.

Lilienthal, David E., *TVA—Democracy on the March*, Harper and Brothers, New York, 1944. An able defense of the Tennessee Valley Authority and of planning in a democratic society.

Poston, Richard Waverly, *Democracy Is You*, Harper and Brothers, New York, 1953. Techniques and procedures for local community planning.

Poston, Richard Waverly, *Small Town Renaissance*, Harper and Brothers, New York, 1950. A lively description of the experiences of small communities involved in the Montana Study.

Sharp, Thomas, *Town Planning*, Penguin Books, Further Revised Edition, Harmondsworth, Middlesex, England, 1945. A lucid discussion of town planning in England; the author takes note of the disappearing distinction between town and country.

CHAPTER 14

The Community and the Future

1. Possible Patterns of Change: Rural and Urban

With respect to population size of place of residence, the American people are becoming increasingly "urban." With reference to general social characteristics, it is perhaps more accurate to say—as we have said in the preceding chapter— that the distinction between the rural and the urban is breaking down. What does this mean for the future of the American community? Although prediction would be dangerous, due to the many uncontrolled forces involved, we can make some tentative guesses and express a few fears and hopes.

(1) *The future of the city.* What is the future of the American city? Many people have theorized that cities are doomed to disappear: due to the wrath of God for their wickedness, as a result of the use of electricity and rapid transportation and communication, and because of the danger of concentration in modern war, among other reasons. In our country, however, with concentration still a major trend in our population statistics (in spite of something of a counter trend) the predicted effects of God's wrath, of war, or of technological change seem hardly to have been felt at all.

With the advent of the atomic age and atomic war, we face the question: Will the new mass destructiveness of war bring a stop to the development of cities? Not enough time has elapsed to allow the development of basic theories concerning the effects of the harnessing of the atom on urban life, as T. Lynn Smith and C. A. McMahan point out, but there are currently two schools of thought. The first is that the city will, in the future, be about the same as now, but with important problems solved and major bottlenecks removed. There will be, however, no fundamental changes in the urban scheme of things. The second holds that the atomic age will witness a great dispersal of population and decentralization of industry. Just exactly what the patterns of change and the new urban forms will be is not specified.

The first of these lines of thought is perhaps utopian, and the second over-pessimistic. Smith and McMahan, cautiously enough, indicate that whatever changes occur in the next few decades are likely to be merely accentuations of present trends: (1) development of "immense, straggling suburbs," with lower population densities than are at present typical of cities, and (2) loss of many social characteristics cities have had in the past; there is likely to be a greater homogeneity of people, ethnically and culturally, because foreign populations of the over-sixty age group are rapidly dying off, because the city is no longer dependent on rural migration for the maintenance of its population, and because such rural migration as will continue to come will be from regions themselves becoming constantly more homogeneous.[1]

But some feel that the metropolis is a hateful thing, a manifestation of human illness of spirit. In a book called *Cities Are Abnormal*, Elmer T. Peterson takes the usual posi-

[1] Smith, T. Lynn, and C. A. McMahan, *The Sociology of Urban Life*, The Dryden Press, New York, 1951, pp. 790-92.

tion of the critics of urban life. He writes that the changes now taking place in the pattern of the city will destroy it. There are, in contemporary America, powerful motivations which will eventually humble the city: (1) a desire by individuals for material security, (2) a longing for "spiritual peace," which drives people out of the crowded city into the open country, and (3) all the results of electricity which make possible decentralized industry. The real question Americans are faced with seems to Peterson to be, "Can we wrench our thinking into the realization that learning to live with nature is even more important in the long run than learning to live with ourselves?" [2] But such thinking as this is modified by even such a hardened critic of cities and city life as Lewis Mumford. In his magnificent *The Culture of Cities,* he has this to say:

To describe the modern community one would have to explore in detail the potentialities of life for modern man. In brief, the care of those whose labors and plans create the solid structure of the community's life must be to unite culture in all its forms: culture as the care of the earth: culture as the disciplined seizure and use of energy toward the economic satisfaction of man's wants: culture as the nurture of the body, as the begetting and bearing of children, as the cultivation of each human being's fullest capacities as a sentient, feeling, thinking, acting personality: culture as the transformation of power into polity, of experience into science and philosophy, of life into the unity and significance of art: of the whole into that tissue of values that men are willing to die for rather than forswear—religion. The culture of cities is ultimately the culture of life in its higher social manifestations.[3]

[2] Peterson, Elmer T., Editor, *Cities Are Abnormal,* University of Oklahoma Press, Norman, 1946, pp. 3-5, 24.

[3] Mumford, Lewis, *The Culture of Cities,* Harcourt, Brace and Company, New York, 1938, p. 492. Reprinted by permission of the publisher.

Such is the thinking on the future of the city; it is speculative, but more than speculation only, for the divergent trains of thought are based on different interpretations placed on current data. And it is much easier to describe what is currently happening to American communities as far as rural-urban population shifts and concentrations are concerned than it is to predict the future.

(2) *Recent population shifts.* In terms of population distribution, the United States is a highly urbanized country, although not the most highly urbanized among nations. Landis and Hatt, drawing on the seventeenth Census of the United States and statistics published by the United Nations, present figures to show that, in terms of percentage of urban population (unfortunately, not perfectly comparable for different countries), the United States ranks fourth among major nations, with 59.0%. Our country ranks fifth with respect to proportion (29.4%) of her people residing in cities of 100,000 and over. In the first ranking, the United States is preceded only by the United Kingdom, Denmark, and New Zealand, and in the second by these three plus the Netherlands.[4]

It is interesting to note that, while there is a correlation of industrialization of the population and urbanization, it is not a perfect one by any means. With respect to amount of commerce, the five highest ranking nations are the United States, United Kingdom, Australia, the Netherlands, and the Union of South Africa; however, the United States is not included in the first five in manufacturing and construction: Switzerland, Belgium, United Kingdom, Sweden, and Denmark.[5] That the position of our country in these respects should be reflected in her communities is, of course, inescap-

---

[4] Landis, Paul H., and Paul K. Hatt, *Population Problems,* Second Edition, American Book Company, New York, 1954, p. 484.

[5] *Ibid.,* p. 485.

able, for the sum of the population characteristics of a nation is the sum of the population characteristics of the communities in which her people actually live.

Census statistics reveal the extent of the trend to urban residence which has persisted for many years in our country. In 1910, 45.7% of our population was defined by the Census Bureau as urban; in 1920, 51.2%; in 1930, 56.2%; in 1940, 56.5%; and in 1950, 59.0% (or, by the new definition of "urban" used for the first time in the seventeenth census, 64.0%).[6] What is more, there is also a trend toward concentration of population in the larger urban areas as compared to the smaller. Figures for 1910 and 1950 show significant changes in proportions of our population living in places of different size:

	1910	1950
URBAN TERRITORY	45.7	59.0
1,000,000 or more	9.2	11.5
500,000 to 1,000,000	3.3	6.1
250,000 to 500,000	4.3	5.5
100,000 to 250,000	5.3	6.4
50,000 to 100,000	4.5	6.0
25,000 to 50,000	4.4	6.3
10,000 to 25,000	6.0	8.3
5,000 to 10,000	4.6	5.2
2,500 to 5,000	4.1	3.7
RURAL TERRITORY	54.3	41.0
1,000 to 2,500	4.6	3.6 [7]

---

[6] *Statistical Abstract of the United States,* 76th Edition, Washington, D.C., 1955.

[7] *Ibid.*

A major proportion of our population increase from 1910 to 1950 accrued to places of large size. The shift in numbers of rural and urban communities from 1920 to 1950 also is significant:

	1920	1930	1940	1950
Number of urban places	2,722	3,165	3,464	4,023
Number of rural places	12,855	13,433	13,288	13,235[8]

Here again we see a trend toward concentration of population in large communities. The reasons for such shifts are closely related to the increasing industrialism of our nation. It is a commonplace to say that the people of rural areas reproduce themselves more rapidly than people in urban areas. This is still true in America, but the relative fertility ratios of urban and rural communities have been changing strikingly in the past fifteen or twenty years. From 1935 to 1940, net reproduction rates were .726 for urban populations, 1.150 for rural non-farm and 1.661 for rural farm populations; for the period 1942-1947, corresponding figures are 1.085, 1.465, and 1.859. Percentages of increase are, for urban populations, 49, for rural non-farm, 27, and for rural farm populations, 12, for these two periods.[9] Thus, while the reproduction rate differential between urban and rural peoples still persists, it is slightly less of a differential than previously, and there is no significant indication that the trend will be reversed in the near future.

What are the reasons for the difference in urban and rural rates of reproduction? These explanations have been offered: (1) the basing of life on competition and status in the city;

---

[8] *Ibid.*
[9] Landis, Paul H., and Paul K. Hatt, *op. cit.*, p. 227.

(2) the anonymity and freedom from social controls in urban communities which gives an even greater air of romanticism to courtship and marriage than elsewhere in America— marriage, for some, comes to be construed as solely a romantic association of a man and a woman, not to be allowed to interfere with career or profession and to be dissolved if romantic attraction disappears; such an attitude, to the extent it actually exists, leads to impermanence of families and hence stands in the way of fertility; (3) the emphasis on pleasure and sensuous aspects of living, rather than on duty, in metropolitan areas; (4) the emphasis on family in rural life; (5) the differences in rural and urban values—in the former, "work, land, and family," in the latter, pleasure, consumption, and status; and (6) such factors as the later age of marriage and commoner use of contraceptives, which are direct results of competition for success and status in urban life.[10]

(3) *The future of the small community.* The lessening of differences in fertility ratios in rural and urban communities during the past few years has been the effect of a constant diminution of the gap between city and country life. As modern transportation and communication more and more "citifies" the culture of smaller or more isolated communities, and as urban people increasingly move into suburbs (the fastest growing areas in most parts of the country) or seek country haunts for leisure or residence, a more nearly common culture will be the result. Whether this means a deadening social conformity and a nation of mechanized communities of culturally sterile citizens—with an Orwellian *1984* as its horrible extreme—depends upon the foresight and wisdom of the American people. With careful planning and provision of creative opportunity, it

[10] *Ibid.*, pp. 233-37.

can mean, instead, a new kind of soil in which the human individual can be nourished in cultural plenitude, decency, and freedom.

But, even though the barriers separating the rural and the urban are fast dissolving in our country, there still remains the valid distinction between larger and smaller communities. It may well be, as some believe, that our future as a democratic nation lies in the welfare of the small community —of 50,000, 20,000, 5,000, 1,000, or a few hundred people. The family is too small and the greater society too large to be "the preserver of basic culture," but the small community serves this function well. Furthermore, local communities are suppliers of people to be "consumed" in cities, and so provide the basic character of the city and the nation. But we, in America, have taken the community for granted, have neglected it, and abused it.[11]

Small communities are feeling the same forces of change that affect larger areas, but they present a particular kind of challenge to Americans of good faith who wish to plan for the future.

It is not an oversimplification to say, then, that the most challenging aspect of the present transition in the United States from a planless society to one that is to some extent rationally planned centers around education—and diffusion of knowledge—and that nowhere is the need and desire for education and enlightenment more obvious than in our small communities.[12]

There is no question that the harmonious, isolated life of our small communities will be largely destroyed in the

[11] Morgan, Arthur E., *The Small Community*, Harper and Brothers, New York, 1942, pp. 57-59.

[12] Hayes, Wayland J., *The Small Community Looks Ahead*, Harcourt, Brace and Company, New York, 1947, p. 204. Reprinted by permission of the publisher.

years to come; indeed, the process is already far along. The problem is whether the change shall be uncontrolled or planned so as to utilize the resources of the small community to satisfy human desires and needs.[13]

People in rural areas are feeling the impact—a mixed blessing, to be sure—of the present trend toward economic decentralization, the development of big government, and the growing recognition by religious, welfare, and educational agencies of the problems of the small community. Wayland J. Hayes, a careful student of rural life, concludes that the future of small communities will be determined to a very large extent by the kinds of adjustments made by these social agencies.[14]

2. The Road Ahead: Community and Freedom

There can be little question that the future of American local communities will depend to a great extent on the kinds of social planning we do as a nation. Community life, without national prosperity and peace, cannot be expected to be full and rewarding. On the other hand, the citizens of those communities which join with others to participate and plan on a large scale will be contributing strength to the very foundations of our democratic system. "The supreme choice in contemporary society need not be between laissez faire individualism and dictatorship; the course that can be experienced progressively, locally and on a larger scale, lies toward freedom with and through planning." [15]

Community planning requires a liberal outlook, but that is in the American tradition. America, Gunnar Myrdal ob-

[13] *Ibid.*, p. 205.
[14] *Ibid.*, pp. 206-26.
[15] Hillman, Arthur, *Community Organization and Planning*, The Macmillan Company, New York, 1950, p. 357.

served, is a conservative nation, but the principles she has conserved are liberal.[16] And it is true, also, that, more than any other nation, America has formulated the idea of the importance of liberalism for an industrial culture. Even the "leader" in America has traditionally been an idea, not a person, and the collection of values in the leading idea is called liberalism. But liberalism, with its emphasis on human dignity and personality and on individual participation in social experience, can only succeed through cooperative planning.[17] And, as we have previously said, planning is not the sole prerogative of the larger society, but must have a community base, as well.

Some people have gone to extremes in the expression of their faith in community. Brownell, for example, blames two world wars and the death of 30,000,000 men, the depression, regional and world famines, deflation and inflation, and the execution of masses of people, among other things, on "the decline functionally and qualitatively of the human community" which is replaced by "thin functional associations" such as chain stores, baseball leagues, booster clubs, professional associations, and the college department.[18] While there may be some measure of truth in such a statement, it smacks too much of dogmatism, ideologies, and panaceas. But, at that, Brownell may well be right when he says our chance for survival depends on our making the community central in human lives.[19]

The future of the American community is intertwined with whatever the future holds for the whole American

[16] Myrdal, Gunnar, *An American Dilemma,* Harper and Brothers, New York, 1944, p. 7.

[17] Meadows, Paul, *The Culture of Industrial Man,* University of Nebraska Press, Lincoln, 1950, pp. 150-51.

[18] Brownell, Baker, *The Human Community,* Harper and Brothers, New York, 1950, pp. 18-19.

[19] *Ibid.,* p. 294.

nation. The trend of things over the past half-dozen years is not encouraging: the great shift toward concern for loyalty, conformity, and security, the fears, the doubts, the questionings, the loss of faith in our time-honored institutions, and the loss of faith in man himself. A perspicacious and eloquent observer of the American scene puts it this way:

Two things become increasingly evident as the sickness of our American democracy approaches its inevitable crisis: one is the surpassing genius of the founders of this Republic; the other is the transience of even the greatest of political resolutions. It was the supreme achievement of the generation of the American Revolution that it solved the most difficult of all constitutional problems, the problem of the reconciliation within one society of the conflicting human desires for freedom and for community. It may well be the shame of our generation that with us that resolution fails.

A free society is, of course, a contradiction in terms. Freedom means individual freedom: above all, freedom of conscience and freedom of mind. Society means community of some sort: not only of membership in the community, but loyalty to the community. Only where all men think and believe alike does the contradiction disappear; and such societies, as history has demonstrated over and over again, are not alive but dead.[20]

In America men were to create community not on the basis of their likeness in race, political doctrine, or religious worship, but on the basis of freedom to share experience in common. Their basic loyalty was to the right to be free. Freedom, therefore, was first and loyalty second.

But what have we been doing in our American communities and even in the nation as a whole? Since shortly after World War II, we have been whittling away at our old

[20] MacLeish, Archibald, "Loyalty and Freedom," *The American Scholar,* Autumn, 1953, p. 393. Reprinted by permission of the publisher.

loyalty: we have had a great shift in the direction of conformity, belonging, and security and away from our old
passionate embrace of the principle of individual freedom—
and the frightening thing is that this shift resembles another
shift (not to the ultimate end thus far, most fortunately)
occurring in the Europe of the 1930's and 1940's.

Archibald MacLeish says that we have convinced ourselves
that, since Communism is a faith, we, in order to withstand
it, must also have a faith. We must all believe in something
in common or perish. We come to desire conformity for an
illusive sense of security in an insecure world.

Perhaps it is in the free-flowing, informal conversation
that Americans have traditionally carried on in their communities, the tangy talk of everyday, that the current pressure
to conform makes itself most strongly felt. "Listen to America talking and you will hear it. The old independence is
gone. Fear is in the silences, in the things that are left un-
said." [21]

What we really have lost is faith in man, without which
faith in individual freedom is a mockery. Without trust in
man's capacity to live a sane, decent life, we can no longer
believe in our institutions. Perhaps, as MacLeish decides, the
major fault has lain with our education: we have failed to
educate our children in the things of spirit and mind, not
only in the lower schools but even in the universities.

Generations of schoolboys taught only techniques and tools produce generations of men to whom only techniques and tools are
important, men who have no comprehension of their own resources or those of their neighbors, men who know nothing of
those great conceptions of human destiny, those patterns of life

[21] Smith, Bradford, "The Making of a 'Communist,'" *The American
Scholar*, Summer, 1953, pp. 337-45.

and death, which our kind has produced over countless generations.[22]

Education takes place not only in schools, but in family and community as well, and it seems safe to venture the suggestion that the process of coming to our senses will involve a new faith in community life and family life as well as a new concern for education in the things of spirit and mind. We cannot turn the job over to the society as a whole,[23] for American citizens live their lives in communities; nowhere else can men come to know themselves and their fellows more intimately and completely than in communities. It is here, first of all, that faith in man can be re-created for Americans, and it is here that loyalty and freedom can once more be put in their proper relation. If Americans fail to maintain and to build democratic communities, they will fail to maintain a democratic nation.

SELECTED REFERENCES

Hayes, Wayland, *The Small Community Looks Ahead,* Harcourt, Brace and Company, New York, 1947. An interesting presentation of the case for planning in the small American community.

Landis, Paul H., and Paul K. Hatt, *Population Problems,* Second Edition, American Book Company, New York, 1954. This leading text contains valuable discussions of population change in the United States.

[22] MacLeish, Archibald, *op. cit.,* p. 398. Reprinted by permission of *The American Scholar.*

[23] Carle C. Zimmerman warned years ago that centralization, especially of government, tends to break down the community realism emphasized by localism, and to replace it with "nominalism, formalism and individualism in the local community." See *The Changing Community,* Harper and Brothers, New York, 1938.

Mumford, Lewis, *The Culture of Cities,* Harcourt, Brace and Company, New York, 1938. A fine volume on the history and culture of cities by an outstanding student of urban life.

Nisbet, Robert A., *The Quest for Community,* Oxford University Press, New York, 1953. A thoughtful book on political power and social organization in contemporary society.

Peterson, Elmer T., Editor, *Cities Are Abnormal,* University of Oklahoma Press, Norman, 1946. An emotional volume presenting one school of thought with reference to future community planning. The title adequately indicates the point of view advocated in the book.

INDEX

A

Accommodation mechanisms, 177-178
Achievement, human, 7
Activity, human, motivation and, 135-138
Adams, Donald K., 6
Aggression, 178-179
Agricultural communities, *see also* Rural communities, 43
Aiken, Harvey, 242
Airplanes, 76
Alertness, element in personality, 109
Alorese, 101
American dream, 61-63, 148, 150
American Society (Williams), 223
American way, 61-63, 85, 148
Analysis
functional, 7
structural-functional, 8, 15, 22
Anshen, Ruth Nanda, 189, 190
Arbitration, 177
Assimilation, 178
Associations, 256-258
changes in structure and functioning of, 72
Athens, Tennessee, 163-170, 248
Atomic bomb, 67
Attitudes, 111-112, 180
toward authority, 111-112
toward reality, 111-112
toward security, 111
Automobiles, 76, 129, 162

B

Baptists, 230, 231
Barker, Ernest, 237
Becker, Howard, 222
Behavior
aggressive, 178-179
community, processes of, 155-181
deviant, 5, 115, 144
human, organic base of, 94-96
social, 6, 182
Belief, 9, 26
Benedict, Ruth, 101
Bernard, Jessie, 181
Biological needs, 14, 15, 55
Biotic community, 18-20, 21, 69
Boy Scouts, 20
Brahmins, 146
Brookover, Wilbur, 214
Broun, Heywood, 265
Brownell, Baker, 47, 292
Buchmanism, 223
Burgess, Ernest W., 31
Butte, Montana, 263-267
Buttram, Jim, 164, 165

C

Cadence, element in personality, 109-110